WHO WAS
SOPHIE?

WHO WAS SOPHIE?

The Lives of
My Grandmother:
Poet and Stranger

CELIA ROBERTSON

virago

VIRAGO

First published in Great Britain in 2008 by Virago Press
Reprinted 2008

Copyright © by Celia Robertson 2008

A CIP catalogue record for this book
is available from the British Library.

ISBN 978-1-84408-189-9

Typeset in Goudy by M Rules
Printed and bound in Great Britain by
Clays Ltd, St Ives plc

Virago Press
An imprint of
Little, Brown Book Group
100 Victoria Embankment
London EC4Y 0DY

An Hachette Livre UK Company
www.hachettelivre.co.uk

www.virago.co.uk

For my mother

Carpenter looking
at a dead swallow

Person
with her
mouth full
asked a
question

Look me in the eyes!

'*The familiar when met is stranger than strangers*'

JOAN ADENEY EASDALE,
AMBER INNOCENT

Relaxation drawings.

I wont look.
Tell me when
you're ready.

CONTENTS

INTRODUCTION

1973. I am swinging on the front gate with my brother James (me aged six, him four), licking the taste of traffic off the railings. A man walks past and says hello and James tells him that our granny is 'sick in her mind'. My mother comes rushing down the stairs to call us indoors.

She was our family secret, like something dark and buzzing kept in a box. Other families did not have mad grandmothers who washed their hair in margarine and cut up their nightgowns. I never told people at school about her, partly because it seemed too complicated to explain and I was sure no one would understand, and partly through a dread of what might happen if I broke the spell.

There was another reason, too. In the back of my mind there was always the fear that I too might unravel and spin off into nothing. I did not want to think too much about that.

As we got older, our mother told us about her; the good bits and the weird bits, shielding us from the worst. It was difficult to grasp who she really was or what had really happened to her. On one hand she was the brave creative spirit who had written poems and lost everything; on the other she was the person who sent angry letters scrawled in mad biro, which seemed to fizz by themselves on the hall table and made my mother cry. Between the poet and the witchy old lady lay a blurred wasteland. The sadness of it made me feel sick.

She was there throughout our childhood, just out of sight, her shadow cast across family life. We saw an image of her, refracted through my mother, unclear and dreadful. Nottingham, where she lived, was a mythical, frightening place where I imagined it was always raining.

At the same time, my mother somehow managed to make us understand that our grandmother was a special, rather amazing person, albeit damaged and impossible to deal with. This complicated knowledge was a burden, as if we were learning to hold something very dense and heavy. Other kids in the playground would laugh about straitjackets and psychos, chanting 'They're coming to take you away today!' and 'He needs locking up!', stuff they picked up from TV, and I would think, But you don't know! It's real!

It was at once real and totally imagined.

My mother would not give Sophie our address. In order to establish her own family life and to protect herself from constant visitations, all post to or from Sophie was handled by a solicitor. Likewise, for years she did not have our phone number.

As children, we began to recognise the envelopes quite early on and knew that they heralded a difficult day. Several letters might fall out at once, or just one. Reading them now – those that were not ripped up in exasperation and self-defence – provides a vivid picture of Sophie's life in her seventies and eighties. She had always been a fine letter writer and even these chaotic pages contain moving details and flashes of brilliant observation. At the same time, I can see exactly why they span my mother into misery, guilt and rage; they are repetitive, haranguing and often written when Sophie was drunk or had lost her magnifying glass. The words crowd illegibly into corners or scramble across one another or skitter off the page completely. One feels mad just trying to decipher them.

My mother visited her twice a year. A date would appear circled in felt tip in the family diary beside the single word, 'Nottingham', and tension would build as the day approached. My diary entry for 25 October 1983 recalls the atmosphere:

A mixed day starting with rows all round. Jane and I had a head-on clash because we weren't on time for the opticians . . . we didn't speak all the way to Kidderminster . . . Jane had landed herself with a parking ticket (she said it was our fault) & so lunch wasn't too happy either – she started crying. I think she's rather low anyway because she's got to go and visit her mother soon.

She would leave early in the morning, distracted and grim, and return the same evening, exhausted and volatile. It was the only time we saw her smoke, the evening after a Nottingham trip.

Looking back at those years, we did talk about it but there was nowhere for the distress and guilt to go. Sophie lived as she did and made demands on Jane. Jane could not adequately deal with her demands, partly because they were often impossible and partly because she found the situation too upsetting. There was no solution. Life crashed on.

We lived on the edge of a small country town in Worcestershire, just where the houses began to thin out, and occasionally had travellers knocking on the door, asking for refreshment before they continued on their way; vagrants and misfits who were walking or hitching to Wales. Mum would invite them in. I remember a big weather-blasted woman wrapped in a cape, newspaper and plastic bags. She was eating bread and jam in the dining room when I got home from school one day. Another time, a fragile teenage boy spent the night on the sofa. On 13 November 1983, aged sixteen, I wrote in my diary:

> A tramp came to the door for a cup of tea. We gave him some cheese on toast and sandwiches too before he left for Leominster, having told Jane his thoughts on nuclear weapons, smoking and life in general. Jane told me about her mother. I try to imagine myself in that situation where my mum is like a stranger to our shared past – I can't do it. Jane is still suffering from the visit. Sophie is very lonely and poor. As Jane says it is a horrid place where she lives. She read me one of her early poems.

It was perhaps a way of helping Sophie by proxy; this hospitality extended to complete strangers, which she was unable to offer her own mother.

I remember feeling that these people were themselves but also significant, symbolic characters, who belonged to the pages of a children's story book. They were somehow related to our grandmother and therefore, somehow, related to us.

I first met Sophie in the eighties when I was about seventeen. She was living in a dilapidated council flat and had moved all her belongings, her bed, her stove and a bowl for washing into one room. A complicated, web-like arrangement of string snaggled across the windows and was attached to the door with drawing pins. This, she explained, was to catch burglars. She had sprinkled talcum powder on the sills in case intruders got in and left footprints. The main piece of furniture was a desk that she was using as a dresser – the compartments meant for ink and paper filled with a pat of butter, a tomato, half a loaf of bread. She cooked us a cake made of margarine and chocolate in a frying pan on top of her Baby Belling and insisted that we filled the kettle very slowly 'to avoid too much gas coming out of the taps'.

The reality of seeing her was both shocking and a relief; for someone who had loomed so large in my imagination, she was tiny. Despite her disturbing milky eye, she had a dreamy smile that could make her look suddenly young and she looked disconcertingly like my mother.

I tried not to feel appalled by the squalid little room, by the pile of ripped fabric and clothes on the bed, by the faint smell in the air. At the end of that first visit, just as we were leaving, she held me back by the arm to whisper, 'If you want to make a baby, you must do it! Don't let anyone stop you! Don't let them hurt the baby!' Her urgency made me queasy; I'd barely kissed anyone, let alone tried to make a baby. I escaped from her grasp and bolted to the car.

From then on, I would sometimes join my mother on her visits up to Nottingham and, once I had passed my driving test, I would go on my own or with James, butterflies in my stomach as we headed up the motorway. It was never as bad as I expected. The trick was to live in the moment with her, to walk the tightrope and ignore the drop of her past. If you looked down and recognised the loss, you would go spinning head-first into dizzying sadness.

Sophie would come to the door, beaming sweetly at us, her hair newly dyed yellow with turmeric rice, grains still caught in her fringe. She retained an old-fashioned sense of hospitality and occasion and would make us tea, slowly and precariously. She would find some milk, maybe even some biscuits or bread, and we would sit around the table and talk. Once we had wine in mugs. I was surprised by how much she laughed.

Our visits usually took the same pattern; tea or a drink at her place, lunch out, then a pub. She was always desperate to get out and into town, but preparing to do so was a tortuous process. We would wait while she slowly finished dressing, applied make-up, then laboriously checked that everything had been turned off and was safe. She would then bundle most of her possessions into a series of plastic bags that had to be lugged around with her all day, in case someone broke into the flat while she was out. Finally, there was a taxi ride, called and waited for with growing anxiety, the rigmarole of doors and seatbelts and working out how to get through the snarling one-way system, hoping she would not suddenly feel trapped and demand to be set down in the middle of a busy main road.

She disliked anywhere too quiet or genteel so we always ended up in the city centre, often at a bistro near the theatre called Punchinello's, which involved a steep flight of steps down to the basement restaurant, and extremely difficult trips up to the lavatory (as she got older, Sophie would crawl up the stairs on hands and knees to get there).

She would be wearing electric pink lipstick, fishnet stockings, complicated shoes that she had made out of cardboard and string, a nightdress under a coat tied with an old ribbon. She would proudly introduce us to the waitress with a gracious wave, order lots of food and eat it with relish, repeating the introductions whenever anyone passed our table.

Once, we misjudged a place from the outside and ended up in a tearoom with chintzy tablecloths and a sniffy waitress. The meal became an excruciating endurance test. Everything Sophie said sounded obscene, things got spilt, disapproval hung thick in the air. It was one of those occasions where we all went into slow-motion, putting on coats and hats to leave, bumping into one another and dropping gloves as the manager stood holding the door open with a tight, impatient smile. Far better to eat at a cheap lively café with people who responded to Sophie as if she were just another customer and waitresses who asked her if she was enjoying her meal. Then it could be fun.

The onward journey to the pub had to be undertaken at an agonising pace, as she insisted on walking but could only take tiny steps. We crept along the sides of wind-scuffed parks with lorries roaring past our shoulders, or shuffled through blaring concrete malls, holding on to Sophie as she inched her way towards some distant hostelry. She would launch herself into four streams of moving traffic, waving and smiling, and then cross the road at the speed of a tortoise on her two sticks, the sea of halted cars waiting patiently for her to get to the other side. 'Oh, don't mind them!' she'd shout against the engine noise. 'They all know me here!'

By the end of her life, Sophie Curly was essentially a bag lady you might have walked past as she sat on a park bench, or ignored as she looked for something over and over again in her handbag. She was blown about the streets of Nottingham, a crumpled figure, half frightening, half pitiful. She harangued the officers at police stations, spent her pension on beer and lace, fell out of taxis, fell down stairs.

In her will she left all her effects to the Chief Constable of the Nottinghamshire Police Force. Politely grateful, if slightly nonplussed, he passed them on to my mother. Two cardboard shoe boxes tied with pink ribbon, containing:

- A map of the world, which she used to have taped to her wall.
- Two pocket dictionaries, one French, one German.
- A copy of the *Communist Manifesto*.

- A strip of passport photos of her smiling.
- A bundle of letters from her solicitor; a bundle from social services.
- Cards and letters from her children and grandchildren.
- Several pocket diaries and hand-stitched notebooks full of sums and shopping lists.
- A glass brooch, pink.

The boxes sat in a cupboard for five years before I looked at them.

While she was still alive, I would never have tried to piece the story together. She was fiercely protective of her privacy and did not want to be interfered with. Being written about would have angered her. Certainly by the time she was an old woman. Her younger self might have laughed and thought the idea preposterous. In some ways I feel that I have betrayed her, but I wanted to bring her into the light from the shadows where she had been for so long. I wanted to honour her, take everything out of the box and put it back again, known.

'Unless you tell it as it is, what's the point?' said my aunt Polly when I went to talk to her in Australia. But how does one 'tell it as it is' when the story is the life of another person? Finding the truth is like the process at the optician's when you get fitted for glasses. You stare at a blurry poster on the opposite wall in a darkened room while the optician drops a series of lenses into your spectacle frames. With each one the blur shifts and changes, popping the figures in and out of focus, sometimes rendering you completely blind, until, eventually, your eyes reach a consensus and you can make out a clear series of letters.

Who was my grandmother? What exactly did happen to her?

We are all, ultimately, unknowable to one another. Love disguises the fact and biography tries to ignore it. Mother to child, husband to wife, friend to friend, subject to writer, people are essentially mysterious. My grandmother in particular. Although I have been walking about with her in my head for over five years, she remains elusive and her story incomplete. Hers was a life with holes in it and some bits will always be indecipherable, like the last line of the poster at the optician's, which I've never been able to make out.

This, then, is as close to 'as it is' as I can get; a portrait of my grandmother, my version of her several lives.

CHAPTER I

KISSY SMACKY

Sometimes she gives a jump in the hall
And speeds away to a phosphorescent land.
She feels like a dancing transparent ball,
And she spins round in a bright light, like a strand
Of golden card in the wind, or a top.

from 'Getting Away Only to Come Back',
J.A.E., 1928

Perhaps it was inevitable that my grandmother would spend her life absenting herself. Not running away exactly, but not quite belonging to the present she found herself in. It was a trait that those close to her came to find either irritating or sad. As she got older, she became harder to pin down, dreamy, disconnected.

In the first photograph I have of her, taken when she was about six months old, there is no suggestion of this. Round and serious, she sits propped against cushions, a bright-eyed baby wrapped in white, hands and feet emerging from swathes of gown and blanket. She could be anyone.

At two, wariness occupies her solemn face as she sits for another portrait, against a brocade curtain. She is solid, bored and potentially mutinous.

The next picture shows her self-conscious at six or seven, standing in a hallway in front of a grandfather clock. In a short, wide smock-dress and white calf-high socks, she does not really want to be there. Smiling nervously, weight coyly on one leg, she rests one hand on a toy bulldog, presumably instructed to do so by the photographer. Her other hand is slightly blurred, caught as she scratches her head at the last moment.

It is only in a photo taken when she is about ten or eleven years old that one begins to sense her becoming her own person. She has long, shiny hair in plaits tied with satin ribbon and looks directly at the camera. She is intelligent, intense and already slightly mysterious.

It was her mother, my great-grandmother, Gladys Ellen Easdale who first made it necessary for Joan to slide sideways to somewhere else. One cannot tell Joan's story without first telling hers, for she had so much influence over her daughter's development. Nor can one ignore my great-grandmother's own version of the past since it is her journals and memoir, *Middle Age*, that provide the only detailed account of her own and Joan's childhoods.

Ellen, who did not like to be called Gladys, was the youngest child in a large, eccentric middle-class family, growing up on the edge of Hampstead Heath at the end of the nineteenth century. Her father, the Reverend Walter Adeney, a devout and learned man, was a non-conformist minister and a professor of comparative religion. Her mother, Mary Hampton, was an independent and unconventional woman, a passionate traveller who, despite having eight children, had ventured as far as the Holy Land – she had a leaf from the Mount of Olives and a bottle of sand from the Desert of Arabia to prove it.

Religious and self-absorbed, the Adeneys inclined towards

Gothic drama, sharing a strong belief in ghosts and a tendency to whip one another up with thrilling fears. A particularly exciting family anecdote, told and retold to the children as absolute truth, described how their dead grandmother's ghost had walked through the kitchen and terrified the cook before going into their grandfather's room and having a conversation with him as he lay in bed. When they moved to a new house, Ellen's mother insisted she could smell burning flesh and hear the sound of a shovel scraping outside in the middle of the night. She also believed that the large portrait of Gladstone, which hung in the hall, had shown a 'psychic revelation' by developing a halo.

Ellen and her siblings – four brothers and two sisters – played as a big, noisy pack, running free on Hampstead Heath and charging up and down the staircases of the family home in North End. A favourite game involved one of the brothers pretending to be mad and chasing his siblings around the sofa, gibbering and screaming at them until they became hysterical.

None of them could go to sleep without first checking under the beds for burglars, and there were constant false alarms when both adults and children would become convinced that someone had got into the house. Armed with lamps and a poker, they would regularly creep downstairs to search the cellars, only to discover that the intruder was an owl, a faulty door or, on one occasion, a trailing dressing-gown cord.

The Reverend and Mrs Adeney were keen exponents of the outdoor life, and wheeled around Hampstead on an early tandem tricycle – a contraption consisting of two upholstered armchairs mounted on high wheels, which enabled the riders to steer, pedal and peel an apple at the same time. They would take their offspring out on rambles, cycle rides and picnics in Kent and Surrey, and for several years undertook ambitious camping trips. The entire family travelled in gypsy caravans and camped at the side of the road in three huge army tents. During these holidays – which might last a month – the Reverend Adeney would hold open-air Sunday services in whichever county they had stopped in, and the children would go to sleep on rolls of bracken, listening to nightjars. Ellen's love of nature and her passion for the countryside – which she, in turn, passed on to Joan – can be traced back to her parents and these blissful expeditions.

Her uninhibited sense of romance and self-indulgence were also traits Ellen inherited from her mother, a woman whose approach to life tended to be poetic rather than practical. Mary Adeney was prone to dark moods and terrible headaches, which would regularly confine her to bed. If she was displeased about something, she would not speak for two or three days at a time, keeping up what Ellen described to Joan as a 'black, gloomy, unbroken silence' and directing 'vibrations of hate' towards her children. Her sizeable family and the strains of being a minister's wife were no doubt enough to make her periodically depressed, or at least to seek refuge from the outside world. She became obsessed with the idea of building a rural retreat, and she spent considerable time looking for the perfect site. Out walking in Ashdown Forest one day, she fixed upon a pink cloud in the sky and followed it for two miles until it stopped above a field. This, she announced dramatically, was where she would live and die. She had a little house built on the exact spot and named it The Prelude, after Wordsworth's poem.

In 1903 Ellen's father was appointed resident principal of the Lancashire Independent College in Manchester, an establishment that provided education and training for non-conformist ministers, who were denied access to Oxford and Cambridge because of their beliefs. Much against their collective will, the Adeneys left London and moved north to take up a house within the college grounds, where family life soon became fused with the life and routines of the institution. Ellen and her sisters inevitably attracted attention from the students, whom they, in turn, professed to find both boring and inferior. The girls would flounce into the hall for morning prayers and sit demurely in their pretty frocks, only too aware of their captive and admiring audience, while their father gave his sermon for the day. The service over, they would flounce out again, chivalrous young men leaping up and falling over one another to get to the doors first.

It was at a musical evening held at the college that Ellen, now in her early twenties, met Robert Carse Easdale. Ten years her senior, Robert was an Irish dye salesman born in Belfast. His own childhood had been an unhappy one; his mother had died in childbirth and he had been brought up by a fiercely Calvinist aunt, whose beliefs were so literal, she had held his finger in the fire to teach him what the flames of hell would feel like. Feuds and rivalries had split the family; Robert saw little of his father, a former textile and dye manufacturer, who now lived like a hermit in a shed in the grounds of his ruined estate. The large house was used as a barracks, the surrounding park overgrown and the river running through it polluted by the factories he had built on its banks. A tall man with a long white beard, he would sit outside on a stone to receive visitors before retreating into the shack where his possessions totalled a bed, a chair, a table and a map.

According to Ellen's memoir, Robert was self-educated and well-read, an intense, romantic man with a beautiful singing voice. He courted Ellen conventionally, through concerts and poetry, but their relationship was sustained by brief secret meetings in the college grounds, where the couple spent their time together inventing an imaginary island. This elaborate shared fantasy, which involved a devised language and a complicated system of symbols, was a place to which they would 'send their spirits'. When Ellen was away on extended family holidays they would exchange long letters, detailing their spiritual meetings and adventures on the island, which had become the perfect distraction from actually getting to know one another. Although she had already had several suitors, fallen in love more than once and suffered the hurt of one beau breaking off an engagement, it seems that Ellen remained naive about men and marriage. Reading her version of events, one cannot help thinking that she was also flirtatious, easily flattered and unrealistic. She believed that, if Robert became her husband, married life would be a simple extension of their romantic games and of her privileged, happy childhood.

Founded on whimsy, the relationship soon became uncomfortably real. The couple were married by the Reverend Adeney on 6 June 1908, with Ellen still not entirely sure of her own feelings. They then travelled to Devon, where they stayed at an inn and endured an excruciating wedding night. According to Ellen's memoir, Robert ignored the elaborate supper laid out for them, refused to speak to her throughout the evening and became almost catatonic in the bedroom. They suffered in silence for the rest of the honeymoon.

Returning to Manchester, they settled into an ugly modern villa near her parents and Robert took a good job with a dye firm. This was not exactly how Ellen had imagined married life. It was in a state of shock and with little practical knowledge that she gradually worked out how to run her own house. She was so used to living in a family of ten – and so new to domestic tasks – that the first time she had to buy coal she ordered two tons of it; the delivery swamped the villa's little coal shed and she had to beg her parents to take most of it into their cellars for her.

Ellen and Robert appeared to have a great deal in common. They spent their time together playing chess, going for long walks or singing at the piano. To others, they seemed to be the perfect couple; attractive and talented, and soon the focus of a busy social circle, they were kept busy hosting musical soirées and play-readings in their front room. Privately, however, neither was happy or comfortable; once the music had stopped and the guests had gone home, they were incapable of communicating.

Ellen gave birth to a son, Brian, in 1909 and nearly died in the process. She had always been fragile and her health was further weakened by pregnancy and the delivery itself, which was both protracted and agonising. Brian was a sickly child, diagnosed with asthma at the age of two and kept under constant watch lest his condition deteriorate. Ellen struggled to keep him well, and her perpetually distracted state did nothing to help her failing marriage. When she asked for advice from a specialist, the doctor suggested she have a second child to act as Brian's companion. It was not certain that she would survive childbirth a second time but she went ahead, determined that the new baby would be friend and guardian for her precious son. Joan Adeney Easdale, my grandmother, was born on 23 January 1913.

The marriage, meanwhile, had become mired in suspicion, fear and misunderstanding. Robert was extremely emotional and, although kind and gentle at times, was likely to weep a lot, lapse into prolonged dark silences or explode with sudden rage. He became bitterly jealous of any contact between Ellen and other men, at one point insisting she burn a gift of autumn branches sent by a male friend and later forcing her to terminate her close platonic friendship with the much older William Hale White (who wrote as Mark Rutherford). Ellen, who was naturally flirtatious, seemed unable to reassure her husband that these attachments were entirely innocent. She had always been sheltered and petted as the youngest in her family and was now at a loss in the face of Robert's violent mood swings. Her health suffered and she took to running off with the children to stay with her family whenever she could.

No record of Robert's side of the story survives; even as an adult Joan had trouble persuading her relations to talk about him. Was he an alcoholic? Was he physically violent? Was he mentally ill? My own guess is that he could have been a combination of all three. What is certain is that he and Ellen were totally mismatched and struggled miserably to make their marriage work. The situation was not helped by both Easdale children suffering illnesses that necessitated long periods of recuperation in southern England, leaving Robert alone in Manchester, where he became paranoid, lonely and increasingly hostile.

Ellen and Robert eventually decided to separate in about 1916, when Joan was three years old and Brian seven. They would never be divorced – Robert did not believe in divorce, presumably for religious reasons – but the break was final. Ellen and the children moved to London and a legal arrangement was drawn up whereby Robert could visit the children once a year. He would stay in a nearby guesthouse and see them during the day, but it seems that this arrangement did not last long.

Remaining in Manchester, Robert became increasingly peculiar and more and more interested in spiritualism. His sister later told Joan that he would occasionally come round to her house for a game of chess. After the game he would sit in the garden for a long time with his eyes closed and, if asked what he was doing, he would calmly reply that he was 'mostly in the other world'. He emigrated to San Francisco in 1936 and Joan never saw him again.

In her memoir, Ellen claims that she was able to achieve the split without the children realising what was happening. She formally told them about it three years later and believed that they had come through the experience completely unscathed. But this was wishful thinking on her part; while they might not have understood the details of the separation, they were only too aware of the pain and disruption it caused. In a letter written when she was eighty-two, Joan could still recall her early confusion and distress at losing her father:

> I remember in my own case, when as a two or three year old, I used to run to the front door in our new home (in Hampstead Way) if there was a knock at the front door, thinking, 'Who's that – is it Daddy? Yes – it's probably Daddy – he must be arriving home from work – or come to see me and my brother.'

Robert was rarely referred to, and then only as a demonic figure who had been cruel to Ellen and wished the three of them ill. Servants were instructed to intercept letters and to reinforce this image of him. It was hoped that both children would gradually forget him altogether, but Robert's absence was a source of unhappiness to Joan well into her adult life and she would eventually come to question whether he had really been as bad as her mother insisted. She never forgave Ellen for his departure.

For much of their childhood, Joan and Brian lived with their mother in a house in Hampstead Garden Suburb, where they had the run of the communal garden. Their Adeney cousins lived a short drive away and there were constant games and activities, holidays to the seaside and trips to the theatre. Ellen had been left four thousand pounds by an uncle, which was topped up to five thousand by her mother so that her share would equal that of her brothers. This meant she had enough money to live independently and could employ some domestic help. Exhausted, yet relieved, by the break-up of her marriage, she was happy to stay in London, even when the air raids of the First World War came so close that her bedroom door blew in and a hole was knocked through the neighbours' wall. According to her memoir, the children would race to the windows to watch flashes of gunfire and falling bombs and Joan would long for one to fall in their own garden so that they could go and look at it.

They spent a lot of time with Ellen's side of the family. As an old woman, Joan would recall long summers among uncles and aunts and grandparents, whose large houses were packed with treasures and smelt of tiger skins.

As their mother had hoped, Joan became both a friend and a protector for Brian and had a strong sense of responsibility for him from early on. The children spent hours together, inventing games and languages, dressing up, putting on plays and articulating a cast of twenty-three soft toys, who became part of their daily life for many years. Ellen recalls a few of these creatures in *Middle Age*: Colin the big bear; Trotsey the white cat ballet dancer; Benjamin and Lucy, two naughty monkeys dressed and wigged by Joan; Philip the paralysed, hysterical bear from Brighton who had to be put out on the steps in a shoebox for sun treatment and who suffered screaming fits and Jemima Apocrypha Allah the wise philosopher ape. Each of these creatures had a defined character and history, and each was absolutely real to the children. No meal was served without several of them sitting at the table and they would take it in turns to join family holidays and trips to the ballet. They even read a specially produced weekly newspaper.

In addition to this menagerie, Brian and Joan were obsessed by an equally real array of imaginary creatures. There were the Swon-gars, gushing, dramatic beings who would mass on the horizon and commentate in an excited throng. One referred to them with the stress on the second syllable, with slightly popping-out eyes and one's mouth dropped open – 'Aaah! The Swon-gars!' Then there were the Schoolshes, sad, wispy, gliding things that lived in the shadows and wept. At fourteen, Joan wrote a poem entitled 'An Attempt to Explain What a Schoolsh Is', describing how these animals slipped through abandoned orchards and hung about people's houses, crying because they would only die if let inside:

> Schoolshes are made up of feeling,
> But they are never joyful
> Because they can never finish
> Anything that they try to do;
> Everything is unaccomplished.
> They choose to go in the dark
> Against anything pale or white,
> For then they are not easily seen
> As they are so pale themselves.

Joan was still writing poems about Schoolshes when she was seventeen, an indication of how the imaginative world she shared with her brother survived well beyond the normal limits of childhood. It was more than just play and fantasy; their games provided an essential escape from sadness, tedium and the constant attentions of their mother.

From the beginning, Ellen was convinced that her son and daughter were special and felt that it was her duty to bring their genius to light. She believed that she had passed on to them her own deep passion for music and poetry as they lay in the womb and that the bright star she had watched through the window during Brian's difficult birth had been a cosmic indication of his brilliance.

She encouraged them both in the arts, reading and music, but her treatment of the two children was quite different. Brian was enrolled in the choir school at Westminster Abbey, while Joan received very little formal education. Brian became a soloist, was pushed through his music exams and encouraged to participate in every school activity. Joan, in contrast, was given plenty of books to read and occasional haphazard tutorship in 'some of the Rudolf Steiner education' from an uncle when they visited him on holiday. Remembering this in her eighties, she described it as 'very gentle and very expensive at the same time', adding that '[Uncle] Cuthbert used to talk a lot about "the id"'.

Why this traditional division between the education of son and daughter? Ellen was not normally guided by convention. She had attended school herself – and loved it – and her own mother's attitude had always been relatively enlightened when it came to treating her girls and boys equally. However, it seems clear that Ellen did not see the schooling of her own children as an automatic right. Rather, it was something to be bestowed at her discretion, and she no doubt would have justified her decision to treat her son and daughter differently on the grounds that they had differing characters and constitutions. Brian, her favourite, was the oldest, a boy and had a clear talent from a very young age. (At two years old he would conduct his aunt in time as she played the piano and would demand to stand on a chair and lead any band playing in the park.) Ellen adored him and their relationship was simple; his success was a source of pride and a reflection upon her. Joan provoked a far more complicated reaction. Her mother's impulse was to promote her yet simultaneously hold her back. Ellen over-identified with Joan, appearing glad when her daughter's life mirrored her own but resenting her for where she was different. Not giving her a proper education was part of the complex series of rewards and punishments she meted out according to her own emotional needs. She was probably unconscious of what she was doing and might well have claimed that her actions were based on solid maternal instinct, but one cannot help seeing her motives as selfish. On a very basic level, Ellen was afraid of being left behind. Under the guise of concern for her daughter's health, she ensured that Joan would remain her companion for as long as possible; she would not outstrip her mother in terms of knowledge or capability and she would not fall under the influence of any other adults for some time.

Joan's childhood was dogged by illness and the restrictions imposed by her mother in order to prevent it. As Ellen herself confessed, she was always convinced that anyone ill was about to die, a fear she claimed to have inherited from her own parents at a very early age. She had been born while her mother was still grieving for another daughter and she believed that she had felt 'the anguished beat of her suffering heart' from within the womb.

Determined that Joan was weak, Ellen would wrap her up in layers of mufflers and shawls, even when she was completely healthy or the weather quite warm. And her ministrations were not always gentle. Once, when Joan was little and had a high temperature, her mother insisted she be wrapped in sheets soaked in boiling hot water to draw the fever out. Joan screamed so loudly during this process that the maid refused to continue with it.

Another destructive aspect of Ellen's behaviour was her readiness to cancel treats and excursions at the last minute, in case Joan found them too much of a strain. The resulting emotional whiplash – of promised pleasure followed by bitter disappointment – was a pattern Joan became used to but always resented. She was unable to relax and enjoy things because she never knew when they might be taken away.

The most wounding of these changes of mind occurred when

Joan was about eight years old. A talented dancer from a very young age, she had begged for ballet lessons and Ellen had finally taken her for an audition with the renowned Italian master, Enrico Cecchetti. Cecchetti had been one of the greatest dancers of the nineteenth century; he had trained Diaghilev's Ballets Russes, been private tutor to Pavlova and taught Nijinsky. Now in his seventies, he was one of the most sought-after ballet teachers in Europe and professional dancers would flock to his studio in Shaftesbury Avenue. On seeing Joan dance, he proclaimed her advanced for her age and told her mother, through an interpreter, that she should start classes at his school the following week. However, once the initial brush with fame was over, Ellen decided that the daily journey from Hampstead would be too tiring for a fragile child and she cancelled the lessons before they had begun.

Joan was devastated. Not only did she long to be a dancer but she had also secretly hoped that this would be a way of meeting her father again, imagining that he might come to the ballet one evening and see her perform by chance. She would dance brilliantly, he would recognise her on stage and, overcome with pride and love, he would seek her out after the show.

Whether Ellen's decision was based on a genuine concern for her daughter's health or was just another impulsive unkindness, the crushing disappointment had a lasting effect. Ten years later, Joan wrote a poem entitled 'A Sadness':

> The infinite sadness that barred my heart,
> And that which tied my arms and feet
> So I might not dance,
> Was dark, like a velvet flower and sweet
> As one with petals torn apart
> Left to die in a summer rain.

Even as an old woman she could not forgive Ellen for her decision and her anger was still raw when she talked to me about it in the late eighties.

She spoke too of her mother's constantly changing affections – one minute kind, the next hard – which meant that Joan could never predict her reactions or feel entirely secure. 'Kissy smacky' was how she described her.

Once, as Ellen was returning home from buying a special dress for Joan to wear to a party at a doctor's house, Joan came running out to greet her in the rain, thereby pre-empting the grand entrance and revelation. Ellen immediately told her that she could not go to the party after all, saying that it was her own fault and that she should have stayed inside and not spoilt the surprise.

Another time, she egged Joan on to write a nasty letter to one of her friends, urging her to be as insulting and outrageous as possible. Ellen then insisted she post it. Hearing the envelope drop into the post box, Joan realised with horror that this was not just a thrilling game, that her friend was actually going to read what she had written. It was only once Joan had worked herself up into tearful hysterics of guilt and dread that Ellen suggested they waylay the postman and ask him to give the letter back.

In the spring of 1926, when Joan was thirteen and Brian seventeen, Ellen bought a house in Crouch, a small village near Sevenoaks, and the family moved to rural Kent. Set back from the road in its ample garden, Crouch Farm House was solid and atmospheric, with space enough for Brian's two pianos in the living room. Surrounded by hop-fields and orchards, Ellen felt she was making a completely new start. She was about forty years old by this time, and in the throes of a love affair with a mycologist called Professor Ernest Salmon. Over a decade older than her, he had featured as an exciting figure in her childhood, smouldering darkly from beneath a hat and reading poetry aloud on country walks. The age difference had kept them apart, although he had voiced his sadness at her marriage, and had since been involved with her sister Hilda. Now that Ellen was separated from her unsuitable husband, they found an intense spiritual understanding and became lovers.

Professor Salmon had spent many years at Kew Gardens and was now a fellow of Wye College, the University of London's School of Agriculture in Kent, where he worked on developing hop strains and studied, among other things, celery blight and apple scab. He would travel up to London and whisk Ellen and the children out on glamorous treats or take her alone for trips into the countryside.

The Professor became a regular visitor to Crouch Farm House, spending most weekends and holidays there, planting the garden with bulbs and exotic flowers from all over the world. It was an unconventional set-up but Ellen refused his proposals of marriage – she knew that Robert would not contemplate divorce and she did not want to hurt her sister's feelings by making her unofficial relationship public. She cast her wedding ring into a lake, took the Professor into her home and decided to concentrate on the future.

Ellen and her children spent most of their waking hours together, talking or walking or presenting work to one another. She not only believed in their unique brilliance – 'both B & J have the mind of the Mystic & can see & know & hear what very few can' – but she insisted they show it off. Tireless in getting her children noticed, Ellen chased contacts, encouraged them to write letters and threw numerous musical parties. Their private puppet shows became public performances, Brian's piano playing became concert material and Joan's plays and poems were read aloud to visitors at every opportunity. She also ensured their continuing literary education by filling the house with books; boxes of volumes would arrive from Tunbridge Wells and they would spend whole evenings reading aloud to one another from Blake, the Brontës, Housman, Hardy, Lawrence and T. S. Eliot.

Ellen had always thought she might end up as a writer herself, having often been told in her youth that she looked like a writer. 'I don't know why,' she wrote in her memoirs, 'but all these older men who became my friends seemed to think I would become another famous writer – I can't explain it – I had a large brow and did my hair in the middle and wrote stories to amuse myself and read a lot.' The idea that one's hairstyle had as much sway over one's literary development as one's reading seems typical of Ellen's peculiar affectedness. Yet her literary activities cannot be dismissed entirely. *Middle Age* was published by Constable and she would go on to write two novels, one of which – *Don't Blame the Stars* – she had published by the Fortune Press under the name Francis Adoney.

At Crouch in the early thirties, however, Ellen's energies were channelled into her daughter's writing, and she was convinced there was a direct connection between Joan and the spirit of some Literary Great. She described in her journal how, in the middle of the night, shortly after Joan's conception, she had woken to see the figure of a man leaving her bed, having sexually possessed her unconscious body only minutes before: '. . . one wonders – wonders over so many things – one is half aware of, half conscious of mystic things – Could some spirit form have conceived in me the spirit life of Joan – the life of her genius?'

Likewise, she thought that her own intense love of music had filtered through to the unborn Brian, and that both her children were visited by the spirits of literary and musical figures who would somehow inspire them from within. The Adeney belief in psychic phenomena was clearly as strong as ever; when Brian was reading

D. H. Lawrence's poems in 1931, with a view to setting them to music, Ellen wrote of his virtual possession by the writer: 'Did Lawrence get under the eaves of his brow? It seems like it.'

The truth was that both children were genuinely talented. Brian was a gifted composer and wrote his first opera, *Rapunzel*, at the age of seventeen. Three years later his *Death March* was performed by the London Symphony Orchestra, conducted by Malcolm Sargent. His mother's belief in him was well-founded; he would go on to become a well-known composer of film scores and win an Oscar in 1949 for the music to Powell and Pressburger's *The Red Shoes*.

Similarly, Joan was intensely creative, a good self-taught artist and a shrewd observer of those around her. She was constantly inventing stories, writing poems and drawing pictures. One of her sketchbooks survives from the Crouch Farm House days and is now in Reading University Library, left to posterity by her forward-thinking mother. Packed with drawings, it shows Joan's considerable range. She drew the everyday things she saw around her at Crouch – a silver birch tree, a glass of flowers, 'Brian lying in weird position on settle' and 'Carpenter looking at a dead swallow'. These straight pencil drawings appear alongside careful, precocious pictures of fashionable ladies in frocks, girls called Harriet and Phyllis languidly toying with their beads, figures who might sit happily in *Punch*.

And then there is something entitled 'The Scandal Sheet of Zony Delaras', a series of caricatures of society types, their portraits in watercolour above paragraphs of gossip. This acidic collection features the faintly moustachioed Miss Frances Hencock, a lesbian novelist; the suavely popular actor Maurice Tranker (star of *Love in a Tool-shed*) who appears to have murdered his main rival; Stavia Glandinia, a wild poetess whose latest shock tactic is to get married; a boxer who regularly beats up his wife; a young composer called Vaf

Gungza who keeps over two hundred pigs and is beginning to look like one himself; and an illegitimate black child who cannot be hushed up. These sketches are both juvenile and knowing, and show how alert Joan was to the hypocrisies and complications of the adult world.

Her drawing book is also scattered with doodles; funny little angular figures jump across the page, Blake-like naked bodies dance beneath stars, a woman with an impossible squint demands 'Look me in the eyes!'

Among these, two sketches stand out as suddenly less playful; 'Dire Terror', a man's grimacing face, and a picture of a young girl kneeling, head in hands, labelled 'They will not understand'.

Ellen's insistence on being so deeply involved with her adolescent offspring's lives is both touching and repellent. In some ways, she was simply revelling in their talents, enjoying their early success and anticipating an exciting future in which they would achieve public recognition. Having struggled to bring up two sickly children alone at a time when separation was not socially accepted, she was now able to relax and enjoy their company. On the other hand, she had no particular activity of her own with which to balance her interest in Joan and Brian. Nor did her relationship with the man she called her 'spiritual husband' last: after a miserable period of rows and tension, Professor Salmon moved out in 1930. Released from what she described as 'the prison bars of the ego', Ellen was now completely free to concentrate on Brian and Joan.

This of course meant that the children were under even greater pressure to provide their mother with companionship and entertainment. They were her project, as she confirmed in her journal in 1931: 'Both of them busy with their creations – and I – I with mine – after all B and J were created by me!' In her diary she admitted to spying on Brian through a chink in the door-jamb as he conducted to a gramophone record. This was clearly not an isolated incident; Joan wrote a short poem when she was sixteen, describing being watched in a very similar way:

> A little black eye
> Came to spy
> Through the crack in the door.
> What did it see?
> You and me
> Sitting upon the floor.

Under these circumstances, how could Joan and Brian grow up normally?

As adults they would become highly critical of their mother, but Ellen's own diaries admit to very little conflict. In her view, the three of them shared an idyllic existence where poetry and music flowed against a background of rural delights. They walked most days, tramping through the woods and fields surrounding Crouch village, picking armfuls of primroses and bluebells in the spring, resting on hayricks in summer, gathering fruit and berries in the autumn. They were passionate about the landscape and soon knew every copse, stream and path within range of the house.

This went beyond a simple enjoyment of the countryside. It was an immersion and belief in Nature as a moral good, a version of the eighteenth-century Romantic idealism they read about in the poets, something that verged on religious worship. The landscape, the seasons, the country people were all imbued, for Ellen, with an innate spiritual power. She and the children steeped themselves in any rural experience, unashamedly swooning like Keats and Shelley when the fancy took them. When the thyme was out on the Downs they lay in it until drowsy; on clear nights they star-gazed or walked by the light of the moon. Ellen even recorded how, early one August morning, Joan went straight from bed to roll naked in the dew-soaked grass of the orchard.

The search for 'authenticity' was something deeply entrenched in the Adeney family culture. In 1951, Joan would describe her grandmother's travels as a quest for acceptance 'in the shepherd's hut on the mountain side or in the gallant smile of the robber or among strangers in a hotel lounge'. Ellen, like her mother, was fascinated by gypsies, believing that their way of life made them truly free. In her journal, she describes walking with Joan through a travellers' encampment, awed and envious, stopping to hear the fiddler play and being transported by his music. Similarly, she would rhapsodise about farmhands sowing seed or cutting hay – she relished their strength and the way they took their time – and she often referred to the liberating simplicity of their lives. Joan absorbed her mother's admiration for and envy of 'real people' from very early on. Decades later, she would actively seek them out and attempt to join them herself.

Much of Ellen's diary-keeping consisted of breathless descriptions of sunsets, trees and views, and her joy at simply looking at them. In April 1931 she described picking white violets and being overcome with rapture: '"O!" I cried, "I can't bear it – it's too lovely. I don't think I can go on."' A month later she wrote of being in a fruit orchard: '. . . all this so ravishingly beautiful – the scent of the cherry blossom giving one far more ecstasy and excitement than any lover's kiss in all the world. No, I know now absolutely and convincingly that Nature is my deepest, truest love, that from communion with Nature I get all my great happiness – and all I want and all I need . . .'

The passages verge on the preposterous but the Easdales seem to have enjoyed a complete lack of self-consciousness. Who knows what the village made of them, this trio of bohemian outsiders, who galloped about in strange clothes and put on puppet operas in the village hall. On one occasion they even borrowed an enormous Victorian bath chair from a neighbouring farmer so that Joan, invalided by a wasp sting to her thigh, might not miss out on the family constitutional and could be pushed through the country lanes by her brother.

Although the Easdales were not at all well off (and at one point had to resort to painting china to make ends meet) it is clear from the journals that life at Crouch was packed with activity and social events. Ellen loved to have the house full of young people and Brian's musical friends were regular visitors up from London. The composer Herbert Murrill and the pianist Norman Franklin were among those who would come to work on scores or to practise for hours on end on the two pianos. Joan's close friend Geoffrey Dunn also spent a lot of time at the house. He was a singer and collaborated with her on various projects, including *TB* – an operetta in one act about a consumptive. Birthdays were celebrated with home-made damson wine and piles of food. They drank beer at local pubs, visited friends' houses for supper and dances and indulged in fancy dress whenever they could.

Ellen threw several notable parties at Crouch Farm House. Brian's twenty-first birthday party in the summer of 1931 was particularly memorable, '. . . with its 50 guests & his 6 young men friends & Joan's 2 girl friends . . . Herbert Murrill playing Jazz opera on the piano in the orchard that warm afternoon & we lying about, the day after the party, resting under the plum trees.'

It was on this occasion that the general manservant Goodenough was packed off to the woods to search for glow-worms, in the hope that he would find about two hundred – enough to light up the garden for the evening. He returned with just two.

A few weeks after this, a musical evening with over thirty guests filled the house. Ellen's description of the event gives an idea of just how bizarre some of her acquaintances were:

> . . . [there were] people sitting on the floor and on the stairs, strange unusual people – 'Paddy' who arrived with her galaxy of young poets and an actor and sinister Dr/Mr Strauss with his great eye glass measuring up the proportions and figures of people to compare them with his lunatics – and his hypnotic sinister face (for he hypnotises) looking round all of us – Paddy clasping my hand and whispering absurdly to me about him and 'my perfect form'. Christopher Christian, a young poet like Shelley with his Great Grandfather's marvellous cloak, sitting on the floor with his back to everyone and two light candles beside him – absorbed in listening to the Bach.

Ellen found her guests completely thrilling – and the weirder the better. She continued,

> . . . the French family Petit Pierre's feeling ghosts all over the house . . . taking out their crosses they always wear to protect them from the supernatural, telling me wherever I am, spirits will be – as if I trailed ghosts after me like the train of my garment. Rex looking strange and dark and sinister too – and Celtic Mary Stanley Smith, the friend of the Irish poets, exclaiming, when introduced to the French boys – she saw forms on their heads and their cloven hooves and ears sticking out and Mary Payne and I seeing all this revealed as she told us . . . and Brian looking beautiful and in good form and music – music – on and off all the time – and Joan reading her poems to Brian's music . . . Mary P. said she never was at a party so electric with Personalities.

The Easdales clearly accepted the supernatural as part of everyday life, in parallel with both their belief in Nature and a low-level Christianity. Ellen was convinced that one of the rooms upstairs at Crouch was haunted, and she regularly 'felt' auras and 'sensed' the past in certain buildings. Describing the end of an evening spent at a neighbour's house in September 1931, she wrote, 'Before we left, Frida [Brian's girlfriend] gave a little cry – she saw the ghost of a little child in white pass quickly by her in the hall – and Joan, without knowing this, a little later said – 'I saw in my imagination a man in brown tweeds standing by the door – the house seems full of ghosts this evening, all moving about.'

Spiritualism was highly popular at the time, but whether they ever went as far as attending seances, I don't know. It was more that their awareness of spirits leant a frisson of excitement, a dark edge and a complexity to life. There were fewer boundaries – it was not a complete surprise for the living to have sightings of the dead or for odd things to happen to everyday objects. One of Joan's poems, written at sixteen, is called 'Phenomena':

> In the darkness hovered many things,
> Pale illuminations, rushing wings.
> Heavy tallboys creaked, and tables knocked,
> A plate cracked, and the wardrobe rocked.

This might be a description of a seance but it is more likely an impression of what the house felt like at night. Crouch was cluttered with Victorian objects – old umbrellas, china, dark pieces of furniture – and for Joan they seemed to acquire energies and characters of their own. Her imagination enjoyed the crossing point between reality and something more intense and more frightening. My mother recalls that, as an adult, Joan could make a puppet out of anything; a plastic bag blowing across the street would immediately become a person, rubber gloves skipped and danced. As an eighteen-year-old, Joan wrote a poem entitled 'Chintz', in which a young girl walks around in the landscape of the sofa fabric:

> Alas, it's almost ten years since
> Tabitha went for walks in the chintz.
> The sofa-cover has faded now
> And the fruit has gone from every bough
> That once was rich with pear or quince.
> She used to climb the dark green trees
> And, stretching out, gather these;
> And then she'd run in case a bird
> With purple plumage might have heard.
> Once she went and plucked them all
> And tied them up in her little shawl,
> But as she ran through yellow flowers,
> Past Grecian urns and bosky bowers,
> She heard the rush of wings outspread –
> The bird had seen her as she fled!
> Soft shafts of sunlight in between
> The shadowed leaves of glaucous green
> Revealed no fruits for him to eat,
> With shiny skins and juices sweet:
> And so he chased with pointed beak,
> Flapping feathers, and furious shriek,
> The little girl from the sofa-chintz.
> And Tabitha's never walked there since.

An 'ordinary' perspective was irrelevant.

Of all their gatherings, Brian's Party of the Midsummer Fires was the most spectacular, recorded in Ellen's journal in July 1933. It was held in Oxonheath Park, about three miles' walk from the village, and the Easdales gathered for a late drink at their favourite pub, the Artichoke, beforehand. They then threw themselves into the pagan drama of an event which characteristically teetered on the verge of farce:

Joan had made a Tata man, which she had chiselled out of a block of Silver birch, and an angel man, life size, strange and haunting like a Medieval ghost . . . These were the sacrifices in the Great Bonfire – we all trooped up to the spot and lit it – Then the rites and revelry began – Besoms dipped in paraffin were handed to the dozen folk there, and dipped into the flames they flamed like torches –

They danced in a circle round and then the angel man amongst wild cries was flung on the furnace and next they jumped the fire, each young one – then the Great Cartwheel Brian had tarred and they had covered with straw was set alight at the top of the hill and blazing the young men ran with it, but it fell over and then Brian became as a triumphant Greek hero – he took hold of the pole alone and raced with it flaming like a Catherine Wheel, keeping it under amazing control and balance until it fell into the fire – more wild cups and dancing and then the Tata man was placed in the flames and beat with the besoms – after this, dances were done by each of them and then we all circled round eating off a great basket of fruit . . . and Brian played his pipe and taught us old, old songs to sing about the crops – and we all sang and sang and sang and this went on until after midnight . . .

One of the recurring themes in Ellen's diaries is how happy the three of them were when together back at Crouch, tired after shopping up in town or after a party. She liked to shut the world out and reiterate how they only needed one another. It was difficult for Joan and Brian to contradict her. Years later Brian admitted to his daughter that he would go to the local pub, the Chequers, with its buzz of conversation and darts matches, just to feel like a normal person and to escape the claustrophobia of being at home. He described his embarrassment at having to perform to 'ladies in hats', the sense of not feeling ordinary, of being on show and the constant pressure of having to be perfect. Always the favourite child, he was often the focus of Ellen's anxiety, especially when he was preparing for an exam or concert. She would insist on being both practically and emotionally involved at every step, which usually only complicated the situation. When Sir Henry Wood rejected a score that Brian had submitted for the Proms in the summer of 1931, Ellen described her own disappointment as a kind of grief and declared how 'brave' Brian was being in the face of this 'injustice'. Thus he not only had the routine rejection to deal with but his mother's tearful histrionics as well.

For Joan it was even more difficult to maintain a sense of privacy and a sense of self. Brian was up at the Royal College of Music for much of the week and he was older and male, which meant he was automatically granted more freedom. He also had a girlfriend, Frida Niklaus, whom he had met at the college and spent much of his time with.

Joan, on the other hand, was her mother's closest friend and confidante – they even shared a bedroom – and her notebooks, poetry and diary were all open to maternal scrutiny and comment. As we only have Ellen's side of this part of the story, it is difficult to work out how much Joan resented this at the time. On the surface, she seems to have been happy enough. She loved the countryside, enjoyed the life they shared and was touchingly keen to please other people. Photographs of her at Crouch suggest a girl of great innocence. In one she sits under an apple tree with Brian and her friend Geoffrey Dunne, clutching her knees and laughing at something her brother has just said; in another she stands on a promontory on the Kent coast, staring out to sea in a billowing cotton dress. As an adult, however, she would eventually protest against the role forced upon her by her mother and claim to have found it an unbearable responsibility to be, as she saw it, the guardian of Ellen's emotional welfare.

Uncomfortable in the face of her daughter's encroaching adolescence, Ellen sought to preserve Joan's childhood for as long as possible, as if this might stall change and keep them happily at Crouch for ever. If one were to rely solely on Ellen's descriptions of her at seventeen and eighteen, one might imagine Joan to be a placid and saintly creature, the 'dear, good industrious child' of her mother's journals. She is regularly caught in lamplight, working on her poems 'with exceeding care and devotion, like at the most exquisite piece of sampler'. Her hair was parted in the middle and dressed in two long plaits or drawn back like a Victorian girl's, in the style that Ellen herself had always worn as a child (and which she had been persuaded made her look like Elizabeth Barrett Browning). Joan's clothes were simple and shapeless, mainly frocks she made herself out of curtain lining or off-cuts. And because Ellen was constantly afraid that Joan might catch a chill, she insisted she wear cotton wadding around her waist, which filled in any womanly curves and gave her body a rather lumpen outline. (According to family legend, she was still wearing this binding in her twenties when, on discovering what the padding was, her incredulous flatmates unravelled her from it, setting her free with shrieks of laughter.)

Typically, on a rare occasion when Joan was invited alone to a neighbour's party, the hosts reported back in such detail to Ellen that she was able to write about the evening as if she had been there herself: '[Joan] in her simple spotted muslin frock made by herself for B's birthday party, only costing 10/- . . . it turned out she created a sensation by just being her sweet simple self all amongst very up-to-date young men and women who sat in the dark and flirted outrageously and discussed artificial creation.'

Joan was repeatedly cast as the gauche observer, sitting at the edge of a group and watching everyone else. If this was her natural tendency, then Ellen seemed to reinforce it. In December 1931, when Joan had returned exhausted and tearful from a tea dance where there were not enough men to go round and Brian's girlfriend Frida had snubbed her, her mother wrote, 'No – life does not intend her to have flowers, chocolates, be asked out to restaurants and enjoy the ordinary dance . . . the ordinary everyday things that she wants and I want her to have, are always a humiliation and disappointment.'

On her twenty-first birthday, when the dressing-up box came out and everyone picked a costume, Joan appeared in a white crinoline, garlanded with roses and forget-me-nots, as a kind of Little Bo-Peep character, the epitome of childhood innocence. It was on this occasion, the celebration of her daughter's coming of age, that Ellen chose to read the manuscript of her own memoir to the assembled throng. The birthday meal over, she was encouraged by some of the guests who wanted to hear a sample of what she had written. Typically unaware that this might not make for an altogether riveting evening, she read the entire book out loud. She later wrote up the event in her journal, having clearly relished every minute: 'To my surprise it amuses everyone who listens . . . It took hours and hours to read . . .'

Thus, even at her own twenty-first birthday party, Joan was not allowed to occupy centre stage for very long.

Although Ellen repeatedly claimed that her overriding desire was to secure Joan's well-being and success, I cannot help thinking that she would not have been able to cope with her daughter's complete happiness. Certainly, she seemed to greet any social setback suffered by Joan with a combination of distress and relief.

As to Joan's writing, however, they were both determined that it would reach a wider audience. When she was seventeen, my grandmother sent some of her poems to Leonard and Virginia Woolf at the Hogarth Press.

CHAPTER 2

A VERY YOUTHFUL POETESS
IN HER GARDEN

A goldfinch splashed in the vase
As the echoing voice of Mamma's
Came hootingly out from the balcony
Where the company chattered in glee.

from 'In the Bower', J.A.E., 1930

The Hogarth Press had started as a tiny enterprise, operating from the basement of the Woolfs' house in 1917. By the time Joan submitted her poems nearly a decade and a half later, the Woolfs had moved from Richmond to Bloomsbury and no longer used a hand-press to print the books themselves. Their criteria for publication, however, remained the same; they published material that interested them, often by writers who had been ignored or thought too risky a proposition by other publishing houses. Their list included Vita Sackville-West, C. Day Lewis and William Plomer; how would a teenage girl strike them?

Piecing together evidence from Ellen's diaries, Virginia Woolf's letters and half a letter written by Joan in 1937, it appears that some of Joan's poems were straightforward verses she had written as herself. Others, bizarrely, she had written in character, as a woman she called Garrie Chutneygrove. Where this name came from or why Joan chose to write in the persona of a wild, middle-aged virgin goat-keeper remains a mystery, but it definitely got her noticed. Woolf immediately wanted to meet her, and by October 1930 the Hogarth Press had decided that they would publish her poems. 'The girl poet is my discovery,' announced Virginia in a letter to Hugh Walpole in April 1931, 'she sent me piles of dirty copy books written in a scrawl without any spelling; but I was taken aback to find, as I thought some real merit.' Woolf was not entirely sure where this discovery might lead but was intrigued by Joan and her unlikely background; 'it may be a kind of infantile phosphorescence; and she is a country flapper, living in Kent, and might be from behind a counter. Very odd.'

Like her drawings, Joan's poems are a strange mixture. Some are the playful verbal equivalent of her doodles:

> She was in love with a window-cleaner,
> So every piece of wash-leather
> Made her heart beat keener.
> She was in love with a window-cleaner,
> So she walked under every ladder,
> For doing this he first had seen her.

Others are sharply observed vignettes of middle-class life, as seen by a precocious younger person trapped indoors with dreary relations (no doubt written from first-hand experience of her visits to the more elderly Adeneys);

> They sat in a gloomy morning-room,
> Dusting What-nots and reading Longfellow
> From a leather volume, with dowdy shamrock
> Put in certain faded pages

To mark Aunt Gwenda's favourite lines.
'This is the one,' said Simon licking his thumb
As he came to a pencil-ticked lyric,
'Now listen Emma, dearie,
For this was your Grandmother's-step-daughter's
Child's favourite one of all.'
And he read it aloud in a voice
As sacred as he could put on,
Until Emma's tears began to flow
On to her Uncle's carpet-slippers.
'There, there! How touched she is!'
Observed Aunt Gwenda eating dates from a silver
    dish.
'Just like her dear father as a boy,'
Remarked Sheila sighing as she picked
A piece of dust from the cat's ear.

Between these arch little verses lie poems whose titles alone suggest much darker preoccupations: 'Someone Dead', 'Putrid Pantry',
'One for Bedlam', 'Depression', 'The Lunatic'. Both eerily prescient
and horribly graphic, they are not the poems of a sweet-minded
child.

'The Mad City', written when Joan was fourteen, is short but
nightmarish;

Forty men ran tossing balls
Into shops and out of halls;
Women laughed and threaded
Necklaces of wood-lice.
Some cried 'We're level-headed!
So why think we are not?'

Ninety children screaming loud;
Thirty hags turned and bowed
To the leering mongrel-hounds.
'Madness! madness! we are sane!'
Yelled the terrors down the lane.

'The Curdled Waters Chimed' describes a young woman drowning while ordinary life goes on without her – a couple discuss their spare room, a group of suffragettes write notes on the back of laundry lists, a baby is born. The opening lines would come back to haunt her after Virginia Woolf's death:

The curdled water chimed
In her ears;
The tangled weeds slimed
Her face,
Like silver tears.
She trampled water down
With her feet;
The bubbles whispered 'drown . . .'
To her;
Her life lay nude . . .

Ellen appears to have been untroubled by the sinister undertow of Joan's work. Nor did she seem to register that her daughter had absorbed a considerable amount of domestic unhappiness in her short life. Having witnessed her parents' separation and the stormy break-up between Ellen and Professor Salmon, Joan was acutely aware of how miserable adults could make one another, as she demonstrated in the first poem of her collection:

Round the room walked the Duchess,
Looking at the perspiration gleaming
On her husband's brow.

'You must go,' said the battered Duke,
'Or I must; one of us must go.'

The Duchess lay down,
And from a satin solidity
Of cushions, frayed and golden,
She spoke of marriage
And all its madness.

'Then why did you accept me?'
Asked the Duke palely
From behind his curling pipe.

'Because I was young and ignorant,
Full of romance, and lingering smiles
For memories of dew-drenched pergolas.'
'So was I,' agreed the Duke faintly,
Stroking his blazened chin.
'My mind was full of souls,
And slumbering nightingales
And winding hair.'

The Duchess sat and mingled
With youth and sentimentality,
With one pink ankle slanting
From fawn silk and sombre tassles.

'And so you recall it too?' said she
From the shadows of her mind.

The Duke laughed rawly,
Like the selvedge-edge
Of a new piece of calico,
And smoothed his button-hole and said:

'I do. You do. In that we're alike.
Now who shall go, you or I?'
He looked expectantly
Through eyes like furrowed dates
At his wife, and at her pink ankle,
Which she angled, carefully baited.

'Both,' she said through pride-pinched lips,
And smoothed her drowsy hair.
And added, 'To Birmingham.'

The acceptance of her poems by Leonard and Virginia Woolf opened a door for Joan, who suddenly found herself part (albeit a very small part) of the literary scene. She was sent contracts to sign and proofs to correct, invited to tea at the Woolfs' house in Tavistock Square and asked what colour cover she would like for her book (she chose a cherry pink). A *Collection of Poems* (*Written between the ages of 14 and 17*) was published as No. 19 in the Hogarth Living Poets series on 12 February 1931. Four hundred copies were printed and the book was priced at four shillings and sixpence. Joan was incredibly happy; her work was out in the world and people were reading what she had written. She even had the satisfying experience of standing in her favourite bookshop in

Tunbridge Wells, eavesdropping while a man bought her poems and enquired about the author.

Ellen, meanwhile, was beside herself with pleasure. This was what she had been hoping for all along. On the day the first reviews came out, she dragged Joan round to see the neighbours so early they were not yet dressed.

Like Virginia Woolf, some critics were not entirely sure what they were dealing with and chose to hedge their bets. Clemence Dane, writing in the *Book Society News*, described the poems as 'astonishingly adroit, acute, accomplished' yet was slightly cagy in her conclusion, finishing with, 'If this gift of hers is not merely the May-fly dance of adolescence, Miss Easdale should have an exciting future.' The accompanying photograph, entitled 'A very youthful poetess in her garden', showed Joan glossy-haired and bare-armed, dancing demurely around a Victorian birdbath in a long white gown.

The review in the *Times Literary Supplement* of 30 July 1931 did not attempt to guess the future but praised the collection for what it was:

A great many people write poems between the ages of fourteen and seventeen, and it is not uncommon for these to be agreeable and mildly tuneful. But Miss Easdale's poems are sharp and sometimes even harsh, seldom in the least imitative: and they have the merit which we might expect but seldom find in the works of infant prodigies, for they express the pungent individuality of an unlearned mind.

The publication of her poems signalled a future for Joan that would eventually take her away from Ellen and the tightly cloistered existence they shared in Crouch. Although this day was still some way off, and Joan remained a naive, unworldly eighteen-year-old, the horizon was gradually opening up. There were further invitations to go to tea – alone – with the Woolfs, a trip to Sissinghurst as the guest of Vita Sackville-West, afternoons with the critics Clemence Dane (who bullied her, according to Ellen) and G. B. Stern (who didn't). The *Listener* printed a new poem of hers, the *Bookman* named her one of the five poets of the year and the *Spectator* praised her collection.

Responding to this interest, making trips up to London, attending talks and concerts, Joan began to venture beyond the confines of the Kentish country garden and find her feet in the outside world.

It cannot have been easy, however, negotiating this new territory with her mother always at her elbow, excited at every new development and anxious to read every piece of correspondence. Ellen was completely star-struck by Virginia Woolf, whom she saw as a kind of goddess. After the Woolfs had visited Crouch for the first time in September 1931, she wrote in her journal:

> . . . I did not want to speak or listen or see anyone else – and it's not to be wondered at – is it – when one is with one of the Great Ones – one of the Greatest who – and I will dare to say it – one links in one's mind with Jane Austen and Shakespeare. She drifted through the garden – lingered a moment by the orchard and then they left – like some lovely floating cloud, she seemed to melt into the horizon – a limitless horizon, the kind of horizon that one's spirit seeks after – but her fragrance of spirit is still here in every room . . .

What Ellen did not realise was that Woolf found her silly and vain, and was often cruelly dismissive about her behind her back. When Woolf reported the same visit in a letter to Vita Sackville-

West, she seemed delighted to have found the Easdales as chaotic and shabby as she had hoped: 'The son writes music in one room. Joan writes poetry in another. They have meals whenever it takes their fancy – sometimes in the kitchen, sometimes in the bedroom.' She described Ellen as 'a lavish hospitable sloppy mother', the house as 'tumbledown' and the manservant as 'a half wit, who does all the housework . . . dressed in seedy black'. It was Joan she was interested in, and then as a young poet and an intriguing oddity rather than a friend. 'Joan is the mystery – She looks like a chocolate box flapper, talks like one, about how lovely the lilies are, and the sunset, and the dog, and the cat, and yet produces those strange poems.'

Unwittingly, Ellen (who had spent an entire day in preparation for the visit and was grateful that Virginia seemed to like the lemon cake) quickly became a hilarious figure to Woolf, who described her to Lady Cecil as 'an incredible goose and chatterbox but simple-minded and rather touchingly idiotic . . . now not notably attractive, either in body or mind'. In a letter to Quentin Bell she called her 'the mad woman Adeney'. But Ellen was so entranced that she detected nothing of her sarcasm. Even when Woolf made fun of her in person she remained entirely oblivious, as on the occasion at Rodmell (the Woolfs' Sussex home) when Virginia entertained the gathered company with a story about Ellen and Sir Henry Wood. Returning home afterwards, Ellen happily wrote it all down in her journal, blithely convinced that she had been the subject of a jolly, flattering story rather than the butt of a joke:

She [Virginia Woolf] brought up my interview with Sir Henry Wood, saying, 'She is the bravest woman I know – she went into a big restaurant straight up to Sir Henry who was sur-rounded by a crowd of ladies and said, "Sir Henry, my son is a genius"' . . . then she continued in that charming playful way of hers, 'You see, she has a son who is an unknown distinguished composer.'

Next she talked of the recital, the most interesting she had ever been to – that we were the most advanced family in the world – setting to music no-one else would dare and also the most modern of music – and all this carried on half serious, half humorous . . .

The few scattered references in Woolf's own diaries and correspondence suggest that she saw visits to and from the Easdales as something of an endurance test, that might bring on a headache and would certainly take up precious time and energy. While Ellen wrote, 'One of our Great Days! Virginia Woolf has been!' or 'Joan and I are never done with talking over our visit to Monks House – we feel it becomes more and more wonderful', Woolf summed up a visit with, 'Oh, and we've had the Easdales for 3 hours solid, no 4; as they missed their train' or 'I was beginning to write to you when the whole Easdale family broke in, and we had to spend the afternoon with them'. She was intrigued enough, however, to accept an invitation to see Joan singing a musical arrangement of her own poems at the Bumpus Bookshop in Oxford Street and on another occasion to attend the puppet show that Joan and Brian performed in their shed. These eccentric events seemed to pique Woolf's interest and, although she complained about them beforehand and might leave early, she did turn up.

Perhaps Joan was immune to her mother's social naivety and her embarrassing tendency to gush nonsense in the face of celebrity. Or maybe she was just able to ignore it and concentrate on what was important. She certainly managed to protect and develop her own relationship with the Hogarth Press; the Woolfs brought out a second volume of her poems, *Clemence and Clare*, in 1932. With

only a year since her last volume, there is no discernable development between the two, more perhaps a change of mood. A
Collection of Poems seems both more disturbed and more energetic,
while *Clemence and Clare* is sadder and more languorous. The con-
tents page suggests this in itself, with titles like 'A Person Wept', 'A
Sadness', 'Why Give me Balm Before my Woe?' and 'A Sad Story'.
The title poem is a long, rather fey romance, dedicated to Virginia
Woolf, which the critic of the *Times Literary Supplement* suggested,
no doubt correctly, had been influenced by Edith Sitwell. It seems
more adolescent than some of Joan's other work.

According to Ellen's journal, 'My Will' was a poem that Virginia
had suggested Joan write, almost as an exercise. Joan dedicated it to
Leonard Woolf.

> If I should die when young,
> I'd like to leave among
> My dearest friends
> Such odds and ends
> As these:
>
> My little ivory book,
> In which no one may look
> (For in it lies
> My heart's soft sighs),
> To mother.
>
> My case of green leather
> I think I'd leave together
> With its treasures
> (My girlish pleasures),
> As well.

My brother is acquainted
The things I've drawn and painted,
And any book
That he might brook,
Are his.

I bid my mother send
To each sweet bosom friend,
My shawl and rings
And any things
They'd like.

My dolls' house please reserve
For future dates to serve,
The cherished piece
Of some strange niece,
Perhaps.

My prints, my wool-work chair,
My desk, my writings there –
Pray give all these
To those it please
To keep.

The other piece to note is 'Revelation, A Dream Poem', a lush
vision of paradise as revealed to the poet by a mysterious black guide:

The negro closed and locked the gates,
And led me through
An avenue
Of shrouded trees, where glossy dates

Fell in showers
On sickly flowers
That wafted death with each hot breath . . .

Again this seems heavily influenced by Sitwell. Joan probably wouldn't encounter a real black person for another ten years but, deep in the Kent countryside, she loved the idea of someone exotic and aloof in a distant land.

It was at about this time Joan met the writer Naomi Mitchison and forged what was to become the most important friendship of her life. Brian had contacted Mitchison first, when he wrote to ask if he could make an opera ballet of her book *The Corn King and the Spring Queen*. She was delighted by the idea and they met a couple of times to discuss it. Joan somehow came up in conversation and Naomi said she would love to meet her and why didn't they both come to tea.

Mitchison was a recognised figure on the London literary scene, whose interest was at once flattering and overwhelming. She was an unconventional and provocative woman, a prolific writer of fiction, plays and poetry, a socialist with money and connections, and a fearless traveller. She was also a feminist and mother of six, who openly took several lovers throughout her long-lasting marriage. She was famed for her passion, her politics and her intellectual and artistic friends. Joan and Brian found her charismatic, inspiring and not a little intimidating.

While Virginia Woolf had launched Joan as a writer and was to some extent her mentor, their relationship would remain formal and sporadic. Naomi Mitchison, on the other hand, was both a champion and a friend. She asked to meet Joan because she had read and liked her poems, and it soon became clear that they shared a mutual understanding. Naomi recognised Joan's potential and her need to write. In time, as their friendship deepened, they would turn to one another for emotional as well as critical support and Naomi would send Joan maternity clothes and food parcels as well as manuscripts and reviews.

However, when Naomi first invited Joan and Brian to stay at the large Mitchison house in Berwick-upon-Tweed in 1932 they were a little taken aback by her communist ideas and riotous family. Joan read her poems out loud, Brian played his music, there were endless discussions, big meals and a game of dressing-up that shocked them both as it seemed to involve the *removal* of quantities of clothing and a wild abandon they were unused to.

Naomi first visited Crouch a year later, when Joan, Brian and Ellen were out at their midsummer party. They returned after midnight to find the empty house in total disarray, a frying pan used and discarded on the floor, candles burnt low and gramophone records slewed across the living room among scattered pieces of clothing. Naomi and her lover appeared some time after two o'clock, tousled and friendly, having 'got lost'.

Ellen clearly found this whole episode rather glamorous and was grateful that, despite Naomi's politics, she seemed to 'bring Joan out into the world'.

'The world' was still a little way off, however, and by 1933 Joan was feeling frustrated at living at Crouch. The excitement of being published had worn off, the flurry of interest had died down and she was suffering a great sense of anti-climax. Even her mother registered her unhappiness, although with minimal sympathy and her usual inability to see that it had anything to do with her. Ellen wrote, on 21 November 1932,

In spite of these young people coming and going J is discontented with her life – She resents domestic duties – What can be done? She longs to have a different life and yet when she tries first this, then that; singing at the R.C.M, acting there, visits away, they do not please her. I am convinced it's nothing material, it's a soul-sickness, a soul discontent. She has no religion or philosophy to help her – What can one do with her?

A lack of religion was hardly the issue; Joan was simply growing up. A letter to Naomi on 23 July 1933 shows her at twenty, just as she is pulling away into adulthood. Thanking Naomi for a party the previous night, she is still the young observer, the outsider watching the event from a distance:

> ... A party in a London garden appeals to me very much: people standing about ... and the light sliding through open doors from the house spreads flat and gold on the lawn, or gets tangled in dark and secret shrubs. Then, if one looks up, one sees another world; a brilliantly lighted window right at the top of the house through clear-cut leaves ... Yes, I enjoyed everything so much. I ate two delectable peaches for one thing. And it is so odd when one listens to voices of a crowd of people merely as to a sound; when they have worked up to a crescendo (can't spell it) it makes me want to laugh.

In the same letter she refers to a recent poem, inspired by the orchard at Crouch (both she and Naomi had written about the same thing). 'I wrote a poem about the dark wet grass of the orchard, I will show it to you one day. It is very short and rough. But it came from a very real feeling; utterly different to yours of course – it is full of painful frustration, it is acidly virgin, and an expression of the "growing pains" of youth.'

The inverted commas and ironic summary of the emotional content of her own work are typical of Joan at the time; at once child-like and adult. It is again as if she were describing her own situation from the outside in terms that sound precocious, while at the same time actually feeling the pain she writes about.

After finishing *Clemence and Clare*, she started working on a much longer poem than anything she had attempted before, an extended Gothic fantasy called *Amber Innocent*. The title she claimed to have found in a dream and the rest followed, but it was a slow, lonely project that would take her years to complete. Maybe she knew this and deliberately looked for a parallel activity to keep her amused – or maybe she was suddenly struck with inspiration – but at around the same time that she embarked on Amber (early 1933) Joan decided to write a biography of the Victorian domestic icon Mrs Beeton.

It was most likely Mrs Beeton's *Book of Household Management* that had helped Ellen through her fumblings at running a home as a new bride, and presumably the same copy, or one like it, survived to become the domestic bible at Crouch. Ellen's journals are full of descriptions of preserving fruit and making jam, picking wild mushrooms, baking cakes and bottling home-made wine. One passage in *Middle Age* even complains, '. . . and now Mrs Beeton insists the batter stand an hour . . .'; she was clearly part of everyday life. Just when Joan was beginning to feel trapped by domestic duties, and was no doubt doing more cooking than she had ever done before, Mrs Beeton's portrait was put on display at the National Portrait Gallery in London, stirring up public discussion of the woman she, like so many others, had long held as a personal ally. Whether Joan went up to town to catch a glimpse of the photograph herself I don't know, but she definitely saw a reproduction of it in the

Listener. 'I was fascinated by that intelligent face,' she wrote, in her notes for a talk recounting the process of her research, 'there was a challenge in the contrast between those sympathetic eyes and the mouth, which was a trifle mocking.'

Joan had always loved Beeton's recipes for their precision, detail and language. Now, on seeing a picture of the woman herself, she felt urged to find out as much as she could about her and 'Mrs B' soon became her obsession.

She threw herself into the research, visiting distant villages, chasing through parish records and tracking down surviving ancients who had known her heroine in their youth. She pounded the streets of the City of London, befriending lift-men and warehouse managers in the hope that they would grant her access to any buildings that might have had the remotest connection with Mrs Beeton. 'In Pursuit of Mrs Beeton', a talk she broadcast on the BBC in 1938 gives the impression of a breathlessly exciting investigative gallop. She met a fascinating cast of characters and travelled up and down the country, but there was little hard information at the end of her four years' work. For all the snippets and detail she managed to dig up (and she did manage to find a few people who had actually met her quarry in their time – a man who'd let out her hens as a small boy and an old woman who'd done her washing) Joan felt at a loss.

'I remember travelling around in a train on the outskirts of London all day,' she wrote in her talk. 'Through the window loomed the Crystal Palace. As a skeleton of a crinoline it appeared, embodying that Victorian past whose characters hovered illusively, just beyond my grasp.'

Joan's Beeton project had also caught the imagination of Virginia Woolf who, early on, became very enthusiastic about it, if not a little envious. On a trip to Rodmell on 7 August 1933 (recorded, as ever, by Ellen) conversation flowed 'about ice – boiling water – freezing – clothes – and Mrs Beeton mostly. VW longs to write it herself. She suggested the book in two parts – fact and fancy . . .'

Fancy was fast outstripping fact, as most of Joan's key witnesses were either dead or dying before she could get to them and, unbeknown to her, the kindly assistance offered by Mrs Beeton's son was nothing of the sort. Woolf had managed to arrange for Joan to meet him but, as Ellen wrote in July 1933, 'The day spent with Sir Mayson Beeton was disheartening as he gave little encouragement regarding the biography.'

What Joan did not know was that Sir Mayson Beeton positively loathed the idea of anyone poking about in his parents' history, and was especially suspicious of this virtually unknown twenty-year-old girl with her notebook. As Kathryn Hughes now reveals in her own biography of Mrs Beeton, there were family secrets he wanted kept hidden and any attempt to uncover even perfectly innocent information made him deeply uncomfortable. Polite but reticent, he blocked Joan's every move. Ironically, in the light of Sir Mayson's suspicion of her, Joan's schoolgirl zest was born of a combination of naivety and ignorance. Her unworldly enthusiasm and self-belief, fuelled by the early success of her poems, meant that she could not imagine that the project might involve anything more complicated than being told what there was to know. She had no idea that information was being hidden from her, simply that she was finding it quite difficult to make progress. Sir Mayson Beeton apparently felt sufficiently threatened by her excavations to give her a separate heading in the index to his personal archive. Although the archive no longer contains any material relating to Joan – and maybe it never did – a space for it is clearly and disparagingly labelled 'Miss Easdale's efforts'.

Sir Mayson Beeton effectively stifled Joan's project and her mother's journal tracks its demise. In February 1934 both Joan and Ellen went off to find Mrs Beeton's first marital home in Pinner and Ellen gushed,

> How she progressed will all be written in her book – but it began with me noticing an old gardener and suggesting she ask him and it ended with her seeing an old, old woman of about 90 who had actually met Mrs Beeton – taken in her washing and worked for her and getting too the Beeton Dictionary signed by Mrs Beeton's own hand – it was all very thrilling . . . We had lunch in a little café where Joan scribbled away at her notes on her adventures – it's really very exciting this pursuit.

Three months later, 'J is getting along with Mrs B . . . but it's hard work piecing it all together and making it interesting.' By the end of 1934 Mrs B is described as 'such a task!' and then, three long years after that, Joan is 'disheartened because she cannot get Mrs B published'. She gave up on the biography at this point, although her defeat proved only temporary.

Amber Innocent and Mrs Beeton were not Joan's only preoccupations in her early twenties. She had also fallen in love with a young man called Norman Stuart – a rather tongue-tied chemist she had met at Herbert Murrill's wedding in 1933. He was possibly gay and he was certainly unhappy – he killed himself several decades later. It is not surprising, then, that he made an awkward boyfriend for Joan. He started visiting Crouch for intense conversations with her; the two of them would read poetry together by the light of a glow-worm until three in the morning and march off for long, inarticulate walks in the woods.

It was in the middle of this tortured affair that Ellen, showing spectacular insensitivity towards her daughter's feelings, took Joan to Europe for eight weeks on an extended jaunt which neither of them enjoyed. Norman failed to turn up at Victoria Station to see them off, which left Joan miserable for the entire trip. It rained in Florence, she got ill, spent her whole time pining and waiting for post from England, while Ellen felt neglected and cross that they were not having more fun. In the two months they were away, only one letter arrived from Norman Stuart and it offered little consolation: he had been unable to come to wave goodbye as he felt he was on the verge of a nervous breakdown. This news only served to deepen Joan's despair. The troubled tour ended in Paris with a flurry of cultural treats and a series of parties. At one of these, according to Ellen, 'Joan endured agonies being introduced by Mrs Heisch as a prodigy who writes poetry – and I had the usual trial, being asked if it wasn't wonderful being the mother of two geniuses – Lord! Lord! Lord!'

It was time for Joan to move on.

CHAPTER 3

NEW PAGES

Then on she walked, a little ahead of herself
In eagerness for reaching somewhere . . .

from *Amber Innocent*, J.A.E., 1939

By 1936 Joan was living in London. I imagine her walking to Belsize Park underground station on a bright June morning: dark-haired, slim, attractive but not yet elegant. Wearing her new silk stockings – she spent her first real money on two pairs, one emerald green and one cyclamen pink – elated as she heads into town for a day's reading at the British Library or to attend lectures on Elizabethan poetry at London University. She notices that the leaves on the trees are still translucent, picks out the coloured ribbon on someone's hatband, chooses to walk in the sun. She is enthusiastic and determined. A young woman, yet still unformed. Meeting the world and laughing at it.

Fittingly, her mother's voice gives way to Joan's own at this point in her story. Ellen's journal petered out in the mid- to late-thirties, while Joan started writing long letters to Naomi Mitchison. Naomi's replies have been lost – or deliberately destroyed – but she kept Joan's half of the correspondence and left it to my mother. While Joan's poems, her scrapbook and her letters to the Hogarth Press are fascinating evidence of her character as a girl, her own version of life at Crouch and her own account of events in her childhood went into a diary that she later burnt. It is in reading her letters to Naomi that we finally hear her voice and see the child become an adult.

Although the details of Joan's move to London are blurred, it seems that she first lodged with Brian and Frida, who rented a flat in a house in Hampstead. The artist William Coldstream and his wife lived in the same building and it was through this connection that Joan met a young woman called Jill Rendel, one of Coldstream's models and the great-niece of Lytton Strachey. Jill and Joan became great friends and within a few months had moved out together to a flat in nearby Parkhill Road.

Life was fun. In other parts of the country, in other parts of society, the Depression was laying communities waste with misery and deprivation, but among the artistic circles of North London life continued as usual. Joan had little money but she could afford to share a crumbly flat and to spend her time writing, going to concerts and the theatre. She relished being single and deflected any questions from Naomi with girlish nonchalance: 'Chaps? O I just don't think of them these days. The ones I could really fall for, the ones who could make me *grow* and *learn* are all just out of reach in some way or another, and the ones that are in reach make no mark.' One suitor who tried hard but made little mark was Hamish, an attentive and good-looking young Scot who nursed her after a bilious attack, cutting her a chess set out of cardboard, making her wafers of toast and reading her poetry out loud, 'his scotch accent tumbling over and over like boulders'. For all his endeavours, Joan remained unmoved. 'I get waves of warmth for him occasionally just because he is a human being, and because his presence reassures me that I am one too,' she wrote. When he suggested she might become his lover she roared with laughter and immediately reported the conversation to Naomi: 'my feminine frailty is such that I am gratified that he threw out the phrase "if you become my mistress" – it's like a bottle of coffee essence to put into the cupboard, though you know you'd never go near it and you haven't any real coffee in the house'. He soon gave up.

Another beau fell in love with a cousin that Joan introduced him to. And she still saw Norman Stuart for intellectual discussions and painful cups of tea.

She was not yet ready for a lover or a husband and was quite happy to be collecting new friends and experiences without the emotional pressures of a relationship. The pull from her family still dominated and took up a lot of her energy, compelling her to make regular visits to Kent to see her mother and assuage the guilt she inevitably felt at having left home. Likewise, she still worried about Brian, the big brother she had been brought up to feel responsible for. He had married Frida in 1933 and Joan had voiced her doubts about their future together to Naomi, even as she sewed her bridesmaid's dress of pink organdie a week before the wedding. In her letter of 5 October 1937 she wrote to Naomi,

> I had an upsetting dream the other night that I'd had a baby but had forgotten all about him for about a week, I'd left him behind in the old flat which I'd removed from, and now in the new flat I woke up in horror remembering him and convinced he must be starving or dead – I pulled on a frantic assortment of clothes and rushed out into the darkness to look for him, dreading the little emaciated form I would come upon . . .

This dream was surely about Brian, and Joan's own feelings of guilt that she had recently 'abandoned' him by moving out and round the corner.

Despite her fretful sense of duty towards her family, Joan made the most of her independence in these pre-war years. In October 1937 she went to West Wittering for a short holiday by the sea. She loved the combination of grey skies and mudflats, the odd shaft of sunlight and 'the disturbing whistles from the little birds'. The melancholy and emptiness appealed to her and she described the landscape to Naomi with her usual eye for the macabre: 'There were huge patches of blood-red, fleshy little flowering things, like little bloody fingers extending out of the earth to pull down insects and possibly people.' Knowing nobody in the village and not having booked ahead, she ended up spending her first night in a room over a butcher's shop, '. . . very comfortable, but faintly, ever so faintly, smelling of meat'. She then found a boarding house, 'where I am allowed to stick to my pet fad of baked apples and cream for breakfast'. Perfectly happy on her own, she spent the week writing and going to bed very early.

She also spent several holidays at the Adelphi Centre in Langham, Essex, an eccentric establishment set up by John Middleton Murry and, among others, Cuthbert Adeney, Joan's uncle. Murry – critic, writer and the former husband of Katherine Mansfield – wanted the Centre to be a permanent and self-sufficient place of socialist learning. Based in a large country house, it provided summer schools where like-minded people could gather for intellectual and political debate and lectures while living together as a group. Participants had to contribute to the domestic arrangements as well as the intellectual. The Centre was a troubled establishment from the beginning, wracked with ideological conflicts and difficult personalities. Murry's third wife loathed the place and the people involved in it; the atmosphere was fraught and Murry perpetually on the verge of giving in and closing it down. Joan enjoyed the talks and the ethos of the summer school, and was quite bowled over by a few of the speakers, but found the marital feuds excruciating, especially on the occasion when she was Murry's house guest for a few days and found herself the sounding-board for both him and his wife.

Joan seems also to have been working out her ideas on religion during this period. She placed herself within a Christian context yet was not convinced by the conventions of the Church, which she felt were too narrow and encouraged division. 'I feel the orthodox Christian stops short at Christ,' she wrote to Naomi in March 1938, 'and that isn't fair to Him, any more than Marxists are fair to Marx when they abide by him as their ultimate.' What gradually emerged was a strong personal faith in which she believed that each individual had a responsibility to the whole and where one's actions on a small scale could have an effect on all of mankind. She was very much influenced by Blake, finding morality in the detail of everyday life. She felt passionately about Good and the human power to change things, with Christ leading the way as an example.

'Why aren't the good men good enough?' she wrote to Naomi, again in March 1938, referring to Hitler's seizure of Austria, '... every calamity in this world seems to me a personal failure. The bad men aren't so bad, they're just utterly mistaken, and it's somehow the good man's failure that he can't get at them.' This fundamental generosity towards other human beings was something that she would demonstrate throughout her life. And although her faith would vary in its structure and its intensity over the years, it would always be an essential part of her.

She was also very much influenced by Naomi's socialist ideas and endeavours, although she was never politically organised or directly involved herself. Where Naomi was engaged in the committees, meetings, and practicalities of politics, Joan was often bursting with outrage or distress but rather muddled as to the exact details of a situation. Despite these differences, they were united in their belief in love, the human capacity to change things, female strength and the value of the written word.

*

65

Joan had sent a radio drama sketch to the BBC in January 1937, suggesting they could use it in a variety programme. The sketch was rejected but something in her writing caught the interest of producer John Richmond, within a few months he had commissioned her to write a play about the violin-maker Stradivarius. It did not seem to matter that she was no expert on the subject, only that she was keen and could write. This turned out to be the first of several pieces she would create for Richmond in a style he described as 'imaginative reconstruction' – short plays with incidental music, loosely based on fact and produced as entertainment.

The work suited Joan and she loved it. Writing to Naomi in October 1937, she enthused, 'It is so stimulating to be writing stuff that isn't just going to go putrid in the drawers of my desk.' After several years of working in isolation on *Amber Innocent*, she responded eagerly to Richmond's support and reassurance. Under his guidance she met most of her deadlines, edited her work and felt professional (although she was apt to return borrowed scripts bent in half or crumpled up). She was thrilled to have to go on fact-finding missions to the British Museum – 'my beloved B.M.' – where she would spend hours digging up information on violins or eighteenth-century French etiquette, fascinated by the detail of subjects that he threw at her out of the blue. Radio was the perfect medium for Joan – a place of the imagination where anything might happen, at once vivid and not really there.

The initially formal relationship with Richmond soon relaxed into a warm, respectful friendship, in which he coached her through her youthful extravagances, gently steering her towards writing viable plays, and she, despite her usual scattiness, bad spelling and botched typing, turned in a series of interesting scripts. She wrote lively, esoteric pieces with great verve and a certain disregard for normal radio conventions.

As they became friends, their correspondence, which was essentially about work, began to reveal glimmers of what was going on at home and in the wider world. 'I am sorry to hear you have had an accident with the sardine tin, but I must say I admire your wrong-handed writing', wrote Richmond in May 1938. Joan then submitted a drama about hand-held fans on 12 September 1938 with a note that read, 'I hope you approve of the modernisms being combined with the 18th century style – I have not attempted to be realistic . . . P.S. I write this while awaiting news of Hitler's speech. So excuse tension.'

On another occasion she advised him to 'Think twice about going in for pigs!' – 'Pigs are being reconsidered' came the reply, at the bottom of a letter urging her to write another play.

It was Richmond who commissioned Joan to write a play about Mrs Beeton, no doubt prompted by the knowledge that she had already amassed a quantity of material on the subject. Having despaired that anything would come of her years of research, she was now able to give her heroine what she called a 'rebirth'. *Mrs Beeton* was a serious biographical drama and Joan was thrilled to be back on the case. 'I've got good news for you about Mrs B', she wrote to Naomi. 'She has been received most cordially by the BBC and will bring me twenty-five guineas.'

'Mrs B' got a much colder reception, however, from Joan's old foe, Sir Mayson Beeton. Ever-defensive of his mother's life story and the reputation of his father, he was livid at the prospect of Joan's play being broadcast and did his best to have it withdrawn by the BBC. He also enlisted the support of the Reverend E. E. Dorling, another relation who objected to the artistic freedom Joan had taken with family names (the two men were outraged that she should refer to Elizabeth Mayson as 'Eliza' and Harry Dorling as 'Henry'). They insisted that she had misrepresented some characters and slandered others.

A crisis meeting was called at Broadcasting House, just five days before the play was due to be aired, with the aim of heading off Sir Mayson's threat of legal proceedings. Beeton himself did not attend but was represented by the Reverend Dorling, who joined John Richmond, Joan and two others to thrash out a solution. Joan was asked to justify her actions in having gone ahead with writing about Mrs Beeton 'in the face of express prohibition' from her son. She fought her corner hard and had the producers on her side, although their main priority was less to protect her than to placate the angry relations, smooth ruffled feathers and get the programme broadcast with as little fall-out as possible. It did not go unnoticed that Joan had allowed a few inaccuracies into her script. An internal BBC memo from the executive producer, a few days after the meeting, reads, 'Obviously Sir Mayson Beeton had got his knife into Miss Easdale, and I do not think we can profitably go into the rights and wrongs of that side of the case, but it does suggest that we must watch Miss Easdale's work carefully in future.' In the event, the BBC apologised for any offence caused. Tactful letters were written, Joan agreed to make some alterations to her script, Sir Mayson Beeton and the Reverend E. E. Dorling reluctantly approved the revisions and *Mrs Beeton* was broadcast as scheduled on the Empire Programme on 9 November 1937.

So what of the play itself after all this fuss? In many ways it is typical of Joan at the time; unsophisticated, fun, full of enthusiasm and humming with the love of her subject. She had poured every piece of research into the first draft, with the result that it was hugely long and had to be radically chopped to fit its half-hour slot. Richmond sat up with her past midnight to get it down to size, and she was disappointed that the resulting script felt hewn about, with missing scenes making for unsubtle relationships and character development.

To the modern reader, the plot is heavily pointed and over-stuffed with information, but the whole thing bowls along and demonstrates Joan's penchant for eccentric detail. In one scene the young Isabella Mayson is interrupted by her future husband as she simultaneously fries pieces of lamb and recites Thomson's *The Seasons*:

(Fade in background of frying)

ISABELLA: Well, if the butcher won't saw down this chine bone, I shall have to do it. *(Vigorous sounds of sawing)* O – Samuel Beeton!

S. O. BEETON: Please don't let me disturb you. I am charmed by the sight which confronts me.

ISABELLA: As a rule I don't allow people in the kitchen when I am cooking.

S. O. BEETON: I will behave well, Isabella. I will sit down quietly and watch you from a distance.

ISABELLA: You may come a little nearer if you like. Only mind your elbow doesn't go into those eggs, for they are to be added to the mashed potato.

S. O. BEETON: Er – tell me, what is this formidable looking instrument?

ISABELLA: A cutlet-chopper. You see, I use it to beat the cutlets flat. *(Sounds of chopper whacking meat)*

Characteristically, in Joan's eagerness to make the scene vivid she somehow makes it slightly over-charged. She would have loved the sound effects, and in other parts of the play one senses her relish in getting the historical and domestic detail exactly right. A barrel-organ plays in the background of the young Isabella's childhood (a cliché in radio drama today perhaps, but not for Joan) while in another scene one lady asks another if she has 'burst her hooks' – popped open her tight bodice. The best example is a scene set at a garden party, where the ladies with collapsible crinolines are asked to collapse them for the egg and spoon race.

As a challenge to the integrity of Sir Mayson Beeton's parents or family, the play seems totally innocuous. Joan had indeed got a lot of the detail right but remained completely unaware of any dark secret. Rather than discrediting the family, she had written a naive dramatic homage.

The last three years before war broke out were some of the happiest of Joan's life. Her buoyancy derived partly from her new independence in London and her positive working relationship with the BBC, and partly from her falling in love with her flatmate Jill's brother, a young geneticist called James Meadows Rendel.

Jim was shy, very intelligent and somewhat surprising. He kept a pet chameleon and had a passion for the ballet – if he wanted to see something at Covent Garden he would queue for tickets at dawn. He was tall and thin and had very long legs. In one photograph, he bends to light a cigarette between long cupped hands, his chiselled face serious under short dark hair and a floppy fringe; in another he kicks up into a headstand on a summer lawn.

Jim's father was Colonel Richard (Dick) Rendel, a professional military man who ran a farm between the wars. His great-uncle was Lytton Strachey and his mother's sister was Frances Partridge, the

Bloomsbury diarist and writer. Although his background was far more conventional than Joan's, he too had grown up in the Kent countryside, bird-watching and ice-skating on ponds, only about thirty miles from Crouch. He had been sent to school at Rugby and then studied biology at University College, London. In one of the strange coincidences that ran through Joan's life, Jim had done his Ph.D. in genetics under J. B. S. Haldane, the great left-wing geneticist and writer, and the brother of Naomi Mitchison.

A convinced atheist and rationalist, Jim was open to any new idea that would stand the test of scientific thinking. He valued literature, poetry in particular, and to the end of his life he loved T. S. Eliot. He liked and respected Joan's work, instinctively knew how important it was to her and did what he could to give her space to write in.

Joan always said that she first fell in love with Jim's jacket as it hung on the back of the door, an inanimate object that she typically imbued with character. He turned up with his pet chameleon one day, having been expelled from his Uncle Vincent's house, and was soon sharing Joan's bed.

Writing to Naomi in April 1938, she describes their early sexual relationship with uninhibited honesty. It was clearly a challenge she was determined to rise to, approaching the initial consummation with a naive practicality: 'Both my visits to Dr Wright were v. successful. I know just the correct angle to wear my cap. When I went to Boots to buy it I found myself instinctively drawn towards the bathing caps, and then I thought, no, I didn't want that sort.'

On what she calls their 'wedding night', dressed in her 'wonderful lobster-pink chiffon nuptial nightie', she felt it her role to be kind and supportive, as it was the first time for both of them; 'My calmness was such that I suggested a paper game of heads, bodies and legs (him, his sister and me are specially good at this), but there wasn't time for it . . .'

It was not an easy induction, but they persisted. Ellen welcomed them down to Kent to stay in the spare double bedroom and Joan was very positive about her new-found womanhood, as she explained to Naomi:

> I look forward to when everything is adjusted because then I shall feel less distracted and sleepy and more able to read and write properly. But I am very happy. It won't be long before he gets home again – he comes home smelling of dog-fish. Soon it will be fifty pounds of frogs – but maybe it's formalin.

At some point during the spring or summer of 1938, Jim proposed. He had been offered a job, breeding ducks at the Harper Adams Agricultural College in Shropshire, and this would mean having to live in a small village near Newport. The college would be offended if they were not married, so it was up to Joan to decide. It was her first major adult decision and she found it a miserable process. Describing her dilemma to Naomi on 10 October 1938 she wrote,

> I've been through agonies, knowing me you'll be able to imagine it. I was in darkness and wretchedness not being able to make up my mind and of course being terribly serious-minded and going through my heart and mind with a tooth-comb till I could have vomited . . . I was in tears not knowing what to do or what I wanted, for I had now got to decide to break or stick.

Instinctively, she knew it was a question of freedom and identity. While most young women of the time would have leapt at the chance to marry the man they loved, she had already witnessed the collapse of her parents' marriage and suffered its repercussions. Having at last spread her wings as a writer in London, she was loath to surrender her new-found independence. And she knew that, however unusual Jim was, she would still be expected to run a home and to combine her work with the inevitable tasks of being a wife.

For him, however, it was a pragmatic solution:

He said that virtually all I had to decide was whether I wanted to go on living with him, for to him the marriage certificate meant nothing and I should be as free after-wards as before. I said all the things I could ever imagine wanting to leave him for, he said I need not feel bound or caught, and I could go to London whenever I wanted for work etc.

As the threat of war loomed, she felt pressurised both by Jim's parents, who were impatient for them to marry, and by her own mother, who thought she should turn him down (presumably because her own marriage had proved such a disaster).

It took Joan weeks to decide. She returned to London alone with a single ticket and her trunk and 'went into the desert'. Eventually, after much deliberation, she sent Jim a postcard which read, 'Buzzles says yes.'

By 19 October 1938 she was happy once again. Optimistically, if slightly defensively, she set out her reasons for marrying in a letter to Naomi:

Yes, I know I'm getting married at a time when it's hardest because the new tradition is casting its first fore-shadow. I'm in for the time when the married woman has to live a double tempo. It isn't so much she's denied her separate identity & career, she is rather expected to achieve something as a co-bread-winner, but tradition of the home regime hasn't changed yet; indeed there's something buried deep in her very nature which makes herself, as much as any onlooker, take it for granted that she will still be the one to do most washing up, to house-keep & count the linen. So she lives at a double tempo. If she has anything worth giving, she can still create & give it – why, you're proof of that – If marriage makes a talent go under then the talent's damn well not worth preserving. Talent's the wrong word though – All the same it means con-tinual rack, a continual harrowing, and a painful conflict of loyalties. I know we're going to be more tied than we say we are. But I'd rather be a woman tied than a woman sitting untied in a Hampstead flatlet with a divan and a kitchenette. At the same time I'm not marrying because I can't face being lonely, for I've lived alone for one and a half years & shall always be glad I did it . . . it's simply now that I actively want to marry Jimmy & have his children; I love him, & I want to be with him.

They married on 22 October 1938 at the register office in Wellington, Shropshire, and straight away moved to the small, windswept village of Edgmond.

I drive to Edgmond on a wet day in November. Until today it's been a village that didn't really exist, impossible to find, like a place in a dream. The name always sounded odd to me. It made me think of Edmond in King Lear, made me want to over-pronounce it and pull a face over the O.

I can't find the cottage where they lived – where they got on with the neighbours so well that Joan made a hole in the hedge and laid a little brick path so that they could visit one another easily (the grandmother popping through to talk about death and discuss pictures in the *Daily Mail*, Joan taking a plate of roast chicken back the other way). The cottage where they froze all winter but where, in a sunny corner, they sat outside for spring meals. Where Joan tried hard to have supper on the table for when Jim came home from work. Where they were young and in love and still learning about one another.

Ellen visited once and declared it quite the dreariest place she had ever been. Naomi sent an armchair as a wedding present and a rug.

There are lots of cottages that might be it – smartened up with bright gravel in the driveways and new wooden gates and brass name-plates and new cars. That one? Red brick, tiny, pock-marked, with a yew tree at the gate and a mini-bulldozer grinding the garden to flat mud? Maybe. I hadn't thought the village would be so sprawling, or how many of these cottages would line its narrow roads. No one has heard of Laurel Bank.

But the Lamb, the largest pub in the village, is still there, dominating a road junction. It's huge and almost empty. Lunch takes ages to arrive and is accompanied by loud rock ballads piped to speakers above each table. This is the bar where Jim and the road sweeper from next door discussed their gardens and played in darts matches, where Joan felt happy on crowded evenings and promised everyone she'd throw them a party once she had been paid for her next play.

Jim's work started almost as soon as they arrived in Edgmond and he was kept more or less constantly busy breeding ducks. This involved feeding them, setting and turning their eggs and studying the genetic changes from one generation to the next. He and Joan had little time together, apart from evenings or the odd bleak bike ride. Joan was amazed to find that the very next village, only a mile away, was called Adeney and was the place where her family had lived in the sixteenth century. This was enough to convince her that she was already speaking differently and had reverted to the Shropshire accent of her Adeney ancestors.

Occasional visitors came to stay – Jim's parents and sisters, Joan's old friend Norman Stuart – but they were mainly alone that year.

They would read, listen to the radio, talk. The new Mrs Rendel was besotted with her husband, though it clearly felt strange to be sharing her life with someone.

'I think it's very advantageous not to start a baby in the first year of being married,' she wrote to Naomi. 'One is having to work out so much together as husband and wife, without a third party looming. It's queer how one can never sink back for one moment's respite at any stage in finding out how one should live. One makes up one's mind one isn't going to trespass on anyone, and one does trespass.'

The same letter closes with a description of Jim coming home from work:

> At just that moment, as I reached the end of the page, Jim walked into the sitting room, beaming, saying, 'I now know what's wrong.' His hands, black with motor grease, were full of the insides of his bicycle, and he sat down and started to fiddle with them. Of course I was enchanted but I said, 'Please not over the carpet, darling,' and hugged the back of his neck. It's perfectly awful how much I love him – too much now, I sometimes think. It's awful when one feels oneself growing almost clumsy with loving and no longer so illusive and vampish!

Joan's frustration with herself was slowly becoming apparent. She had hoped that a lack of distraction and a part-time maid would allow her to concentrate on writing *Amber Innocent*, but in practise she found it hard to work with any consistency or ease.

I can't quite understand it, but I think there's a clamp on me somewhere. Ever since I came into this cottage, I have felt very urged to write poetry – acute & shining images have come to my eyes & mind on & off every day, the words already there, but inexplicably I can't muster the courage to abandon the household things I'm doing & go & write. Jimmy wouldn't mind how late a meal was, how many cakes were burned, if he returned from work to find me writing a poem, or writing anything. I somehow have an awful weakness of mind about it – a fear of actually bringing myself to the point . . .

It was not as if the household ran smoothly at the expense of her writing, more that she felt caught between the two roles and unable to fulfil either. For one so keen on Mrs Beeton, Joan's domestic arrangements verged on the chaotic; in one letter she reports sprinkling salt into her typewriter while cooking spaghetti, in another she has just found a tea towel reduced to ashes in the saucepan, having let it boil dry on the stove. On another occasion she is totally preoccupied with the maid who has burst into tears while making the morning coffee and is unable to explain her distress.

'It's nothing to do with being married – I was like this long ago,' she wrote, '. . . I feel it's the same clamp on me which makes me slow in dressing in the morning, undecided about what to wear, afraid of the cold, unable to run a house with real method. I am always busy – horribly occupied, with moving things from one place to another place, but I am unmethodical. I think I shall die feeling I have wasted my time.'

This is the first suspicion of her unhappiness at herself and of how hard she found normal life. Having time and space to think was not necessarily helpful as she spent it cursing herself and her lack of focus. Also, as so often in her life, Joan found herself out on the edge of a social situation. Beyond the immediate neighbours, of whom she became very fond, she found village relations quite peculiar:

> Edgmond's ice-age society continues to amaze me and I, I think, continue to flabbergast it. However, callers continue to descend on me, dropping little white cards like bird-lime everywhere, and I go to incredible tea-parties – the last of which was marked for my having shocked everybody by saying I was thinking of joining the Co-Op. But the little curate who was present defended me so heartily against the haughty condemnation of the local auctioneer's wife, supporter in some way of the conservative association, that she nearly shrivelled up and fell under the table. I can't resist going to these tea-parties because they are always so terribly funny.

She clearly found the village men more entertaining than the women, most of whom she thought dull and repressed. Astonished at the segregation of the sexes, she could not understand why the women could or would not go to the pub as she did. She also disliked what she saw as their tendency to gossip, and was convinced that the men were better-natured than their wives. She enjoyed being the only woman socialising at the Lamb, being bought pints of beer at the darts match and talking about it the next day with the coalman. These were 'real people' and she relished the sense of liberation it gave her to socialise across class and gender. But as her first year of marriage went on, she found the isolation of the village increasingly difficult to deal with and longed to be back among old friends in London, especially when impending war became a national preoccupation. Jim could at least engage in discussions with his colleagues, but Joan felt at odds with the other college wives in her position:

> . . . [the men] could spend a whole afternoon talking about something to do with science – but on the same afternoon, in the same room, what do I talk about with the wife of the man to whom Jim is talking? Our maids, homes, latest callers, our trades people, dress-patterns, babies, what to do with hair that is splitting at the ends – And all these things seem very important and are no effort to talk about – I babble away and listen fascinated, but I simply long to talk of other things also! . . . Once I had to explain my looks to a woman because I'd been crying over something to do with the news and she looked at me very bewildered and then I felt her decide that Mrs Rendel was probably rather highly strung.

Someone nominated her for membership of the Women's Institute – the hub of female activity in Edgmond, it seems – but here again she remained an amused observer:

> I thoroughly enjoyed it and found it most depressing. Somebody gave a demonstration in bread-making in a bowl that was too small, and the audience either giggled or sat up stiff with scorn or embarrassment and pity, while the bread-maker, very red-faced, slopped it all over the edge and exclaimed, 'O dear – O dear.'

Then the bread stuff, which was supposed not to stick to the basin, was passed round, and it did stick to the basin . . .

Next, I was asked to judge the egg-cup flower show, then there were refreshments, when people chatted, and afterwards an entertainment – Mr Somebody's wax-works – just a little too painful.

Next time I go I'll try and make a few suggestions – I would like to know why, on such occasions, one of the so-called educated women is always asked to judge a flower show?

Joan's correspondence with Naomi was a lifeline, a reassurance that she was not really as isolated as she sometimes felt. Naomi was also finding her feet, having moved to the country in 1938, although her domestic set-up could hardly have been more different. She and her husband Dick Mitchison had bought a large castellated house on Carradale Bay in Kintyre, Scotland. It had extensive gardens and grounds, big trees, farmland, cottages, shooting and fishing, and it looked down an avenue of rhododendrons that ran straight from the garden gate to the sea.

Carradale House would become a beloved place for Joan, the setting for many holidays and happy times as well as a place of refuge. For over ten years she and Jim would visit as often as they could, taking the train up to Glasgow, then the ferry and doing the last leg of the journey by bus, grinding along the single-track road to Carradale village. Many of Joan's letters begin or finish with her longing to be at Carradale, thanking Naomi for a visit or planning when they might next get there.

The house was still a magical place when I was a child, an inherited pleasure. I remember the first time we arrived there, when I was about five, staggering into the dazzle of the hallway after hours of driving through the dark. My brother and I had been told so much about Naomi and how special she was that, seeing her and Dick sitting in big armchairs, we got confused – I thought she was the Queen and James thought her husband was God. They did, after all, live in a house with turrets.

There were pictures by Wyndham Lewis hanging on the walls, kippers for breakfast, mulberries in the garden, attics and cellars to explore. There were always lots of houseguests and political arguments at the dining table. A gong sounded for meals, a hatch led up onto the roof. And, sometimes, if we were lucky and the tide was right, we might be taken out netting fish in the bay, Naomi sitting in the boat under the moon and the fishermen muttering in the dark.

I still dream about Carradale. It filled your head. It permeated Joan's later poetry.

Despite her persistent worries that she was not working properly, Joan finally finished *Amber Innocent* in a burst of concentrated activity in March 1939. She wrote to Naomi a few days later, 'I shall never forget the night I finished *Amber* – we rushed off on our bicycles trying to find a telephone to wire you then!' She was briefly torn between Naomi's offer to recommend her to Faber, and Leonard Woolf having casually said 'Send us the poem' when she had seen him the previous autumn. Loyalty to her publisher won out; 'I felt the old fold of the Hogarth Press pull at my heart strings,' she explained to Naomi. In the face of war, she was impatient to have her poem seen and published as soon as possible: 'I didn't want to have to wait, having finished it – it's all I can do and the horror of this world makes one feel one must throw out one's own small cry upon the wind without delay, one feels in a fever!'

She sent the manuscript to the Woolfs with a note that read,

'Here is *Amber Innocent* at last. If there is still a world left to wait in, I shall be waiting anxiously to hear.'

Leonard replied two months later, saying that they liked the poem very much and planned to publish it that autumn.

It is worth looking at *Amber Innocent* in some detail as it is Joan's most substantial piece of surviving work and one of her last. It would also turn out to be oddly prophetic.

The sixty-page narrative poem describes the experience of a young woman, Amber, who leaves the large, shadowy house of her cruel brother-in-law Mark to venture out into the world on a modern odyssey.

Mark, a widower damaged by the Great War, is an embittered man who wishes Amber ill. His daughter Megathy is a sickly, negative child, wasting away in a turret, old before her time. Amber escapes them and exchanges the Gothic fears and hostility of their domain for a series of strange encounters and frightening experiences in an unnamed city. Her journey involves a train trip, spending a night in a city park, encountering road-menders on a hot day, watching a military band, meeting a war veteran. In a state of exhaustion she arrives at an old stable, the home of Mr and Mrs Lapwing. When Mr Lapwing opens the door she collapses at his feet and has a sudden vision of eternity, which strengthens her for the future. The Lapwings offer her refuge and unconditional friendship. She stays in their loft. Megathy (now much older) comes to visit her briefly and talks about her own lack of faith and interest in life; they argue and Megathy disappears again.

Having hidden away in the stable for several months (or years – the time frame is deliberately ambiguous), Amber returns to her brother-in-law's house to find that Megathy has committed suicide. Mark dies in a final confrontation with Amber and she is left to fight a rapacious white lion. Alone, she faces despair. She returns to the

top of the turret and the stones of the building dare her to surrender
to death and to throw herself into oblivion. She refuses and resolves
to go on living.

In a letter to Naomi and in the blurb for the cover of the book,
Joan explained that the name Amber Innocent had come to her in
a dream a decade earlier; she had woken knowing that she had been
telling a story but could remember nothing more than the title.
'The process was rather as if the shapes were already there but I
could not see them until I had drawn them,' she explained to Miss
Nicholls, manager of the Hogarth Press at the time. Joan admitted
to not knowing exactly what the poem meant and not wanting to
analyse it too much. While her romantic suggestion that the idea
had come to her in a dream sounds like something Ellen would
have said, the struggle to write *Amber* had been real enough. In
another letter to Naomi she laughingly suggested that Freudian
readers might have a field day with her imagery and could no doubt
give everything a sexual interpretation if they wanted: 'I imagine
that the turret, the stairs, the railings, the train, the wash-house, the
lion, the gardener, in fact everything in the poem is simply stiff
with scope for people so inclined. They would probably be quite
right, but that would not alter the rightness of other interpreta-
tions.' For her, the job was done. She had written *Amber* and she did
not really want to explain it as well.

It had taken seven years to write the poem and Joan was a very
different person from the nineteen-year-old who had started it back
in Crouch in 1932. No wonder she wrote to Naomi in April 1939,
'I still champ and will always champ when I think of Amber's
unevenness. For I know it's uneven.' How could it not be? Months,
if not years at a time, had gone by when Joan had not even looked
at it. She had lost heart, been distracted by other work, by love, by
household preoccupations, added to it sporadically and then, with a

final surge of energy, managed to complete it at the age of twenty-six. My own copy comes from Carradale House and is inscribed with the dedication, 'To Naomi, Who made Amber go on again.' Joan's final push to finish it had been due, in some considerable part, to her friend's encouragement and a particular conversation they had had while weeding a flower-bed.

Although Leonard's brief acceptance letter was enthusiastic, it is clear that the decision to publish had not been unanimous. John Lehmann, who had taken over Virginia's stake in the Press to become partner-manager in 1938, had serious doubts about the poem and, according to his autobiography, argued strongly against its publication. His taste was for the new writing of bright young poets like W. H. Auden, Stephen Spender, Louis MacNeice and C. Day Lewis, poets with whom he had an established understanding. Highly educated, modern and male, they were politically-engaged, well-travelled and looked forward rather than to the past for inspiration. A scribbled note in the Hogarth files, presumably Lehmann's immediate response to the poem, reads, 'I think it has a most remarkable quality . . . but 1. a bit too Tennyson, 2. terribly long, 3. nobody buy it.'

Despite his misgivings he eventually gave in after the Woolfs agreed that they would pay for any financial losses the book might incur. In the letters he sent out to potential reviewers, Lehmann described *Amber*, somewhat ambiguously, as 'a most extraordinary bit of work'.

So it is. Difficult to understand on a single reading, it leaps forward in jolts and starts, has no consistent metre or style and is crammed with allegorical symbols, strange characters and vivid images. It may lack cohesion but many of the individual sections are simple and direct, and much of it has a luminous cinematic clarity.

The poem is ambitious, highly imaginative, weird, profound,

often beautiful, sometimes bathetic. Parts of it are startlingly fresh and strong, while other sections are clumsy in order to force a rhyme or to accommodate certain words.

Joan's education had ostensibly been an inculcation in poetry – almost as a religion – and *Amber* reflects this. Written with an intensely romantic sensibility, demonstrating Joan's passion for the eighteenth-century poets (and Blake in particular) it also combines stream of consciousness with a style heavily influenced by T. S. Eliot and the early modernists.

The result is remarkable. Uneven it may be, but it would be mis-guided simply to dismiss it, as J. H. Willis does in his book, *Leonard and Virginia Woolf as Publishers*, as an aberration, a mistake on behalf of the Hogarth Press. Willis seems to think it might have been pub-lished as a charitable feminist exercise by Virginia or as a favour to Joan, the Woolfs' one-time protégée, but they were not charitable publishers; they clearly saw merit in it.

Thematically, *Amber Innocent* explores several of Joan's most compelling preoccupations. One is the idea that time is a dimen-sion beyond the simple linear concept of past, present and future. As Eliot had in 'Burnt Norton' a few years earlier, Joan insisted that these were not separate states but that they could co-exist, were stacked one on top of the other to be experienced simul-taneously. She believed there was a morality in the fact that one was connected with the whole of time and not simply the particu-lar present one found oneself in, that this demanded great human responsibility. Her language becomes almost biblical as she sets out this belief:

> Say that we are scribes to the written page,
> Yet what we write shall never be blotted out.
> Say that we are here and that we have gone before

And as we shall be are we now and were we.
So should we be more careful.

Say that the bread upon the table is also in the van,
And that the wheat in the bread is also in the field
And in our mouths as it is sown.
Then would men not despise the moment, which is also
eternity.
Not until we acknowledge the moment as eternity
Shall war cease and life have meaning.

She also challenges the convention of physical space, playing with the idea that one can contract distances into one another or expand a single line into something three-dimensional. When Amber experiences eternity on reaching the Lapwings' house, time and space explode in a moment:

There is a space called the threshold,
Immeasurably long or unaccountably short,
But it is crossed, and all that is remembered
Is where we have left and where we have arrived.
But Amber did not cross, she stepped in to the threshold.

'Have you journeyed long?'
'Yes, and Christ how tired I am.'

The light switched on. A burning white
Slew the values of her sight.
A quick omniscience, an utter blankness,
Revealed eternity rolled in a second.
The man, the hall, the stairs and all

Had diminished beyond the reach of vision,
Or else enlarged till atoms were
Holes within holes – again, oblivion.
And this is all there is to know.

. . . Amber had fallen on her face –
The floor was so cold and lovely a place'

With hindsight, I cannot help interpreting much of *Amber* as a foretaste of what would happen to Joan herself. It charts the long journey of a woman who remains the watchful outsider, who has relationships with other people but is never entirely comfortable with them, who seems to absorb the world through every pore of her body and yet stands apart from it. As a child and as a young woman Joan had managed to escape to her own dimension when the realities of life became too much. As an adult, 'the threshold', the place between worlds, the slip of somewhere that does not really exist, was still the place she sought to be.

The territory of *Amber Innocent* is dreamlike, at once recognisable and distorted, concrete and nightmarish, reflecting the way Joan processed physical experience. She retained the visual perspective and acuity of a child, was both an expert witness and someone who went beyond simply seeing to inhabit what she saw, turning it inside out for the reader, taking them to her viewpoint. Thus, the gardener encounters Amber as he is first netting strawberries and sees her from upside-down, towering above him:

Through the arch of his legs
He saw Amber approaching. An immense figure
Which, had he thought, might have been a goddess.

87

She lengthened to the upstairs windows of the house
And out of sight, except for her legs and shoes.

As Virginia Woolf did, Joan would often become absorbed in describing some tiny detail or private activity and would lead the reader to see the same thing: spilt milk caught in the creases of an old woman's shoes, the underside of leaves in a garden, children hiding between baskets in a wash house, picking flakes off the copper boiler with a pin. When Amber is waiting for the Lapwings to open the door, she is briefly engrossed in the painted surface in front of her, finding significance in the most ordinary object:

The door had once been painted green,
Now it was blue, and blemished here
Where stray fingers had burst the tempting blisters.
Its countenance was lined. It had the wear
Of every caller's absent-minded stare.

A few lines of the poem had already appeared in the *Adelphi Magazine* in May 1937, as part of an article Joan wrote entitled 'Holes'. In this short essay she explored her fascination with the idea that nothing is really solid:

If an object were magnified to an exaggerated degree, it would become nothing, and likewise, I told myself, if it were diminished to the nth degree again there would be nothing. I looked down at my knee, and in the weave of my dress I saw the same theory illustrated. There were small holes between each thread of material, and could I but see, I should find more holes within each thread, and the threads around those holes would contain more holes. Somehow I felt sure that in the end the holes would win. Likewise, I was full of holes, the table beside me was full of holes . . . So-called reality was only a matter of focus.

Later in the same essay, she describes how the inspiration for Amber's vision of eternity came from fainting in the kitchen,

> I had cut off the tip of one of my fingers and, unfortunately, in washing the wound I had lost the bit of flesh down the drain. It was not until about ten hours afterwards, when it was being redressed, that I fell into a brief but most complete black-out. Actually, I remember no psychic significance in relation to this perfectly ordinary occurrence. I just felt that it had been a physical foretaste of death, and, as I lay on the floor in regained consciousness, I regarded the biscuit tins under the kitchen table with an abounding love such as I had never felt for them before.

Joan's absorption in the physical – to the point where physical sensation becomes psychological experience – is essential to Amber's sense of self. At several points in the poem she separates her mind from her body or becomes so involved in one aspect that she loses the other. The opening verses describe her standing at a window, her whole face buried in the velvet curtain so that she can see nothing at all but feels the warmth of her own breath and the nap of the fabric against her eyelashes. After a long time she is brought back to herself by her brother-in-law's voice:

> Amber turned back and trod in the world.
> 'I thought only the curtains were dark,
> I forgot the room,' laughed Amber with laughter

Round and unreal, which she could not feel.
But within her person –
For now she had stepped down from her face
Into the whole length of her body – she was crying,
'Dear God,
    Dear God, protect me!'

A similar dislocation occurs when she washes in a basin in the turret of the house and encounters herself as another person,

She leant over the water and met her face,
A little removed she watched herself.
The familiar when met is stranger than strangers.

In the future, this separation would become much more of a reality for Joan; in the poem, it remains an interesting sense of experiment.

Another theme explored in *Amber Innocent* is the idea that the kindness of strangers is the perfect kindness. The Lapwings are unknown to Amber but they take her in, feed and comfort her, without demanding anything in return. Their uncomplicated generosity leaves her free to go on her way when she is ready. Likewise, her exchange with the gardener is simple and strengthening, and enables her to leave the grounds of the house feeling happy and complete. For the rest of her life Joan held that this was the purest kind of human relationship, in contrast to what she had come to see as the oppressive and ultimately destructive love that a parent has for a child. Writing about the poem to Naomi on 3 April 1939, she explained, '*Amber Innocent* is perhaps a denial of father and mother . . . the turning away that seems always cruel but has to be gone through. When the child seems to smite the parent by turning its back and going away, but the child does it or the parent would eat up its spirit.'

When she witnesses the spirit of Mrs Lapwing's unborn child, skipping in Blakean innocence in the hallway, Amber urges it to enjoy this freedom before birth. The verse becomes a lacerating attack on a mother's love, Joan's anger barely disguised:

> The miniature figure, the self's precursor, unmanacled,
> Danced in the thin ray of light,
> A perfect form,
> And Amber said to it,
> 'Dance before the net is made
> To net you in,
> Dance before your joys are diarized
> And your mother says, "Tell me everything."
> Dance before your suffering is her ire
> And she like the she-wolf bites your paw off
> To think to put an end of, to think you'll have no more of
> Pain, but only pap, sweet pap
> And no more pain, so safe,
> So safe in momma's lap.'

Likewise, one cannot help interpreting Amber's bitter explanation of why she has had to leave Mark's house to find her way in the world as a long-overdue justification of why Joan has distanced herself from her own mother:

> Because you encroach, as strangers never would,
> Not because your closeness understood as you think
> closeness should,
> Not because you were close as you would be, I left you.

I left you because your closeness is not knowing,
Because your knowing is not knowledge
And therefore never kindness.

. . .

'It is the eternal stranger that I seek.'

It was not until she had submitted *Amber* that Joan felt she had
come of age. Its publication signalled freedom and adulthood. It also
liberated her to think about her father, to confront the idea of him
as a real person rather than the 'fiend' so hated by Ellen. 'I have
never thought so much about my father as of late,' she wrote to
Naomi in June 1939, describing how she had been questioning her
uncle and aunt about Robert's true character and trying to talk to
her mother on the subject. She desperately wanted to know more
about him, yet could only glean from his sister that he had been 'a
very lonely and rather austere man, very proud, and slipped into an
utter back-wash'. Ellen remained terrified of his memory and did not
want to discuss him, so Joan was left as confused as ever. 'I feel I
must write to him – if only to wipe out the memory of a very hard
little letter I wrote him, refusing to see him, when I was thirteen. Yet
I still hesitate . . . I turn it over in my mind and think, *I* and *Brian*
are the children of this man . . . I get terrified and absolutely in a
tangle about hereditary problems then – I imagine the worst in him
and apply it to myself or I look for the worst in myself and – Oh, I
get in an awful muddle.'

She would not, in fact, contact her father for another few years
but at least she had finally defied Ellen's veto on the subject.

Amber Innocent, which Joan dedicated to Jim, was published on 25
September 1939. The dust jacket for the poem, drawn by Vanessa
Bell in pen and ink, depicts a tall woman in a long pale dress leaving

a black doorway to head up a flight of turret steps that disappears out of sight. The woman holds a candle in front of her, sending cross-hatched shadows ahead and up the stairs.

Owing to the outbreak of war just three weeks before, and uncertainty about paper supplies, the reviews were delayed for a month or so.

Vita Sackville-West wrote to John Lehmann the day after *Amber* was published: 'I have read Joan Easdale's new poem and am much impressed by it although I am not sure that I quite grasp all its implications and symbolism. What a strange atmosphere she contrives to suggest and how good certain bits especially are such as "Dina" and "The woman in the train", which is really terrifying. Thank you so much for sending it to me.'

Naomi, determined to review *Amber* herself, had written to Lehmann early in order to get hold of a copy. She also wanted Stephen Spender and Naomi Royde Smith to read it. Her piece in the *New Statesman and Nation* was a chance both to laud her friend's work and to take a shot at the male-dominated modern poetry she so thoroughly disliked. She opened with brazen drama: 'From time to time poetry takes a new turning . . . At present there are a number of minor poets along the Auden lines, some of them with moments of real authenticity, but in the main boring; it is obviously time for the new turn. I believe it is to be found in this book.'

Royde Smith's reaction was somewhat cooler. In her review for *Time and Tide* she described Joan as 'entirely a poet, not so much sensitive as sensitized to the physical and emotional phenomena of life', but she suggested that the plot of her 'verse novel' was somewhat obscured by the poetry itself. She also wrote that, 'If Mrs Woolf had, early in her career, decided to write in verse, this is very much the kind of book she might have produced.'

The *TLS* reviewer noted that Miss Easdale's poetic imagination had 'grown remarkably both in depth and subtlety' since the publication of her last volume and called the poem, 'an unusually original attempt to crystallize the meaning and movement of a girl's life, the unfolding pattern of her self-awareness at a new and deeper level'.

They went on to say, 'Miss Easdale may owe something in her exploration of this new dimension to the pioneer work of Mrs Woolf and others, but her discoveries are as much her own as is the sensuous refinement of her imagery and the somewhat sombre reflections upon life which filter through it . . . The whole poem distils with a delicately vital art the sufferings and searchings of a rare sensibility.'

Sadly, Joan did not have long to enjoy the relief and exhilaration of having her poem published. Just when she seemed to have reminded the literary world of her existence and established herself as an independent adult, the preoccupations and practical challenges of the Second World War took over. Although valiant in the face of the exhausting and sustained anxiety to come, Joan, like so many others, would find herself under pressures that were ultimately damaging. Certainly, she was never to recover the joys and successes she had found in the thirties and the cracks that eventually appeared in the fifties can be traced to her struggle to keep going during the war.

She was only too aware of her weaknesses as she wrestled with the duties of being a wife and then a mother while needing – but failing – to function as a writer. She entered the forties with typical determination but it turned out to be a long and destructive decade.

CHAPTER 4

_____

UNDER SIEGE

Domestic tides swelled from room to room
With rush of voices, brush or handle-broom.

from *Amber Innocent*, J.A.E., 1939

Jim and Joan were at Carradale with the Mitchisons at the outbreak of war, gathered around the wireless set in the drawing room. 'Joan cries at her husband's feet. I go over to her,' Naomi wrote in her diary on 1 September 1939, as Germany invaded Poland. The announcement that Britain was at war with Germany came two days later: 'At lunch Joan said she was on a small island of sand with everything cut off before and behind. I said I had been feeling the future cut off for some time. We all agreed it was queer to feel the past so cut-off, everything had a different meaning now . . .'

Jim's contract in Shropshire had come to an end and the Rendels were glad to return to London, despite the looming international crisis. Jim started work at the genetics lab at University College, breeding drosophila fruit flies under J. B. S. Haldane, his old genetics tutor. Joan was soon busy on her own project; within a month of war being declared and *Amber* published, she was pregnant with her first child. I try to picture what it was like for her, waiting for hostilities to start, anticipating horror and yet trying to get on with life as normal, dealing with gas masks and the blackout and morning sickness. No letters survive to illuminate those first months of waiting or what Joan felt about impending motherhood. I imagine she found it fascinating and probably wrote a great deal to Naomi, who was pregnant with her seventh child at the time. Sadly, Naomi's baby girl died of a heart defect at just a day old. Perhaps she didn't want to keep Joan's correspondence of the previous months, or maybe it just got lost. The missing letters would not only have detailed the pregnancy but the other major event in the Rendel's life that year – a serious injury Jim suffered during an experiment.

With the advent of war, the authorities had become increasingly interested in how they might harness ongoing scientific work to outwit the enemy. In the early summer of 1939, during peacetime trials, the submarine *Thetis* had sunk off Liverpool with the loss of ninety-nine lives. Haldane had since attracted the attention of the Admiralty by conducting various experiments on how men might survive such disasters in the future. Over the first few months of the war he enlisted the help of various colleagues and acquaintances, who joined him in the quest to investigate the physical and mental limits of the human body under deep water. In a series of potentially lethal experiments, they submitted themselves to conditions of intense pressure and extreme cold while breathing various combinations of gases. Jim was recruited to this small team of guinea pigs in early 1940 and they worked throughout the spring and early summer of that year.

The experiments took place at the London works of Siebe Gorman, a company that developed diving equipment, on Westminster Bridge Road. Participants were locked into a horizontal steel tank and subjected to increasing pressure, to simulate being lowered to increasing depths. They were to do crossword puzzles, solve mathematical problems and recite limericks until they could no longer continue, at which point they were to knock on the tank wall or communicate through the small glass window to ask to be released. Subjects regularly suffered intense headaches, blackouts, convulsions and vomiting. During one of Jim's sessions, his signal was either misunderstood or not received in time and his lungs collapsed before he could escape.

The injury – technically known as a pneumothorax – meant that he would suffer pulmonary problems throughout his life. The lung lining had separated from its outer membrane, allowing a cavity to form between the two and compressing the lungs as it filled with air. This was extremely painful and in the shorter term it meant Jim was swiftly demoted from medical grade I to grade IV in terms of war-work suitability. Over the next few years he would suffer a series of relapses and crises where one lung and then the other would 'go' and he would have to be admitted to hospital for lengthy bouts of treatment. This consisted of bed-rest and the application of silver nitrate, which encouraged the fusion of the two layers of membrane. Jim was left vulnerable to illness, unable to lift or carry much and (as he revealed in one of the two questionnaires he filled in for Mass Observation, the social research organisation) feeling vaguely guilty as to his role in the war. The fact that he had been part of a dangerous and important research project, the findings of which would determine the Admiralty's training of submariners in the future, went only some way to reassure him. His partial incapacity inevitably meant more physical work for Joan, and his state of health became a source of intense worry and distress for her throughout and beyond the war.

Jane – my mother – was born in Aylesbury in July 1940 to the sound of the air-raid siren. Two months later, Joan insisted on bringing her new baby to join Jim in London, determined that they should all be together in spite of the dangers of nightly bombardment. A friend recalls Joan's description of breast-feeding during the Blitz, her milk spurting out in time with each exploding shell.

'I saw the birth of Joan's baby in the paper,' Virginia Woolf wrote to Ellen, 'I'm so glad it's over happily. Please congratulate her from us, only we hope she won't stop writing. And let us believe that some day we shall all meet – babies and all – in peace.'

Jim and Joan spent the autumn of 1940 camping out at John Richmond's house in Highgate with him, his wife Sarah and various other refugees from hotter parts of town, having been offered shelter when the air raids came too close to their lodgings in St John's Wood.

A letter to Naomi on 21 September 1940 describes this new wartime existence:

We are leading a queer life, basement from about 7 p.m. till breakfast time. We all sleep in the basement dining room. We get a few hours sleep each night. When it gets specially nasty we go into the kitchen & have endless hot drinks.

I haven't been into the West End or Central London, or the East End. A taxi-man told me he went to his brother's house in Silver Town & it wasn't there – hundreds of families were herded like animals under corrugated iron, in pens. But you have probably heard & read so much about London now that you know more about its condition than I do – I can only tell you what it is like living in London now. But no, I can't tell you that, because it is quite indescribable. One dashes out between raids to do one's shopping & it's as much as one can do to perform the smallest & most ordinary functions of daily existence – so much time is spent simply in

trying to get a little sleep when one can & in arranging everything as best one can to give more of a chance of preserving
life from moment to moment! And yet the elaborate bother of
filling one's stomach goes on – threading ribbon through
baby's nightdresses etc.

Haldane, despite considerable pressure from the university
authorities, refused to give up his department in the face of air raids.
Threatened with having his water and electricity supplies cut off, he
would doggedly turn up to his room in defiance of orders, on one
occasion removing a wooden bar from the door, on another retriev-
ing confiscated apparatus from Bangor in Wales. Jim remained part
of his skeleton staff and would arrive each morning to find fresh
damage from the night before; the Great Hall gone, the science
library destroyed, staff dead and windows blown out.

Back home in Highgate, Joan tried to sustain normality and write
poems between feeds:

. . . our nocturnal basement life with the Richmonds & their
friends is cheerful, fuggy, & maintains a wholesome degree of
sanity, when we all sit around before the big supper wash-up
talking about books, music & the theatre – Otherwise London
conversation & London letters are of nothing but the bombing. In every street, on every corner, from passers-by float the
words, 'bomb', 'windows gone', 'incendiary', 'right in her
garden', 'bomb – bomb – BOMB!' Several windows have gone
in this terrace – or rather the glass has, and the shops in
Highgate Village obligingly say 'OPEN' when they would find
it hard to be anything else. It is difficult to try & fit shopping
in between the warnings – if only they were quite regular it
would be easier, but they do spring an occasional surprise. I

therefore never take Jane beyond the garden, so I've been unable to weigh her (having no scales here). It is so odd, somehow, sitting in the basement room, surrounded by beds of one's fellows, breaking Jane's wind whilst the Nazis fly over-head & the guns gasp & bite. The wind has to be brought up, whatever else happens. Tonight we are a smaller party . . . Jim & I are alone with Hal, a young producer – rather fleecy voiced & sweet. He is swotting up logs, with Jim's help, preparatory to becoming a gunner. Sometimes a Welsh opera singer (passionately communist) turns up & sleeps in the coal hole.

She continues a few days later,

One of the morning raids. Everyone is quite unreasonably much less afraid of the daylight ones. It is such a beautiful morning. A big wind rushing through the leaves. Apples toss-ing about. I like Highgate for being so full of trees and the air, what one gets of it, is good. Nobody in this household feels particularly militant – the most they say is 'there comes another Nasty. How I hate them.' We all wish there could be some sort of a resolution, but feel that what sort is very impor-tant. We are all exhausted and absent-minded. It is difficult to think much about the situation when you are right in it, part of it – doing the jitterbugs on the very horns of the dilemma.

There goes a bomb, or a mine, in the distance. The win-dows shook.

I have never been so forgetful & unable to concentrate before. I have to repeat in my brain, 'saucepan lid, saucepan lid, saucepan lid' as I cross the kitchen or I will forget what I am after – When the planes go to and fro overhead, I often

think of their crew – so young most of them, such babies, &
we so frightened.

. . . Fairly quiet now. A soft bursting of shells in the sky like
hat elastic being plucked.

Joan was frightened by the raids but also excited. She felt fortu-
nate to be at the epicentre of the action, to be witness to what was
happening to the city. 'I want to live through this so that I can write
about it or learn something from it at least,' she told Naomi,
although she found very little spare time to work in. She did,
according to Jane, write an extremely good extended poem about
the Blitz, which Jim thought was the best thing she ever wrote and
one of the most powerful poems written about the war. No copy survives and Jane and Polly can only remember one line, 'In the park
the guns stutter'. It may well have been one of the poems Joan
refers to in her letter to Naomi dated 25 October 1940: 'I'm sending
what poems I've written so far, for you to look after for me. They
have all been written in raids or raid-warnings.' She sent the poem
out to magazines and editors but no-one would publish it. Someone
suggested she should get it printed privately, but Naomi said no, she
was a professional writer and she should hold out until it was
accepted by a proper publisher. In the end, after months, if not
years, of trying, it got lost and Joan destroyed her own copy. It was
one of Jim's greatest regrets that he had not somehow found the
money to get it printed, that in spite of financial difficulties he could
have done so but didn't.

John Richmond had gently but persistently been asking Joan to
write another radio play, on whatever subject she wished. Distracted
by her wedding and moving to Shropshire, by a short-lived plan to
collaborate with her brother on an operetta, another brief fantasy

about making Mrs Beeton into a film and, most importantly, by the completion of *Amber Innocent*, she eventually submitted a play called *Strange Things* in June 1939.

Strange Things posed a problem for Richmond; he liked Joan's writing and he liked her but the play was quirky to the point of being incomprehensible. It was set in an isolated village and the minimal plot turned on a case of mistaken identity involving a ventriloquist and a conjurer – long-lost father and son – reunited by a stuffed owl in a cottage where the clothes rail savagely attacked the ironing board. It was baffling. In a BBC memo of 15 August 1939, Richmond appealed to a colleague for a second opinion and the reply came back, 'I too find it quite attractive, it is unusual and has atmosphere but I wonder if it would act as well as it reads? I doubt it would as the first half is so odd and confusing . . . I imagine many people would become too impatient with it to find it really entertaining. It seems to me that it would be far better as a story than a play.'

Another colleague wrote, 'I think it could be done. Everything must be made as clear as possible in production. I think it should be described and announced as a very mysterious play. Done with odd noises and a good cast it should be entertaining and atmospheric.'

Strange Things was accepted and scheduled for the end of 1939. But, with the outbreak of war, Richmond was moved away from drama production and into news, and his projects taken over by Howard Rose, a very different sort of man. Despite Joan's bright efforts to introduce herself and build some kind of rapport with him, Rose refused to engage with her on anything but a strictly neutral level – she was simply a writer he had inherited from his predecessor. Joan's belief that she was just at the beginning of a serious writing career with the BBC gradually eroded, as her increasingly anxious enquiries about her play were met with increasingly evasive replies and it slowly dawned on her that the production of *Strange Things* might be postponed indefinitely.

On 25 September 1940, jumpy through lack of sleep due to air raids and the new baby, she wrote Rose an ill-judged letter:

Is there any chance of my play, *Strange Things*, being broadcast in the near future – or is it quite unsuited to the moment? I am desperately hard up – with a baby of 2 months, and my husband doing his best to keep us on a very small grant for genetical research. I know it is exceedingly bad taste to embarrass you with this personal relation of facts – do forgive me, I can offer no excuse except that I am sunk in so deep a bog of despair that I'm not afraid to put my foot in any-thing! I am quite prepared to believe that my rather peculiar play can't fit in anywhere at the moment. Do please tell me the kind of programme you would like and I will write one . . .

In his brief reply Rose explained that things had changed con-siderably at the BBC, that fewer productions were now required and that he could not be certain when, if at all, they would broad-cast *Strange Things*. Uncomfortable with her outburst and determined not to allude to her personal circumstances, he concluded, 'There is no special kind of programme that we want – anything that is really first class we are prepared to consider.'

In November 1940, when pressure from the university and increas-ing air attacks on London made it impossible to stay on any longer, Haldane decided to protect both his ongoing research and the results of cumulative years of hard work by evacuating his laboratory staff. The plan was to move the UCL genetics department to the

Rothamsted Research Station in Hertfordshire, just twenty-five miles outside London. The area was already crowded with evacuees from the city and accommodation was at a premium, but Haldane eventually managed to rent a small house in Harpenden. This was to be home for himself, his secretary Elizabeth Jermyn, his assistant Helen Spurway, Jim, Joan and their baby, and a Czech professor called Hans Kalmus, who had fled the Nazis, his wife Nussi and their two small boys.

Joan, excited by the move, wrote in December 1940, 'This is a hideous house, full of pig-stye brown . . . But I am happy, because the atmosphere is thick with creative activity.' She anticipated an invigorating shared life, safe from the bombing, where she would be able to write, bring up the baby and enjoy the energy and companionship of new, stimulating people. But while the other adults were involved in research at the Rothamsted lab, it was expected that Joan and Mrs Kalmus would share all the housekeeping; cleaning, shopping, cooking and doing the laundry for the whole household. They decided to do it on a one-week-on, one-week-off basis, which for Joan meant a week of breakneck panic followed by a week of exhausted recovery.

The house offered little privacy. The overcrowded bedrooms were bursting with suitcases of belongings and piles of personal and work papers, and the communal sitting room was cramped and ugly, the air a mixture of pipe smoke, cooking vegetables, damp wool and drying nappies. Group meals were noisy, with a baby and two boys under the age of ten, as well as several highly opinionated scientists discussing the day's work and the latest war news. Friends and colleagues would stay for a night or two, call in for meals or join the group round the fire for evening cocoa, Haldane holding court in front of the fire, with Mitsi, the white house cat, in his arms.

A photograph taken for *Life Magazine* early in 1941, presumably to illustrate plucky British intellectuals getting on with life as normal, shows the household having tea in the living room. Squashed on to a big leather sofa with Elisabeth Jermyn and Helen Spurway, Jim and Joan look happy and glamorous. Everyone is smiling, Jim about to smoke the unlit cigarette that hangs from his lips, Joan, her hair cut in a glossy bob, beaming at six-month-old baby Jane, propped up on her knee. The picture was not used by the magazine in the end, but it evocatively records that dark wartime afternoon, everyone wearing woollen jumpers and jackets, drinking tea in cups with saucers, enjoying the baby before they all move off to do other things. It gives the illusion that Joan was at the very centre of it all.

In reality, she soon felt out of her depth and unable to participate in the intellectual life of the household. Writing to Naomi, she described going upstairs alone to feed the baby, leaving the rest of the company below and listening to their conversation coming up to her through the floorboards.

Naomi, after one brief visit, was shocked at the conditions her friends and brother were living in and wrote in her diary:

> The house is a piggery: a villa meant to be run by two maids, and with a nasty little kitchen and only one bathroom, inhabited by seven adults, two children and a baby, with no domestic help – partly shortage of labour, partly, no doubt, ideology . . . I admire Joan; here is a poet, moony, elegant, precise in words, a girl who used to wear green silk gloves and very smooth hair, who could spend a week on three lines, now coping with this household, also feeding and looking after the most contented and jolly baby I have ever seen. She doesn't take naturally to domestic service, but she feels that it is a service, to some extent personal to Jack, who has the gift of making his workers love him . . .

What had started as an adventure soon became an overwhelming responsibility, to which Joan felt increasingly unequal. At the end of January 1941 she wrote to Naomi,

I don't know quite what is happening to me. I feel as if my thinking powers have been bled and bled so that they have become weakly and can only concentrate on anxieties. I am in one of the most intelligent environments I have ever been in, but my intellectual or cultural life, has died within me. In fact, I know I never have been an intellectual – I always knew I was completely uneducated – but I did think I had something – something for which intellect is probably the wrong word, but something – which gave me the confidence to express opinions, which quickened my critical faculty, and which made me able to contribute something occasionally really worth listening to. But now I cannot talk. I cannot concentrate properly on what is being said around me.

When I came here first I felt quite lively and chatty if nothing else. Now I feel sober, stupid, closed in, dimmed, with nothing more to say and feeling I am quite unique in my ignorance and isolated for a life-time within it. Why ought I to mind? But why shouldn't I mind? And I do. Sometimes I think that if I were placed as all others in this household are placed (with the exception of Nussi) – with a job which took me out each day and from which or with which I returned to this roof each night, I should feel different.

At present I am working (but not on my job) but on the sort of job which, although I haven't time for anything else, affords me ample time to be supremely and unfruitfully introspective. Bringing up a baby of course is in itself a job and again, owing to the nature of this society, 1941, or of nature herself, it is an isolating one, particularly isolating when one is living in community.

There were energetic breakfast-table discussions about how it was unethical to employ another woman to clean the house, but these arguments were made by the female scientists and technicians who were soon on their way back out to the lab, leaving Joan to do the washing-up and agonise over her own inability to argue her case.

At least she and Jim remained companionable and supportive of one another, despite the constant worries and cramped conditions. In March 1941 Joan borrowed Jill's sewing machine and reported to Naomi, 'Jim is being very sweet and doing some sewing for me on it in the evenings – running up Jane's petticoats etc. It's particularly heart-warming somehow, in a general way.'

Beside the constant housework and baby care, there were wartime shortages and predictable bouts of shared illness to deal with. A snippet at the end of one of Joan's letters to Naomi seems to capture what life was like at the time:

. . . So very glad you are coming to see us. The pheasant and woodcock not arrived yet. We should be most grateful for a hare to help us out with the meat-rationing problem. I think the poem is expert after a fashion, it also has some nice bits in it but I don't know why I'm not so keen on it – it doesn't seem *directly* you. I may be quite wrong. Bring the long poem. Keep the cape . . . Your letter was opened by an Examiner! Perhaps that's why it was delayed – perhaps the pheasant and woodcock have been censored!

In the winter and spring of 1941, half the household went down with a ferocious strain of German measles, which left them exhausted and bed-ridden and the house even more unpleasant than usual. It was Joan who looked after the invalids, called doctors in and arranged for them to recuperate at Carradale. Despite feeling desperate, she was determined not to let people down, Jim or Haldane in particular, so she told herself to stick it out for a year.

It was in this somewhat besieged state, overwhelmed by domestic tasks, anxious about Jim's health, stalled by the BBC and feeling unable to write anything of any worth, that Joan learnt of Virginia Woolf's suicide in March 1941. It came as a huge blow. Although they had lost touch since the publication of *Amber Innocent* in 1939, and had never been personally close, Woolf had always been a touchstone for Joan, proof that she had literary worth and that she should continue writing. With Woolf's death, that endorsement was gone and she felt suddenly and profoundly lost.

On the night they heard the news, Jim took over the washing of the baby's nappies so that Joan might write some form of tribute. She struggled to get it right. The resulting poem is not good, but its very incoherence and repetition reflects Joan's state of shock. With the absence of 'the mountain', her personal landscape had changed, and her sense of identity within it. The poem reads as if Joan is talking to herself, running and re-running her relationship with Woolf out loud, quoting lines from her own youthful poems, which now seem horribly resonant.

ON HEARING OF THE DEATH OF VIRGINIA WOOLF

With your death dies an answer to my voice,
I wake and see removed the mountain
Which distantly fair called me to struggle –

The mountain which listened and spoke and
    echoing not was echoed by many.

On hearing of the death of Virginia Woolf . . .
I'll force myself to speak on death,
Death of the beautiful, unslain,
In a world of pain.

'The curdled waters chimed
In her ears . . .
The bubbles whispered, "drown . . ."
To her'
She knew these words,
She knew,
'In all life lies Elegy, singing.'
She read, she answered,
She said she could not criticise poetry,
But she wrote to me,
And like a mountain distantly fair
She called me to struggle.

How could it be that they should say . . .
How could they say of my poetry
That if she wrote poetry she would write like mine.

I'll rouse a bled mind in war
To write at a table of inferior food, rationed jam,
Bread that looks punched by an impotent hand
And a sandwich spread, the lid shrapnel-proof,
I'll rouse a brain bent by repetition,
Set it listening to a heart whose clustered beats

Have painted funeral flowers upon it,
Bombs, like cornucopias filled with grain
Never smearing men's mouths
And bursting like unwanted love in blows of pain.

Come, come again, death
Hover over my house, powerfully,
With your shape a toy and a man and a boy.
Come, come again,
I'll shout it in your face,
There is one unslain.

Somewhere she lies, among words of death,
Death she had written, death she had read.
And I twelve years ago had written,
'The curdled waters chimed
in her ears . . .
She trampled water down
With her feet,
The bubbles whispered "drown" . . .
To her . . .'

Often I dreamed convincingly of death,
And stood beside a mental tomb,
Leaving it, revisiting it,
And soon I knew that she too must see
My constancy and wonder at it.
'Death, faithful death!' Archambo cried . . .
And Amber, full of it,
Til I, almost frightened, wrote,
'Teach me not first hand, death.'

These and more lines I wrote and thought about her
    reading it,
'Everything speaks of death to those who hear,
In all life lies Elegy, singing.'
I used to send her all my poems to read.
She was a mountain, distantly fair,
Calling me to struggle.

In her death dies an answer to my voice.
O strangest yet, that critics should have said
My poems were her poems had she written them.
I'll let that pass, since she didn't write them.

The sirens go again.
And I am here – small,
With buildings and faces rendered ghosts,
A brain littered with exciting encounters
    once or twice a year –
A whistle on a roundabout at a fair
On my way to Rodmell in August 1933.
I remember that face made me think of a statue
Sensitive to the washing waves of centuries,
I think of the face under the water,
I try to see my words beyond my tears.
I have written of death,
But death remains,
And these words do not.

Joan was unhappy with what she had written, but at least it communicated her sense of loss. More than three months after the event, she sent the poem to Leonard along with a short letter, explaining,

I tried several times to write to you and at last I have decided to send you the enclosed. It is typed straight from the rough draft of what I wrote when I first heard of Virginia Woolf's death. I have made no attempt to tidy it up or send it anywhere because it's such an intensely personal and private expression of how her death affected me and can't be counted as a worthy tribute at all. I think of you very often. God bless you. Joan

A glimmer of hope came for Joan in the summer of 1941 with a request for another play from the BBC. This was possibly due to John Richmond pulling strings on her behalf from Manchester. It was a lifeline, enough to keep her going, and she threw herself into the writing of another enormous project, which, as with *Mrs Beeton*, she then had to wrestle down to radio size.

Mrs Carson sealed Howard Rose's opinion against her. He received it with a brief letter, saying, 'I sincerely hope we like it', and passed it straight into the hands of a reader called Miss Pughe, whose internal report reads, 'This play is about a woman artist who is encouraged by her husband to sacrifice her home and child to her painting on the assumption that her pictures have a message for mankind. It seems to me to be a terribly long-drawn-out affair of soul-searchings and dreary domestic details, and I don't think it's really interesting enough to do.'

Howard Rose replied, 'Yes, all very tiresome. I agree entirely.'

That was that.

Not only did this rejection hurt on a professional level, but it was a brutal dismissal of Joan's own immediate dilemma as something boring and irrelevant. She wrote in protest to Val Gielgud, senior drama producer at the BBC, asking for his opinion and arguing the case for her play:

If I may venture any comment on *Mrs Carson* myself, I should like to say I think it's the most controversial type that I've ever attempted before, and that I believe a great many listeners would find it posed for them a problem, in a setting of 'domestic details' and 'soul searchings' only too familiar to married life and the family, which they would be almost glad to have dragged out for public inspection and argument. The some dozen people who have read my play privately have all been very disposed to discuss, rather violently, the problems and possible solutions arising from it.

Gielgud returned the play with the same grave misgivings as his colleagues. As did John Richmond, to whom she appealed – as a friend – for some kind of explanation, having already come to terms with the fact that the play would never be produced.

I think you'll see exactly why I minded so much when you read what the play's about! It was worth trying though. I hope one day somebody writes something of the same sort and really gets it across . . . I have written a bit of poetry since. Nothing else – no time. I've made my choice and if I had the chance to make it over again I'd make it the same. But I regret that most women are put into the position of having to make a choice: marriage and having children or doing some other work they're fitted for as well.

Richmond responded in his usual discreet way, in a letter that is missing from the BBC archives, suggesting that he sent it to her privately. She accepted his lengthy criticism (whatever it was) and was mollified by the fact that he eventually arranged to produce *Strange Things* himself. Finally broadcast on 27 November 1942 on the Home Service, it turned out to be her last piece of professional writing.

The rest of Joan's war remains hazy, since few of her letters from that time have survived. Her second child, Polly, was born in the summer of 1943. There were further recuperative holidays at Carradale, continued attempts to write poetry and continued frustration at her failure to get it published. She also embarked on an autobiographical novel, which she described to Naomi as 'a most extraordinary hair-raising document . . . far worse than anything in *Jane Eyre*'. She claimed that the book, entitled *Goodbye, Little Girl*, was not for publication but rather to lay certain aspects of her past to rest. It seems to have been an expurgation of her family background, a detailed account of her parents' histories and her own childhood, which she crammed into over seven hundred pages of exercise book during the months of her pregnancy. The novel would remain an ongoing project for the next few years.

Jim, meanwhile, was engaged in strategic work for Coastal Command, under Operational Research, developing ways of detecting U-boats at sea. Having finally received compensation for his damaged lungs he was able to buy a house in Pinner (which, coincidentally, was the town where Mrs Beeton had lived when first married). He also paid for a series of domestic helps, brought in to alleviate the pressure on Joan and allow her time to write, but more often than not causing her worry and taking up more time than they saved.

Jane recalls an incident from the Pinner days that seems to signal the very beginning of things going wrong between her parents. The new house was drab, pebble-dashed and small, but Joan, ever romantic, rhapsodised about it being like a cottage because it had roses over the door. Jim refused to agree. He disliked the way that

Joan would not – or could not – look at life squarely. Life was ugly and difficult and they should accept that. Jane, who was three or four at the time, remembers watching with horror as her father hacked the roses down – angrily destroying what he presumably saw as a poetic lie – while her mother stood by, weeping uncontrollably.

Joan's unhappiness did not go unnoticed by Naomi, who wrote in her diary on 17 February 1944:

. . . tea with Joan at my club. Poor Joan with an acute feeling that she is incompetent, that she just can't cope with things, that she gets everything into a mess (except – a large exception of course) the children . . . It's just because these bloody domesticities are so boring that one inevitably thinks of something else, and then forgets, like Alfred, the cakes in the oven. Meanwhile we all try to be enthusiastic and competent about saving fat and similar idiocies. But it's a bloody shame people like Joan have to. She's not able to write anything. I say never mind, you are storing it up. But—?

Joan may not have been able to get any further work published but, channelled into games and stories, her imagination was as vivid and extreme as ever. She could conjure up scenarios with such an intense conviction that they would appear to a child to be actually happening in the room. My mother remembers a game that Joan would sometimes play with her when she was about four years old. It was called House on Fire. Joan would turn an empty cereal packet into a house, carefully cutting out and folding windows and doors and making a chimney from rolled-up cardboard. She would set the box on the hearth with the end flaps splayed out to balance it, and describe the scene inside:

'And there's the house, all ready and full of people. If you look inside, there they all are, see? All having lunch . . .' She would then set fire to the bottom of the box. It would start to burn and smoke would start pouring out of the chimney. Flames licked up inside and out of the windows. It was beautiful and terrifying.

'Quick! Quick! The fire engine's coming, can you hear it?' Joan would urge. 'Let's get all the people out. Can you see them? Are they all right? Is anyone left behind? Quickly, quickly, rush back in to rescue the last person, don't forget anyone, don't leave anybody behind! Oh, that's all right, they're all out now.' The drama was completely real for Jane, who could hardly bear the sense of emergency and panic and was always left feeling guilty, wondering afterwards, 'What if there was still someone left inside?'

'The Runny Nose That Couldn't Stop' was one of Joan's many invented stories; everyone ended up in boats, paddling about in their own snot. She used a structure she called Nice Nasty Nice: the action might be intense and frightening but the listening child had the reassurance that everything would be all right in the end. She would set the scene, then something appalling would happen, then all would be repaired by a happy ending. On the one occasion Jane asked for a Nasty Nice Nasty story it was completely horrific. Joan held nothing back; terrible, irredeemable things were allowed to happen and Jane was left in tears.

The Rendels were staying at Carradale House when the war ended in August 1945, gathered around the radio with the Mitchisons just as they had been six years earlier. Naomi's diary describes a general sense of exhausted relief when they realised that it was finally over, Jim and Joan 'on the whole happy' despite the news of the atomic bombs dropped on Japan.

As Naomi noted, the people were the same 'but all older and tired'. Her diary for 12 August 1945 reads,

> . . . the girls and I and Joan discussing this business of babies. It really is doing in both Joan and to a lesser extent Ruth [Naomi's daughter-in-law] . . . For Joan and me, our lives are part of our work. The poetic ideas bud all the time, and either live or die. Joan was saying that constantly things and situations were shaping into poems and stories but they never got written down . . . Ruth thought she could combine her work as a doctor with having children. She may yet be able to. I am more doubtful about Joan. She is almost deliberately sacrificing herself now.

CHAPTER 5

_____

ART AND SCIENCE

The night is growing shorter,
The day will soon be born;
The Moon's in her last quarter
Come and dance on the lawn!

from 'Come and Dance on the Lawn!',
J.A.E., 1930

When the war ended Jim and Joan came back into London and lived in Compayne Gardens, South Hampstead. Neighbouring houses had been destroyed completely or stood ripped apart with banisters splayed, wallpapers exposed and bedroom doors opening onto thin air. Geoffrey Dunne, Joan's old friend from the Crouch days, shared the top flat with his sister. Jane and Polly could hear him practising his singing when they played out in the garden.

The next two years proved, as for many families, grey, cold and full of drudgery. Life was a round of coupon-saving, shortages, old clothes, poor food and ill-health. There are few letters to shed light on what was happening in the Rendel household, but Polly remembers her parents having terrible arguments behind closed doors. Jane remembers visits from relations providing a welcome distraction; Joan had developed a close friendship with Frida, Brian's wife, whose little girl

Josephine was Jane's age, and they would sometimes come and stay the night. The cousins were devoted to one another and their mothers would end up in helpless fits of giggles together, laughing as if they were back at Crouch again. Ellen had returned to Hampstead during the war and was now living near enough to take the girls out occasionally – to tea at a department store or to the ballet.

Joan was still trying to get some of her poems published but they were rejected by every editor she approached.

She was dealt an additional blow in 1946, as the result of a botched dental operation. She had been to the dentist for a routine procedure but then developed an infection that spread to her eye, leaving her practically blind on her left side. This gave her a slightly strange demeanour, as she compensated for her lack of sight by tilting her head and turning towards things more than she normally would, so that her right eye could take them in properly. It also meant that she was constantly dropping things and smashing china – the Wedgwood ivy-pattern dinner service, a wedding present from an aunt, was gradually lost to the kitchen floor.

1947 stands out from the general post-war malaise as an important, crowded year for Joan. Events seemed to churn up the past and future together and she struggled to sustain a sense of herself among them. Within a few months, aged thirty-four, she became pregnant with her third child, her father died and the family moved to Scotland.

Joan and Jim spent a weekend with Leonard Woolf at the beginning of the year, a rare couple of days without the children. From bombed-out London where they could buy no soap, the girls had colds and the house was full of dirty washing, Joan briefly found herself back in the place where she had first felt valued as a writer. She described the visit in a letter to Naomi dated 27 January 1947:

It was lovely to be at Rodmell again, worth it in spite of the
emptiness in the moonlit snowy garden where I walked out –
I admit it – in search of Virginia's ghost. I went down to the
lonely room under the churchyard wall where she used to
work. I saw the footpath leading across the fields to the river –
I even called to her, asked her questions, and of course there
was only silence and the snowy landscape – and I felt in the
silence almost a rebuke, as if she would tell me all my great
concern with death was useless (for my thoughts get more
and more wrapped up with death year by year), an unprof-
itable waste of time.

And I turned back to the house thinking that my great
longing to bridge life and death (for I should like to prove
the division, or rather, the snuffing out of the human soul, is
as nonsensical as to say the world is flat) sprang only from
my fear of death – that I was simply trying to get as familiar
as possible with something before I had to meet it face to
face – yet how anyone should not feel the necessity to make
this pre-acquaintance I can't imagine. But the silence in the
garden seemed to infer that we never could make this
pre-acquaintance, and that our duty was to make human
consciousness as tolerable as possible while we yet knew we
were in possession of it.

Joan's spiritual instincts, long suppressed by necessity and domestic preoccupations, were clearly still strong. Free to wander about
alone, without two small girls making demands on her, without
having to get to the shops or cook supper, she reverted to a way of
thinking and a pace that was much more like her old self. Leonard
was an attentive host, feeding them on a haggis from Selfridges and
going through Strachey photograph albums with Jim. In the course

of the first evening they started talking about Virginia and 'all sorts of things which in sympathetic company is such a relief to discuss – the interleaving of sanity and insanity'.

It must have been strange for Joan to be back in the house, to find it the same but gently decaying. She wrote,

> Leonard's ties still hung from a peg in the bathroom and there were primeval looking sponges and tooth-brushes hanging about in nets which looked as if they would turn to powder if you touched them. Everything was almost exactly the same as when I last visited the place about fifteen years ago, only a certain amount of dust had fallen, colours had faded and every kind of weather seemed to have passed unhindered through the walls. Rooms had been changed round a bit and the largest had been given up as maggots had been found in hundreds under the carpet. You could see the bricks were dark with moisture, but a lot of things were still stored there. There was the usual mixture of books and apples everywhere.

This reminder of her old life, of the Woolfs and of her early success, came at a time when Joan was deeply disillusioned with her writing.

'I've come to the conclusion I write badly,' she told Naomi bitterly in the same letter, 'I think I have poetic vision, some good ideas and quite a good grip of dramatic sequences, but I write badly. I begin to think that people are being rather cruel by trying to encourage me at all – you, Jimmy, and Leonard for instance. I shall have to finish my novel, as a sort of therapeutic gesture towards myself and family. But after that, why should I go on? . . . My God, when it's finished I shall just throw it at everybody and say there, and go off to wipe up the tears and blood and never write again.

Polly has come into the room and is saying, What's the matter, Mother?

Surely one ought to be able to do better than this.'

To make things worse, Joan received a note from the Hogarth Press just a couple of months later, informing her that *Amber Innocent* and *Clemence and Clare* had 'ceased to sell almost entirely' and would therefore be remaindered.

She now pinned her personal survival on finishing the novel, as if by doing so she would redeem herself. Its completion would justify the hundreds of hours she had spent on it and the money Jim had spent on domestic help to enable her to do so. More importantly, it would mean she had secured her identity through the act of writing, both making sense of the past and liberating herself from it. As she tried to explain to Naomi in May 1947,

> . . . if I manage to finish my novel as a whole, I fancy I will to some extent be able to start living as a more or less collected whole, aged 35, or whatever I am when I finish it. And from that point I *may* feel *sufficiently* tidied up to be able to focus with greater energy on the present, live with greater care of the personalities closest to me (stand apart, hold onto them less to steady me – and so see them more as they are) and even begin to write stuff that can make a little money! . . . I only know that if I allow myself to be overcome by the difficulties involved, to be wooed with continued success by daily chances of evasion, if in short I never finish it, then my future is unimaginably dark.

In July 1947 Joan wrote, 'I felt again this morning I would like to die, if I could be sure of coming alive again two days later among the same people.' She felt incapable of running the house properly. She had endless arguments with Jim over money and her inability to budget, however hard she tried.

'I feel it is more possible to have your cake and eat it than is commonly believed and that if you save it it will anyway go bad in the end or you will have a stomach ulcer,' she had written a month or so earlier. 'Then I feel heartbroken to see myself as the cause, as holder of the weekly purse, of *Jim* thinking he will never obtain some of the more generous aspects of living, a wider scope for movement on land and sea and in his mind, things that I want too . . . Before he can place any hopes in me as a ship that will come home, I scuttle myself, Naomi, in front of his eyes and say almost fiercely that he must never count on me.'

While Jim fretted over the price of fruit, Joan made seventeen pounds of jam. She yearned to do 'wild and adventurous things' but found herself floundering about in the basement kitchen, cooking four meals a day with hardly a break between them. She wrote of feeling permanently guilty yet unable to see where she was going wrong, overwhelmed by the desire to go away somewhere exciting. She also wrote of being afraid of insanity, although she referred to it as an idea rather than something she had actually experienced: 'I think I may also have discovered why periodically I get eaten up with the fear that one day I shall go mad. It always comes on me most when I am feeling most restricted. I think I look upon madness as a possible loop-hole – a way by which people would be compelled to give me a holiday which was a real change of scene and occupation, if only in the grounds and walls of an asylum.'

It was not only Joan's immediate domestic situation that she was finding difficult. She was also profoundly upset by having to stand as a key witness in her brother's divorce case. She had had Frida and a lover to stay during the war (while Brian was abroad) and was therefore called to give evidence to prove her sister-in-law's adultery. Although each side had agreed that this was the quickest way out of their failed marriage, Joan found it excruciating to be playing so vital a part in the proceedings, providing intimate details and admitting that she had, however unwillingly, been accessory to her brother's betrayal. She bought herself a new hat made of blue feathers to give her courage, and then felt guilty at having spent so much money on it. 'I am waiting a day or two before I tell Jim about the hat,' she admitted to Naomi. 'He knew I had to get it but not that I was getting other things as well, which thank God were all called Utility anyway. The hat wasn't. It really is a beauty.'

Joan was also deeply worried about her father. Throughout the summer of 1947 she received a series of frantic airmail letters from San Francisco, describing Robert on his deathbed. Paralysed and delirious after several strokes, he was dying in the care of a woman who could not understand why neither Joan nor her brother was on hand to help. Since he had no money and was still a British citizen, Robert was not entitled to any hospital treatment in America and his nurse – a Mrs Upjohn – was exhausted and resentful. Joan could only hope that her father would die quickly.

She had vivid nightmares over several weeks and described them to Naomi in detail; in one, Robert's spirit was trying to enter her to evade death and in another she was wandering lost on a muddy road (having been misdirected by her mother) and was looking helplessly in her handbag for proof of her own identity, desperate for evidence of who she was since nobody else knew her except Jim and he was working at the lab.

It was too late for proper communication with her father, let alone reconciliation, but Joan persuaded Brian to send Robert some photos of himself conducting his music to the film *Black Narcissus*. These reached the old man in a brief lucid moment and, according to his nurse, he responded with joy, mumbling about his 'dear, dear son'. 'I had no idea I meant anything to my father at all,' Brian told Joan, who felt she had at least achieved this brief connection between them.

But when Robert died in late July, she was inconsolable and her grief was compounded by the fact that she had nothing to remember him by. The small bundle of his possessions sent on from America, including his precious fountain pen, was lost in the post before it reached her.

Jim's job took the family to Scotland. During his time with Coastal Command he had worked under C. H. Waddington, who had since been appointed Buchanan Professor of Genetics at Edinburgh University. Waddington was also head of the genetics section of the Agricultural Research Council and he recruited Jim on to his team. He wanted his chosen staff to work closely with one another in as productive an environment as possible, preferably in a set-up where they might live together as well. As Haldane had found when he was trying to keep his colleagues in one place, this was a difficult proposition in London, made more so by the post-war housing crisis. Waddington's solution was to buy a large mansion on the southern outskirts of Edinburgh and move everyone up there. The idea was that his research team, technicians, assistants and their families could live together relatively cheaply under one roof in a creative scientific community.

Joan was more than happy to be part of this adventure. Thoroughly disenchanted with the house and life in London, the thought of more space and no cooking appealed greatly to her.

In January 1947 the Agricultural Research Council had whisked Waddington's whole team up to Edinburgh on the train, paid for their stay in a hotel, wined and dined them and showed them round Mortonhall House and its gardens. Joan had written to Naomi, still excited after this glamorous trip:

Of course I can foresee frightful periods when staff will disinte-
grate and wives will have to fill in gaps till they are replenished
with new staff. That sort of thing is bound to happen unless we
are terribly lucky. There will be hideous bogies of every sort and
we are not going into this expecting everything to be perfectly
marvellous. But at present it offers new advantages which we
have never had the fun of trying before and it seems well worth
the undertaking. Yes, it will be like a college, as you say. And
Waddington said this 'would be the first married college of
its kind' . . .

6 May 2005

We edge up a long driveway with speed bumps, past a caravan park
and a field of Highland cattle. My guide George points out where he
once shot a pheasant and it landed outside a Nissen hut and a man
came out and just picked it up and took it inside.

Everything is very green. We park and get out of the car, and suddenly there's the house, lit up in the last light of the evening sun. It's
unchanged from the photographs I have in my bag. Sombre.
Composed. And there's the circular bathroom window in the attic,
from which you'd be expected to abseil in a steel drum and harness
if there was a fire.

The trees are massive – chestnut, oak, copper beech, cherry,
pine. There's a fountain spilling water from a stone lion's mouth.
George looks for the giant monkey puzzle tree he remembers but it's
not there. The lawns have been overgrown for years and then
cleared again, the trees freed but the orientation of the garden
changed, paths re-aligned and lost. The statues have gone but pieces
of pedestal remain in the grass.

The garden is full of blackbirds singing. We find an open bumpy
area, spongy with raised sides; the old croquet lawn. What was once

the kitchen garden has been cleared and now stands empty, short grass running like fitted carpet into every corner of the walled enclosure, making it an outdoor room or a waiting stage. The ghost outline of a greenhouse is scarred on to the brick of the back wall. There are rabbits in the meadow.

At the Stable Bar, where we have supper, they serve swordfish and Australian red. 'I remember when this was the stables,' says George to the waiter, 'I can remember a pile of straw in that corner as if it was yesterday – over fifty years ago.'

We come out of the pub into a purple dusk. Two windows of the big house are lit up, the chestnut trees are silhouetted against the sky. It isn't dark yet, even at ten o'clock, and you can see as far as the hills.

Mortonhall House is a large, square three-storey Georgian building of grey stone, standing confidently in extensive grounds.

Its proportions combine grace and solidity. Fourteen tall sash windows look out over the gardens from under a central pediment. The surrounding land is slightly raised to the front of the house, disguising the lower basement level, reached by discreet steps to one side. Similarly discreet, the chimneys and attic windows are set back on the roof, leaving the façade clear of extra detail.

As one approaches, wide stone steps lead to the large central wooden door under a columned porch.

That is as far as I get on my visit. The house remains divided into private flats.

My guide, George Newell, who joined Professor Waddington's lab aged twenty-one as a technician, and lived up in the attic with the circular bathroom window, even arranges for me to look round one of the flats, which happens to be up for sale. He wants to get me into the main building, to show me the stairway and the views Jim and Joan would have had from their rooms. We call the estate agent and turn up for a viewing the next day. But our plan is thwarted. The flat on offer turns out to be in the basement, where the stores and kitchens used to be, now totally obscured by perfect plaster and tasteful curtains.

When Waddington's people lived here, the shadowy hall was tiled in black and white, a grand wooden staircase lead to the floors above and light filtered down from a high cupola. For Joan and the family, it was a romantic place to come to from devastated London. There was a library with wall paintings and tapestries, a communal drawing room, a nursery, a shared dining room and then flats on each floor, going right up into the attics where the students lived in single rooms.

Post-war practicalities somewhat undercut the architectural grandeur. Each family was given a set of government-issue furniture and a curl of lino for the floor. When they arrived, in the autumn of 1947, the place had not been lived in for some time and was piled with rubbish, the surfaces layered with grime. It took two cleaners several weeks of constant work before a pattern could be discerned on the hall floor and individual floorboards made out in the dining room.

The main problem was how to get the place working as a proper household. These families barely knew one another, if at all, but were thrown together and expected to function as an intellectual and domestic whole. A housekeeper, a gardener, a cook and various other domestic staff were installed by Waddington, but the national shortage of labour meant that the situation was always in crisis, with cleaners walking out, promised maids not turning up and the house teetering on chaos in the meantime.

One of Joan's early letters to Naomi describes the kitchen being at breaking point, the housekeeper in floods of tears, shocked at the constant bad language, the wives not quite knowing who was in charge, everyone still trying to do things their own way. It took several turbulent weeks for the community to settle in and find some sort of routine.

Every domestic decision, complaint and argument would be discussed in a full house meeting and the minutes taken down in a log (long since removed from the ARC archives by someone who realised it was too inflammatory to be left around. George Newell did once get to see it but only once it had been filleted).

The adults were expected to pull their weight with chores, like feeding slops to the pig, working in the vegetable garden or collecting firewood from the grounds. Some were more compliant than others.

Miss Jones, the housekeeper, would collect everyone's ration coupons for the week, do the shopping and cook all meals; impressively efficient, she could cut a pie into thirty-one equal pieces. The household added to its stores with whale meat, which was not rationed and could be bought from the docks, rabbits and pheasants shot in the grounds behind the gamekeeper's back, seagull eggs collected on expeditions out to the Bass Rock and even the odd etherised animal (a rabbit or calf) brought home from the lab.

When the house pig contracted a skin disease and was due to be killed, a special meeting was called. The collective decided they should anaesthetise the animal first, then slit its throat. By the time they sat down to roast pork, every fibre had been impregnated with chloroform, rendering the meat completely inedible.

Dinner was the one point in the day when all the residents of the house would come together. The children finally in bed, the married women rejoined the others and the whole company sat round one long table, Professor Waddington at the head and everyone else changing place from evening to evening, so that they were always sitting next to someone different. It was an opportunity to debate, gossip and entertain.

Foreigners – artists, scientists and dignitaries – would sometimes visit, as Joan describes in a letter to Naomi dated 5 October 1947:

Wad. has been in London all week so J. has been taking the chair again for dinner. We had a Chinese female professor to entertain last night. We took her up to the library after dinner, but the cleaners hadn't got round to it yet and nobody had seen about getting suitable electric light bulbs and the place was so dim and dirty we soon gratefully repaired to the Reeves' flat which was on the same floor. There were about seven of us and quite unexpectedly our entertaining took the form of demonstrating peculiar games, tricks and practical jokes. Our treasurer, for instance, had his hands tied together in front of him and our mathematician went through the contortions of turning the treasurer's waistcoat inside out without removing his (the treasurer's) jacket. It seemed an enormous success with Professor Woo and we spent the evening rocking with laughter.

Susan and Bill Sobey, who were to become good friends of Joan and Jim, met and fell in love while working together at the lab in Edinburgh. Bill lived in the stables and Susan in one of the attics. She remembers Mortonhall as a place 'full of oddballs'. Doors would slam in the middle of the night, shadows climb in and out of bedroom windows. You might hear sobbing in the garden, breaking glass. On hot afternoons everyone sunbathed on the roof.

The building had its own eccentricities. The plumbing would carry music from one flat to another as someone practised the piano, delivering Mozart down the pipes and into the bathroom on another floor. And, because the electricity supply was shared with a local migrant camp, it was often erratic; the lights got dimmer and dimmer on winter afternoons, the radio quieter and quieter.

For Jane and Polly, now aged seven and four, Mortonhall was heaven. There were lawns to race on and roll down, trees to climb, wilderness and woods, grass head high in the summer, thick clipped hedges to run along until you fell in waist deep. There were carefully raked gravel paths to gouge into ruts and turn to mud pies and an arboretum, with the names of each tree tagged to its trunk (a favourite game was to swap the labels around). Someone's ginger cat had kittens (to the amusement of the geneticists) and Jane briefly kept a pet hedgehog. The adults were interesting too; George Newell kept stick insects in the attics, Ruth Friedman made little glass animals by melting pipettes over a Bunsen burner. One of the families had an Italian nanny called Consulata, who would walk everywhere in bare feet. Jane remembers seeing her coming back through the snowy garden to the ice-bound house, carrying a vase of water on her head, having filled it at the fountain.

Where did Joan fit in to all this? Heavily pregnant on arrival at Mortonhall, she gave birth to Alexander, known as Sandy, in November 1947. As with her previous children, having a new baby gave her tremendous pleasure and confidence. She wrote to Naomi from her bed in the nursing home, euphoric after the birth:

> . . . off I went again and found myself swimming downstairs on a stretcher, saying had I really got a son and this was one of the best moments of my life.
>
> I congratulated everybody again and as I was being lowered into my bed, I asked once more if I really had a son, and on being reassured, I exclaimed loudly that it was so nice to have a change of genitals – only to realise by the expression on their

faces of careful obliviousness, that I had said something rather more unusual than they could take and that I was also by this time in a ward of fully-conscious and self conscious, polite people.

While the communal nature of Mortonhall provided mutual support and child-minding for the married women, it was not an easy place to live. The house was extremely isolated and it took forty minutes to walk the property end to end, twenty minutes in either direction to reach a bus stop. The two shared cars available to the thirty or so residents were mainly used to take people in to the laboratory in the King's Buildings and the children to their various schools. The men and single women would pile into the cars and head off to work each day, leaving the married women behind with the babies and younger children.

Intelligent and opinionated, exhausted after six years of war and often sleep-deprived by their young families, these women had not chosen to live together. Inevitably, tensions would build up between them. Arguments flared over discipline and child-rearing, fights between offspring leaked into rivalries between mothers. One mother challenged Joan because Jane had told her daughter, in graphic detail, how babies were produced; Joan raged at someone else for letting Alexander's foot dangle out of his cot and get cold. Polly bit a baby as it slept in its pram, another child continually shat itself and was ignored. Even simple events would quickly become flashpoints between families, as when a present got played with by the neighbour's children:

A feather pillow for the new baby arrived lately with only a banner of paper flying from its bare surface and a straggle of string. Later, however, the Sutherland children took it out of our flat and into the garden where they rent it to pieces and all the feathers flew in clouds over the trees.

When I ask people what they remember of Joan during those three years, the answers are disappointing. Although Susan Sobey recalls her once dancing a rather sexy tango with another lab wife at a party, the predominant memory is of someone kind, gentle and fun but completely subsumed by motherhood and rarely relaxed. People are unable to quite picture her, as if she were always slightly out of focus. The Sobeys still have a piece of yellowed writing paper from Mortonhall, a leftover from some party game. It is a list of everyone's names, where someone has given each resident a joke title for a book they might write. Joan's is simply *Always Rushing Around*. There is something so literal about this, as if she barely warrants a pun or a proper joke; she is barely part of the game.

How ironic, then, that she had actually had work published. Her literary talents and connections remained unknown to most of the other residents, who saw her simply as a mother and wife. She surprised them one New Year's Eve, by reciting some of her poetry but even then most people didn't realise that the poems were her own.

Her artistic skills came briefly to the fore when the children found a Victorian wooden rocking horse in the attics and she helped them renovate it, painting in nostrils and eyes and making a new bridle, but most of the time she was completely absorbed in an endless round of domestic chores. Polly and Jane were left to play on their own for hours while she tended to the new baby or did the washing. For the girls, she was already becoming somewhat distant and vague, although her letters to Naomi remained as engaged as ever.

Jim, meanwhile, was recovering from a relapse when they moved to Edinburgh. He had to go into hospital to have his lung re-sprayed, which was both exhausting and frustrating for him, delaying his start at the lab.

Once working again, he was out all day.

The original plan behind the Mortonhall commune was that individual families would gradually find their own accommodation in Edinburgh and move out. It was not intended as a permanent arrangement, although it did last for about five years, during which time twelve babies were born. Jim and Joan lived there between 1947 and 1949, and then found a house of their own.

In contrast to the graceful proportions and rolling lawns of the big house, 74 Colinton Road was dark and small, in the middle of a terrace between a main road and a canal. Jane remembers it as freezing cold and cramped. Coming into the hall, tripping over Joan's bike, one would be assaulted by smells coming up from the basement kitchen; burnt porridge, and cod heads boiling in the pressure cooker for the dog. In her anxiety to kill germs, Joan tended to over-cook everything and a pall of vegetable reek could hang in the air for days.

Although Jane and Polly were still only nine and seven, they were aware that their mother was often distracted and was becoming increasingly chaotic and clumsy. As Polly recalls,

My mother cried easily, and I would watch her face, anxiously reading her eyes for signs of tears. We would never know why she was crying. She would look away at some distant point, far away inside herself. Her eyes were grey-blue, I think, but even that I can't be sure of but one eye was blind and was a dull opaque grey, which would add to the feeling of her remoteness at these moments.

This absent stare was so familiar but it would fill me with dread. Uneasy, Jane and I would turn away and become engrossed in play or fierce squabbling, which she would for the most part be unaware of.

In an attempt to make herself budget, Joan kept the housekeeping money in a series of jam jars, each labelled 'Food', 'Milk', 'Coal' etc. As the week went on she would tip money from one to the other, borrowing from 'Bills' to pay 'Dinner Money' or 'School' to pay 'Petrol', until she had completely lost track of what she was doing. She would then panic and get upset, knowing that Jim would disapprove. The fact was that money had little reality for Joan; she would worry about it intensely but had no real understanding of how it worked. And she loved to buy things. Jane remembers her cycling off into Edinburgh to buy objects to furnish the house. She came back with a strange padded Egyptian tapestry and a set of china bought from a sea captain; she had been right into the Old Town where, she said, there were still girls with bare feet and babies tied to their backs with shawls.

Inevitably, it was the times when things felt wrong that the children were struck by, and which they still remember. On one occasion Joan accidentally dropped baby Sandy over the front steps into the basement area on to his head. On another, when he was a bit older, she managed to get locked into the lavatory, with Sandy on the other side of the door, and had to call through the window to be rescued by a passer-by. These are not particularly unusual as family anecdotes go, but in Joan's case the domestic dramas were indicative of her state of mind and proof that she was no longer quite in control. Jane turned up at school one day to find no one else there because it was the holidays. Another time, having been in bed with flu for a few days, she came downstairs to check on her pet mice and found that they had all eaten one another's tails because no one had remembered to feed them.

The children began to realise that Joan's interaction with other people could be noticeably odd; she had little sense of what was socially appropriate and was always trying to explain herself to complete strangers. When a parcel of fish leaked through its newspaper and soaked the front of her dress as she was sitting on the tram, she spent a long time reassuring her fellow passengers that it was all right, that she hadn't wet herself and the baby hadn't peed, it was just fish juice.

On another occasion, when the plumber came round to fix something in the bathroom he found a smudged note in close, inky writing, that read, 'Just to explain to people how you mustn't sit on the lavatory seat without taking care. Flush it first because there might be bleach in the bowl which could splash up and sting your bottom.' Joan was disconcerting and occasionally embarrassing, running out to the dustman to give him two shillings and clothes for his daughter and then explaining at length and with great emotion how she wished she could give him more but was unable to do so.

She just about managed to keep the household going. But while she found ordinary tasks very difficult, the rarer aspects of family life seemed to come easily to her. Polly remembers that she was particularly good at providing surprise treats, arriving home from shopping with paper angels for the girls to cut out and stick in their scrapbooks or some new animal for their toy farm. When they were ill she always made them feel very special; she would dim the lights, mash their pills up with jam and bring them books to read. Or, better still, invent stories for them as they lay in bed.

The back garden ran down to a high wall, nettles and the canal. This was the scene of daily games and dramas, with kids fishing for minnows and falling off the wall, getting horribly stung. When workmen came past on a barge one day to clear the bank of obstructions and threatened to knock down the children's carefully built den, it was Joan who ran out to protest.

Another time, she listened carefully to Jane and Polly's story of a strange man they had met out the back, who had no idea that frogs came from frogspawn and who had opened his flies and offered to show them his 'toolie'. With a typical mixture of maternal concern and empathy for the outsider, Joan said they should not laugh at him. They were to stay away from him, but also to 'remember that he is very sad'.

Jim and Joan's marriage deteriorated swiftly at Colinton Road. Where the strange oppression of living in the Mortonhall commune had somehow kept them together, living in their own home showed up the differences between them. Joan was messy and extravagant; Jim was tidy and desperately anxious about money. Joan was increasingly religious and emotional, Jim atheist and contained. Joan wanted to be appreciated for who she was, not judged on how she managed or failed, but Jim could not give her the reassurances she needed because he was so busy with work and so disturbed by the chaos they seemed to live in. They bickered endlessly and were each separately miserable.

Feeling desperate, Joan turned to her mother and the church as sources of comfort and reassurance. Both were guaranteed to infuriate Jim. He knew he had liberated her from Ellen and Joan herself had recognised this, writing in 1939 that it was wonderful to have broken away and to no longer be 'the king-beam, the support paramount' in her mother's life. But where Jim's cool rationality had once been a refuge, Joan now found it hard and uncompromising. As communication between them began to break down she confided more and more in Ellen, writing long, despairing letters about their problems. Some of these she would tear up and flush down the lavatory, leaving the bowl swirling with blue ink. Others survived, page upon page, stuffed into envelopes and posted south. Troubled by her daughter's distress, Ellen sent money and small presents, and even paid for a home help for a while. Jane recalls that her father could not stand his mother-in-law and found it almost impossible to be polite to her. He once shut the door in her face.

It was in Edinburgh that Joan began to attend church regularly and to formalise her very private faith. She wrote to Ellen about her religious ideas and even mentioned wanting to be confirmed – when she was ready and when she had chosen between the Episcopalian and the High Anglican Church. Jim, who remained staunchly atheist, had no patience for this and inevitably felt alienated by Joan's developing Christian beliefs.

Her decision to seek psychiatric help, some time in 1949, only served to make things worse. She felt out of control and isolated, and hoped that by talking to someone neutral she might save her marriage. W. R. D. Fairbairn, one of the leading psychiatrists of his time, was a Freudian analyst who practised in Edinburgh. Jim was furious that Joan sought advice from an outsider and he was hostile to the idea from the beginning, although he did pay for her initial sessions. He also felt excluded from this close relationship with another man – she was seeing Fairbairn once a week for about two years. Suspicious of his motives, unable to believe in the science of psychiatry and angry that his personal life was being discussed with a stranger, Jim chose to loathe him.

Fairbairn was to have a considerable effect on Joan's life. One of his main responses to her distress was that he thought her problems were only exacerbated by her continuing to think of herself as a writer. He therefore told her to sever her literary connections and to give up the constant battle of running a family while trying to be creative. It is a measure of how desperately trapped Joan felt that she complied. After nearly twenty years of intense friendship and mutual support, she began to distance herself from Naomi, turning down invitations to stay at Carradale and sending hostile letters. She also became increasingly suspicious of Naomi's socialist politics and sought to cut herself off from any left-wing connections. Naomi did not understand what was happening and blamed Jim, but he was just as devastated by how determinedly Joan was following her doctor's orders. 'He took from her what I regard as her only hope of salvation – her writing, which is now anathema to her,' he would write angrily to his sister in 1953. Jim believed that Joan's problems lay in her organisational incapacity and not in the nature of writing itself. He had married a poet and he did not believe that she should give up her poetry.

Joan, however, was immensely relieved at being given a way out of her dilemma and she clung to Fairbairn's every word. The impact of this change is clear in her letter-writing. Unlike her letters to Naomi, which flare with imaginative detail and excitement, glancing from one thought to the next, her long-winded communications to Ellen are suddenly earnest, difficult to read and repetitive, as she tries to become the modest, conventional woman she feels she ought to be.

I think it is very sad when men and women become preoccupied and burdened with the feeling they have got to do some particular work by which they will be remembered . . . On the other hand, to feel as complete as possible as an ordinary man or woman . . . is truly wonderful – and to feel the endowments of one's own gifts, to meet with the right encouragement and by those gifts give praise to the glory of God . . .

On Fairbairn's advice, she started painting a great deal. At least she could express herself this way, without the weight of years of self-doubt and rejection pressing down upon her. Jim was initially impressed at how much she was doing and he praised her work as that of a true artist. But, typically, this only fuelled Joan's insecurity; why did he appreciate her as an artist but not as a good human being? Why did he want her to *do* something with her work, rather than just let it be a private activity? In one of her long uncensored letters to Ellen, she reported, 'I said I would never exhibit and he said very sadly, "I am past hoping you would ever do anything like exhibiting."' He felt that he had lost her.

In July 1950, in the middle of this protracted marital stand-off, Jim was approached about a job in Australia. The Commonwealth Scientific and Industrial Research Organisation (CSIRO) wanted him to join their team of scientists in Sydney. The details had not yet been defined, but accepting the post would involve a semi-permanent move out to Australia for an initial three years, a short trip back to Britain, then a further seven years to develop the projects he would have already set up. He would be employed by the Australian government to establish an animal genetics teaching programme at the University of Sydney and to work on a programme of research into breeding methods for cattle, sheep and poultry. It would mean more money and exciting, progressive work.

Jim was immediately keen, Joan anxious. She did not want to contemplate such a move and managed to avoid the subject for many weeks, hoping that some world event might make it irrelevant. She was totally against the idea. They had been fighting bitterly and constantly for months – they had even discussed separation – so why would travelling to the other side of the world make things better?

Joan imagined how lonely she would be, stranded thousands of miles from her mother and the rest of her family, from familiar things and places. She pictured herself struggling without the support of her psychiatrist or the church she had recently found in Edinburgh. What would she do out in Sydney and how would she cope? Jim finally pressed her for a decision in December 1950. With a week to decide, she said no, and Jim capitulated; if she really didn't want to go he would turn the job down.

But Joan's relief was short-lived.

When asked in 1951 if he would reconsider, Jim did so without consulting her. He accepted the job and told Joan he was taking the children to Australia. If she wanted, she could come too. If she wanted to stay behind, she would be alone. Within weeks the whole family was packing to leave.

CHAPTER 6

_____

SOMEONE IN THE ROOF

None can witness when a change is wrought
Til afterwards. Few have heard
The last tick before the clock stops short
Or seen the crack appear upon the ceiling

from *Amber Innocent*, J.A.E., 1939

There was a huge amount to be arranged. Where would they live?
How would they get out there? What about schools? The dog? What
furniture to take and what to leave behind? And what would it be
like? Joan was used to pastoral Kent, the Sussex Downs, the flat
green fields of north Shropshire, the grey-blues of Kintyre. She
could not picture Australia.

She threw herself into preparations for the move and tried hard
to see it as a new beginning. This was a chance to shed the past; she
and Jim could start afresh. As if to convince herself that the future
was what mattered now, Joan decided to eradicate all evidence that
she had ever been a writer. On impulse, a few days before the family
was to leave Edinburgh, she made a bonfire in the back garden and
burnt all her work. Along with her albums of postcards, childhood
diary and early poetry, she destroyed all her adult poems (including

the Blitz poem), her research notes for Mrs Beeton, her BBC talks and plays, her novel (still unfinished), all her notebooks and every other piece of writing she had ever kept. I imagine she burnt Naomi's letters at the same time. When Jim came home from the lab that evening, all that remained was a pile of ash.

It must have seemed the only thing she could do; an irreversible act of surrender, or maybe of escape. Her father had done something similar in 1936; Joan had been told by her aunt that, just before emigrating to San Francisco, Robert had burnt the entire manuscript of his verse translation of Marcus Aurelius. Did she feel compelled to follow his example? Did she feel she had some sort paternal endorsement or was this just a coincidence and a parallel she was unconscious of?

Whatever her motivation, the bonfire marked the end of part of her life; her struggle to be both writer and mother was over. In the passenger list of SS Oronsay, the boat they took to Sydney, Mr Rendel's occupation is registered as 'Agricultural Research'; Mrs Rendel's as 'H. D.' – Home Duties.

Life on board ship would be a challenge in itself. They would be travelling First Class – paid for by the Australian government – and socialising daily with their fellow passengers. Joan needed new clothes for the voyage, a dress for dinner.

After several humiliating shopping trips where assistants tried to persuade her into unattractive satin frocks, she decided to make her own outfit. She bought two silk slips, one cherry pink, one emerald green (still her favourite colours), and made herself a neat little broderie anglaise dress in black to go over the top. She had a matching bolero jacket and, for when it got hotter as the boat edged into the tropics, a sundress covered in pineapples and birds.

The Rendels packed up their belongings and sent them on ahead, then stayed at a bed-and-breakfast in Kent, where they could prepare for departure and say goodbye to friends and family. Leonard Woolf came to tea; Jane remembers him frail and shaking, his tea-spoon rattling in his saucer. Ellen was gently but firmly dissuaded from joining them on the journey. And, at the last minute, Jane trod on a needle in bare feet and had to be rushed off to hospital.

Polly remembers an incident that occurred one afternoon at the bed-and-breakfast, and which illustrates how much of a strain Joan was under during this protracted departure. The owners had gone out for the day and urged the family to make themselves at home and to use the kitchen if they wanted. Joan set about looking through the fridge and became obsessed with some pork chops she found. Deciding they were contaminated, she set fire to them in the grill pan and carried the whole thing, flaming, out into the garden. Polly trailed after her knowing, even at the age of eight, there was something wrong with this. Jim followed behind, bellowing, 'For God's sake!' while Joan insisted, 'But they were completely off! The whole place is filthy! They were off!' The owners returned to find no chops and the kitchen full of smoke.

The *Oronsay* sailed from Tilbury docks on 21 November 1951. It was an immense ship, with thrumming engines, wooden panelling and grand staircases. The Rendels had two good cabins with port-holes.

However hazy and troubling Australia might have seemed from Edinburgh, and however anxious she felt about the future, Joan was happy on the voyage. Released from housework, she was finally able to relax. She could dress up for meals, make new friends or meet other couples for drinks. The days were airy and bright. Flying fish would land on deck, there was the constant invigorating sound of the engines, of bells ringing and of bugle calls announcing the next sitting for dinner. She was enchanted by the luxury of life on board and relished every aspect of it.

In a letter to her in-laws, just a few days into the voyage, she describes the pleasure of being served by immaculate white-suited waiters and of eating whatever she wanted from the incredible range of dishes in the dining room. The children, much to their chagrin, were restricted to the nursery and children's dining hours but Joan could sit up on deck with the other passengers, reading or chatting in the sunshine. On one occasion, hurrying to get the children's costumes ready for a fancy-dress parade, she was joined by Lady McKell, the wife of the Governor-General of Australia, who helped her stitch red stripes on to Sandy's trousers so that he could go as a busman.

Family life was dilute enough to be enjoyable and, suspended between continents, Joan escaped her dreads and felt like a normal woman. She loved the romance of being at sea; the speed and smooth motion of the ship, the colours of the Mediterranean at dusk, the stars at night. Her one regret was that Jim was not keen to dance, whereas she leapt every time 'Dancing on B Deck' was announced. She wrote wistfully to Judy Rendel, her mother-in-law,

> I am reluctant to appear on the dance floor alone as all the married people who dance go there together. In another ten years it won't have the same attraction for me but I have always wanted to have more opportunity to dance and here it is all so beautifully laid on – a lovely floor, a quite respectable little band, an air-conditioned ballroom with two walls open to the decks where you can stroll out and look for the Southern Cross between dances . . .

While Joan longed to dance, Jim preferred to play energetic bouts of tennis, a game she was no good at. He, too, began to unwind as the journey went on. The focus was social rather than domestic and he found himself opening up, talking to new people and forming a friendship with an Australian sheep-farmer that would last for years to come. There were on-board concerts, competitions and treasure hunts laid on and Jim won several prizes.

Granted this respite from normal work, he also had much more time to spend with the children. When Jane found an exhausted bird on board, he told her not to handle or feed it. He helped her find a box, dripped it water from a pipette and in the morning she held it up and it flew whirring out of her hands.

Presumably to give himself some time on his own, he chose not to accompany Joan every time the boat docked briefly at various ports along its way. While she was eager to explore these new places, he said he was not interested, although he did go ashore at Naples to show Jane the city and the whole family visited Columbo. When the boat stopped at Aden, Joan's sight-seeing excursion turned into quite an adventure. She joined four other women in a decrepit taxi, which sped them through the heat and dirt to an oasis. On the way back, the taxi broke down in a completely dark tunnel cut through rock. The ladies sat in black, dusty silence, knowing that there was no passing-space should another vehicle come the other way, holding their breath until the driver finally got the car started again and raced them back to the waiting liner.

The family's first sight of Australia was Fremantle, where the *Oronsay* called before heading east. It was roasting hot and the buildings looked strange and old-fashioned. Advertisements announced, 'Peter's ice-cream: it isn't a fad it's a food!' Voices were new. Back in Edinburgh, listening to an Australian cricket commentator on the radio, Jim had explained that this was how people were going to speak. Now it was for real and it made them feel a long way from home.

As if to signal the end of the holiday and the return to real life, the boat ran into a storm as they came through the Great Australian Bight. China smashed in the galley and the waiters threw water on the tablecloths so that things would not slide off the dining tables. Bunks detached themselves from walls, an old lady was flung across her cabin and Polly was thrown off the top bunk and split her lip.

Next came Adelaide, then Melbourne and the final stop was Sydney, where they arrived on Christmas Eve 1951. From their boarding house in Neutral Bay they could see the whole of the harbour lit up with fireworks and flashing lights advertising Penfolds Wine and Capstan Cigarettes. Boats of every size crowded the water, all sounding their horns and letting off rockets.

Inside, it felt odd to be eating hot tinned Christmas pudding in a dining room full of strangers.

Jim had bought a house in Mosman, a waterside suburb on Sydney's North Shore, which today is a very desirable place to live. In 1952, however, it was a worn, tired district of higgledy-piggledy yards and rickety back verandas. Old people sat in grey rooms behind yellowing net curtains.

The one-storey house was described as 'old' because it had been built thirty years before, and it needed a lot of work before the Rendels could move in. While it was cleaned, repaired and decorated, the family was put up in Cronulla, a distant southern suburb right on the very outer limits of the city.

On a muggy day in March 2005 I take the Illawarra line south out of central Sydney down through suburbs called Kogarah, Allawah, Jannali, Kirrawee, Caringbah.

The plants spilling over walls and balconies are purple bougainvillea, palm trees, flame trees, morning glory, jasmine and jacaranda. I look for the Sydney of over fifty years ago. Is this the view she'd see coming home from shopping in town? Would that house have been there in 1952? Did she see that tree as a sapling?

New development crowds into any remaining space; naked blocks of flesh-coloured brick, big bare stores, an area called Wolli Creek where the trees are being forced back behind executive apartments, advertised on hoardings plastered with smiling young couples drinking orange juice.

But when the train goes over the Georges River, above Scylla Bay, the view is mostly water and boats, houses coming down to the shore through green. She would recognise this.

I get off at Woollooware. It feels a long way from the city. Warm streets run on a grid away from the station, bungalows snoozing behind low front walls, thin lawns, post boxes on stalks, wheelie bins. It's collection day and the street has become an open-air sitting-room of discarded sofas, television stands with bent legs, rolls of carpet, abandoned exercise bikes.

I call in at the Post Office for stamps and ask how long the shops have been here. A large woman with a Yorkshire accent overhears me, says I should go to the primary school over the road because they produced a book on the history of the area last year. The school secretary isn't much interested in my quest but sells me the book. It tells of the whole area being dairy farms until the fifties. The name Woollooware is Aboriginal for 'muddy flat'. It was cleared in the year my grandparents got here. The little school opened in 1951 to cater for the influx of immigrants. The mud was drained for a golf course.

Then I walk to find Sturt Street, creeping up it in the midday glare, hoping that the original bungalow will still be standing at Number 20. But when I get there, watched disconcertingly by two bored removal men from their van, there's a new double-storey red brick house in its place.

When Joan and Jim arrived here the road was still a dust track and milk came fresh in churns. Now it's clearly affluent. Families have four-wheel drives, small boats, gas-fuelled barbecues.

I try to cut down to the sea but my path is blocked, first by the golf course, then by a high school. I edge round a huge rugby stadium, home to the Cronulla Sharks (Let Us Entertain YOU!), and find myself on a long stretch of fast road with trucks kicking grit at my ankles.

The highway runs alongside the school playing field, cranes picking at grasses on the edge of an afternoon netball match.

On the other side, the one nearest where the sea should be, is mangrove swamp. Sinister pools of dark water lie black and shiny in the shade, crowded with trees standing up to their waists. The mangrove tendrils poke fingers up to just above the oily surface. There are insect noises, mosquitoes, stooping birds.

This is exactly as Joan writes in her first letter home to her mother, and what Polly and Jane have described to me. This is the swamp where the dog, Clover, ran off. They found her hours later, completely covered in mosquito bites and shaking with histamine.

It's suddenly very hot. The sun is blazing and my feet are sore. Why am I wearing unsuitable shoes and why don't I have a hat? I don't even have sunglasses. I feel stupidly ill-equipped and English.

Another fifteen minutes of increasing irritability and sunburn and I decide to turn off towards where I guess the sea is. Over a rise, to the end of another blank residential street and I can hear it. Another turn, the asphalt gives out to sand and there it is. The sea! With breakers and surfers and a wide band of yellow beach arcing from the works on the headland far away to my left, past dunes (exactly as she writes in her letter), then on to the beaches and buildings at Cronulla to my far right.

I take my shoes off and paddle where little pink shells roll at the very edge of the water. This is where she walked and where the children played. I head along the beach towards the town, feeling slightly dizzy, as if I might catch sight of them in the middle distance: Joan peeling a shirt over Sandy's head, Polly and Jane bending over something in a bucket.

The cement shark-proof pool is still there, rust bleeding on to the rocks from safety signs. I get distracted taking a photo and a wave soaks my jeans up to the knee.

Later, in the local library, I read that the bushfires of January 1952 were the worst for forty years.

The family arrived to find a prefab bungalow built on the edge of mangrove swamps, wilderness at the bottom of the garden, the place buzzing with mosquitoes. A thin line of wilting petunias marked the edge of the path and the squalid outside privy was shared with the entire local tennis club, who would troop past the window on their way to and from the only lavatory for miles around – a garbage can set in the ground with a bit of fennel at the bottom and a wooden seat on top. It filled up quickly, stank, and was changed twice a week.

With Jim off at the university every day and the girls taking a two-hour train journey to their new school, Joan was left alone with Sandy to make sense of this new world. It was the height of Australian summer and the heat was incredible. In her first letter home to her mother, started on 18 January 1952, she writes,

The roads in the suburbs are very rough, some, as here, not made up at all. Taxis carrying 5 or 6 housewives at a time, who have decided to share (but who still have to pay the full fare) – sometimes myself among them – go along from the shops amid clouds of yellow dust – the ramshackle bus – with rather unpredictable times also. Fibro and cement bungalows

Joan aged about two.

Joan at about ten years old.

Ellen at Crouch.

Ellen at Lyme Regis.

Brian, Joan and her friend Geoffrey
Dunne at Crouch.

Brian and Joan with their dog.

A trip to the beach.

Joan in the garden at Crouch in
1930. The picture was taking by
Goodenough, the family servant, and
appeared in the *Book Society News* in
April 1931, alongside Clemence
Dane's review of Joan's first
collection of poems.

Joan as a young woman.

Brian and his first wife, Frida Niklaus, sitting at the piano for their portrait (painted by Ellen's sister-in-law Noël Adeney).

Jim Rendel as a young man.

Newly married at the cottage in Edgmond, 1938. Joan (centre) and Jim, with Jim's sister Jill.

Naomi Mitchison, 1938.

Carradale House, which the Mitchisons bought in 1938.

Winter 1940–41.
Wartime living in the
Harpenden house. The
picture was taken for
Life magazine, but was
not published. *Left to
right:* Hans Kalmus,
Jim, Joan and Jane,
Elizabeth Jermyn,
Helen Spurway.

Pinner, 1944. *Left to right:* Polly, Joan, Jane, Joan's old friend Norman Stuart.

Mortonhall House, on the outskirts of Edinburgh.

Polly, Jane and Sandy at Mortonhall, 1948.

The strain showing. Jim, Joan and Jim's father Dick Rendel at the family house in Owley, Kent, 1951.

The family on Camber Sands, before leaving for Australia in 1951.

The family on Chinaman's Beach, Sydney, c. 1952.

The children outside
the Mosman house.

A portrait of Sandy (8),
Polly (12) and Jane (15)
taken in 1955, a year after
Joan's departure.

The building that was once
Holloway Sanatorium,
Virginia Water, Surrey.

Polly, Jane and Sandy,
Australia, 1983.

Left: Sophie outside her council house in Brook Street, Nottingham. The picture was taken by Sandy on a visit in the 1980s.

Right: Sophie in the 1990s.

Sophie in the pub in 1998, just a few months before she died.

'Poet, Mother and Free Spirit', the gravestone, designed by Jane.

quiver in the heat like a feverish rash, with patches of bush in between.

Our bungalow here looks across rather attractive purple flats of some short boggy plants, with small purple crabs, herons, curious birds of one kind and another – towards Botany Bay. On the right are sandhills, like a small desert, always changing shape in the wind.

The wind is sometimes as if it is blowing out of an oven.

There are constant power-cuts in electricity – total black-outs lasting several hours, when you can neither cook, wash up, wash clothes (everything heated by electricity), or iron, or even boil a pot of tea. If you are lucky, there will still be some ice in the refrigerator.

The area was rapidly becoming a dormitory suburb, attracting large numbers of foreign workers and people coming in from other areas of Australia. Hostels were bursting, cheap housing spreading by the month, the new primary school had just opened and every-one was trying to put down roots in new, thin soil.

Joan's familiar difficulties with house-keeping continued, with the added challenges of heat and unfamiliarity:

I am slowly getting into the habit of cooking in advance and serving things cold – though curiously enough I think we will appreciate a hot meal from time to time, as people do here! I have some beautiful jellied veal with eggs in it in the fridge now – I cooked it two days ago and it is for tonight –

I am trying not to shop too often. I am going to buy myself a huge bag on wheels which the women round here use for shopping – I will get this out of your present to me. It will make all the difference.

The most mundane details of everyday life were suddenly shocking,

> Daily papers are delivered irregularly and thrown into the garden. The postman comes on a cycle and drops the letters into a little box at the gate and blows a whistle and off he goes. Baker delivers bread in bathing trunks. People are not allowed to undress on the beach, incidentally, so that there are streams of people walking, half naked in their bathing suits, in the streets!

The bungalow contained one book, a copy of *Robinson Crusoe*.

Joan's introduction to the physical dangers of this new country came just a few days after her arrival. Social mores and shopping were one thing, fire something completely different:

> You will have heard of our excessive heat – 105 degrees – and the terrible bush fires – masses of people rendered homeless. Funds are being set up for their relief.
>
> When I was writing to you in the train (going up with the children to meet Jimmy & discuss paint etc in the new home) it happened to be our worst day – the heat became excessive about 10.30 a.m. onwards and I hung out my washing with a wet shirt of Sandy's over my head – the wind was so hot it burned my face and I had to hold my breath – and over our bay, beyond the marsh, the coast on the other side was white with rolling smoke. I was glad to see the water in between. But the heat I was feeling was the sun and the fires behind us which I did not yet know about. Half an hour later it was too hot for me to face fetching the washing in and we had to shut the door over the wire gauze because the hot wind blowing through was so stifling.

The kitchen chairs were very warm, everything was warm and a dress I hung up wet on the back of a chair was almost completely dry in half an hour.

I cooked nothing and we had a picnic meal. I thought of putting off going but decided that once we had got to Mosman we would be cooler in our own bungalow than out at Cronulla. We waited for the bus on our doorstep – buses, local ones, stop anywhere all along the road.

When we were in the train, the children handed me the fan Sandy had given me for my birthday and they told me not to wave it because it only drove the hot air onto us, so I held it between the blast coming in through the window and Sandy and me. Sandy fell asleep and I picked him onto my lap where he lay beaded with perspiration and woke up later much better for it. Jane and Polly were almost speechless. On the other hand, two other little girls in the carriage were jumping up and down, comparing their petticoats under their organdie dresses.

There was a very contented-looking, crimson-faced man, looking cool as a tomato, puffing at his pipe and wearing, as far as I could see, at least three layers of thick clothes. I imagined him perspiring heavily and that was why he was doing well. I wrote my letter to you as long as I could – and whenever I looked through the window I saw sad-looking little shut up homes and, not far away, billows of white smoke. There were fires raging on fronts of many miles at four of the places we passed through – at Jannali, Kirrawee, Sutherland and Como – and I heard afterwards that the temperature at Como was 120! No wonder we felt it! I don't think the children and I will ever forget that journey.

But this ought to reassure you that I can survive the heat

by now. When we motored back in the evening, when the temperature had dropped quite a lot, we saw no smoke where we went but could smell it and we wondered from stage to stage what we should find and planned to pick up Clover and as many belongings as we could fit into the car and return to our empty bungalow at Mosman and sleep on the floor if necessary.

However, all was safe. Jim and I did not feel like going to bed till quite late because of the smell of smoke and burned wood but we were really quite safe – there is a lot of buildings and roads between us and where the fires were and it is nice to think we could always pop down to the water if necessary.

All this may sound rather dramatic and perhaps it's true to say we have been on the finger of chance, but at the same time of course we have been in no danger.

The rest of this first letter to Ellen (which runs to thirty-one pages) is a stoic mixture of the domestic and the emotional, its inconsistency revealing Joan's true state of mind. She cuts from ordinary preoccupations about ants in the sugar and the price of meat, to the barely suppressed miseries of her complicated marriage. The weeks on the boat had been a distraction, a holiday away from what was wrong between her and Jim, but now there was no escaping their problems. Reading between the lines, they were no longer sleeping together and this was Jim's choice, not hers. Sex had always been sacred and essential to Joan's sense of self so the rejection challenged her very existence; she was forced to find a rationalisation, however contorted, to make it bearable. Similarly, she spent much of her mental energy (and much of her letter) in trying to justify her choice in coming out to Australia, both to herself and to her mother, repeating over and over how her purpose now was to build a secure family home and to ensure that the children were happy.

With their emotional life so wretched, she and Jim threw themselves into the practicalities of getting the new house ready. Having started the day at six in the morning, Joan and the children would head for Mosman straight after school and Jim would join them from work to sort out the flooring, check on the decorators or arrange the concreting of the wash house. They would have supper in the garden as the lights were coming on in the harbour below and then make the long journey back to Cronulla through the dark, the children so tired that they would not wake up when Joan washed their feet and hands before putting them into bed.

But there was no escape from her familiar demons. Even as she was writing her first letter home to her mother, Joan panicked that she was wasting time, that every minute spent on the letter was stacked up against her on the domestic front. Time lost, time to be blamed for. And yet, by continuing to write, she was keeping the world at bay, putting off having to engage with her immediate problems. Twenty-seven pages in, she rounds on Ellen and insists that she should not be expected to write such long letters and will write less in future. From now on, she states, she wants to live a practical rather than an intellectual life: '. . . I want to sew all sorts of things and make all kinds of things with my hands – and I want my life to be actual, not matter for journalising. Can't you see that to write a journal would be the last thing I would want to do, even if I had masses of time on my hands?' There are four more packed pages before she can finally bring herself to sign off.

The other element in this long missive is Joan's growing religious fervour. It interrupts her train of thought, slices into anecdotes. She ricochets from explaining the sexual relationship she thinks that all women have with Jesus Christ, to defending an unscientific theory of evolution. Like the physical act of writing, religious phrases and clichés seem to make her feel safe. She walls herself in behind them, and is disappointed that Jim refuses to join her.

I think women are really very dependent morally on men – I can only say that I am – and I long to follow in the paths directed by a husband and to feel that he is ready to accept that we are imperfect and that we need God's grace to help us.

So I read over and over the Epistles of Saint Paul and when I get in touch with more people who feel as I do, it will make a great difference, provided Jimmy does not get too irritated by it – he is intensely jealous of the idea of my being supported by any views which apparently don't seem to tally with the Darwinian Theory of evolution on which modern scientific theory and works is founded.

Where she had once described Jim as being 'so calm and comforting with his genetics', she was now positively unnerved by the nature of his work:

He believes that scientists could take some animals some day and by breeding and selection and selected environment they could produce a man. In fact it seems to me scientists frequently want to prove that they can do what God has done.

Why all this should disquiet me so much I don't quite know – but you see his attitude of priority of knowledge extends over every intimate detail of our relationship. He is always making out I don't even know myself and the feelings of my own body and my own mind.

Joan claimed that realising her inferior status was her highest honour: 'My only mission is submission.' She now believed that the duty of woman was to serve God in her capacity as a good mother and she would find complete fulfilment in her devotion. But, in the face of Joan's fervent protestations, Jim withdrew further from her. He disliked her beliefs and found her behaviour oppressive, unattractive and unreasonable. As those early weeks progressed, the children also thought her strange and off-putting. She had lost much of her playfulness and warmth and seemed constantly anxious. Standing on a chair to screw in a lightbulb, she announced, 'Look at all the mosquitoes round my knees! It's probably because I have my period and they're attracted to the blood.' Jane in particular resented her. Why did she say these things? Why was she so extreme? Surely it was deliberate?

Though instructed not to scratch their insect bites, the children worried at them until they became infected and the walls of the bungalow were soon smeared with swatted mosquitoes. To add to the general sense of squalor, Clover the dog came on heat, attracting all the neighbourhood dogs to the doorstep, where they would howl and pee and bark and fight.

It was an immense relief to move into the Mosman house in May 1952.

The bungalow is still there, although it has been thoroughly modernised and extended; the garden is now mostly taken up with a swimming pool. It stands on a quiet sloping street that runs down towards the bay, hairpinning out of sight to where the ferry docks at Mosman Wharf. The door is open when I approach and a small blond boy races back into the shadows to find his mother.

'I'm just off to work, I'm afraid, so I can't stop,' she gushes, before ducking back into the house, as I try to explain why I'm there and ask if I can take some photographs of the exterior.

A few minutes later, she reappears to apologise and tells me that that was a white lie. She doesn't have to go to work yet; she thought I might be wanting to sell her something. Also, was my grandfather Jim Rendel, whose obituary she cut out of the *Sydney Morning Herald* a few years back? She knew he'd owned the house, was interested in its history.

I am suddenly standing in the front bedroom and then walking down the hallway, past the linen cupboard where the children used to play hide-and-seek. The current owner has four children of her own and two large dogs. The house is full of school holidays and sports shoes. 'We kept the ceilings, you see,' she says, pointing out the patterned plaster above our heads, which is in fact pressed tin panelling painted white. 'We wanted to keep as much of the old stuff as possible, so we got it copied up in Queensland for the extension.'

Here is the walk-in pantry, the stained glass panel, the sliver of a bay view that you can just catch from the kitchen window. The open veranda used to go right round the house; they slept out there on hot nights and Polly kept silkworms in a row of jars until they all turned into moths at once. The loquat tree is gone, as is the mulberry, where the children would gorge themselves on fruit and then pelt one another with the rest.

It is strange to think that Joan was once mistress of this house. That she chose curtains and paint and called up and down this corridor. I try to place her here but it is only much later, as I'm trying to get to sleep that night, that I can finally conjure her up and imagine her coming home to that front door, stepping out of the hot bright sun into the cool of the hall.

After the pioneering crudity of Cronulla, Mosman felt spacious and civilised. The children were much nearer to their schools and Jim to his work. Joan found a church, St Clements, that she could walk to. They were part of a neighbourhood, they had more money than they had ever had before and, for a while, they must have felt they had made the right decision. Joan wrote to her mother-in-law, 'Our prospects are extremely bright . . . we only need to employ discretion and boldness hand in hand, and patience and understanding and we shall build a very good life.'

I have two small photographs of the family on nearby Chinaman's Beach. The first must have been taken by Jim: they sit on the sand at the back of the beach, surrounded by slabs and boulders of honeycomb rock, Jane holding the dog to attention, she and Polly in cotton dresses and cardigans, Sandy in long shorts. Joan sits on a fold-out chair in a sleeveless white frock with a collar, one arm laid across her knee, her face half turned away.

The other, taken by Jane a few minutes later, shows Polly and Sandy, shiny heads together over something on the sand, Jim and Joan both crouching at a small fire with a kettle balancing on driftwood. He's wearing a tweed jacket and trousers, she's putting an arm out to adjust the sticks.

It's a fragile scene. As if, at any moment, the dog will run off, the fire blow out, a cloud pass over the sun.

In reality, things were going badly wrong. Joan was becoming increasingly irrational and isolated. Unable to read the world clearly, she was losing her sense of proportion. Even at the boarding house, when they had just arrived from England, she had been very confused by a couple playing cards. They had been jabbing at one another, calling one another 'liar' and 'cheat', just teasing, but Joan had thought this was genuine animosity and found it distressing. Then, on a family boat trip down the Hawkesbury River, she became desperately upset as they passed a mental hospital on an island and some of the inmates came running down to the water's edge to wave at them; she thought they were calling for help. 'They want to come with us!' she sobbed. 'They think we've abandoned them!'

In the past, Joan had always felt stabilised by her role as mother and by the presence of a baby. She adored children and would have happily had many more. The realisation that Sandy was no longer a really little boy, and that there would be no other child to follow after him, made her profoundly sad and maybe even frightened. She was now in her forties, anyway, but this was another source of friction between her and Jim – he did not want to risk having another baby, while she mourned the fact that once her youngest started school she would be redundant, left alone in the house.

Her grip on the household became less and less sure. With a combination of piety and desperation she wrote to her mother-in-law, 'If I felt I was called upon to produce what is *sufficient*, I feel I could produce my very best, but when I am called upon to be *efficient* I feel utterly hopeless – there seems no mercy in the word efficiency.'

The problem was that she felt that the demands upon her were always set fractionally beyond her capacity to meet them. Hence she felt she could just about cook and budget for the family but found it appalling to have to cater for the dog's needs as well. Clover, the brown and white pedigree pointer they had brought over from England, became a symbol of Joan's struggle with household duties and with Jim. Jim wanted to show Clover in competitions and to breed puppies from her, which he could then sell. He loved the dog, was very affectionate towards her and insisted she be fed proper meat rather than scraps. As he was away at work most of the time it fell to Joan to ensure that Clover remained chaste and safe. Inevitably, given Joan's state of mind and general forgetfulness, she was constantly letting the dog out by mistake, losing her and having to rescue her from sexual encounters with local mongrels. She was jealous of Clover, but also felt sorry for her and was distressed that she could not choose her own mate. Though she claimed not to be able to help the escapes, she also felt it was right that Clover found freedom. Returning home to the latest drama, Jim would be furious, Joan tearful. She complained to Judy, 'for eight months the dog has been making me a slave to it and I get nothing but abuse for my lapses in vigil from my family'.

As Joan found ordinary life increasingly difficult, she clung to the comforts she had found back in Edinburgh – her own, unguided psychodynamic analysis of relationships (inspired by Fairbairn) and, increasingly, the Church. Her rambling letters describe going to services and prayer meetings at St Clements, copying out chunks of scripture and repeating the Gospels to herself to keep the chaos at bay. Jim buried himself in scientific research and the life of the lab to avoid her.

He enjoyed the CSIRO. As with the previous labs he had worked in, it was a lively and companionable place and this time he had a lot more responsibility. The pursuit of knowledge was paramount and, for the most part, it was truly democratic. A bright, over-qualified technician could start by washing test-tubes, join in discussions, prove himself and end up working side by side with his boss on a ground-breaking piece of research. People were excited by their work and Jim was greatly respected – and liked – by his colleagues. A strong sense of male camaraderie existed between them all, and when not locked in fierce intellectual argument they were slapping one another on the back, telling jokes and smoking pipes, playing chess in tea breaks and heading off for picnics and adventures at the weekends. The children were often dropped off at the lab after school and loved the kind, eccentric people who worked there.

In contrast, Joan had few friends in Sydney. She rarely attended these expeditions and most of the people she knew were acquaintances from church or contacts made on the boat, most of whom Jim found tedious. A callow young priest and his girlfriend, whom Joan asked along on a couple of family outings in the hope that they might thaw Jim's attitude towards Christianity, did nothing of the sort. Soon bored and exasperated, he refused to see them again.

For a while, Joan was included in various groups of women who gathered to encourage one another in their home-making activities. She was briefly a member of a sewing bee, organised among those lab wives who wanted to make their own cushions, curtains and bedding. Someone nominated her for the Mothers' Union and she became involved with the Sunday School classes run by the church, doing art work with the children. She was also occasionally invited to attend luncheons at the university by the wives of academics, people she described as 'prudent and discreet ladies', but they did not become friends. As Jim was working so hard, Joan was often alone once the children had gone to bed. Like the good fifties housewife she aimed to be, she would spend the long empty evenings sewing or reading magazines or writing letters home.

When Joan and Jim did spend time together they would usually end up fighting. Both were miserable and neither could see a way out, so each stuck to their corner; Jim to science, Joan to the Bible and social conventions. She quoted the New Testament at him and he would retort that half of St John had been added by a heathen or that most of the world's problems were caused by the Christian faith. She would weep with despair and he would attack her for turning to religion in the first place, methodically destroying her arguments and accusing her of 'woolly thinking'. In a fifty-one page letter to her mother, spanning May and June 1952, she writes,

I am feeling very down today, because last night and the night before, Jim and I disagreed very bitterly . . . When I said, 'When will you ever believe the best rather than the worst interpretation?' he said I was being theatrical and my words were devoid of all sense and meaning. He accused me of 'running away', said I first ran to a psychiatrist, then to the church and then back to my mother's 'fairyland'.

One of the worst fights came when Jim discovered that Joan had removed his private journal from his desk and sent it to Dr Fairbairn as 'evidence'.

How could they return from this point? They now shared so little, apart from the children. Jim interpreted everything she said as preposterous and feeble, while she felt rejected and misunderstood. At precisely the point when Joan needed reassurance and encouragement, Jim was unable or unwilling to give it, no doubt because he was so ground down by the endless fighting and by the strain of coping with her bizarre behaviour. She had been told by Fairbairn that her recovery lay in domestic security, but just when she seemed to be moving towards that ('I was feeling at last we were in a fairly peaceful harbour with reasonable plans ahead of us,' she wrote to Judy in September 1952) Jim started to talk about sailing. Excited by living so near the sea, and encouraged by an enthusiastic colleague, he wondered whether he might sail all the way back to England at the end of his contract. This dream of freedom was something he could think about when the domestic situation closed in about his head, but to Joan's limitless imagination it became a terrifying possibility. 'He spends hours poring over maps and things,' she wrote to Judy. 'It makes me feel quite sick.' The subject became yet another source of conflict: Joan argued against it because it filled her with panic, while Jim thought she was being wilfully negative and discouraging.

The children, meanwhile, buried themselves in books, school and one another. Much of the time Joan was tearful and only half there, looking straight through them. Sometimes she would suddenly focus, gather the three of them into her arms and urge, 'Remember I love you! All you need is love and you will be all right. Love is the important thing. I love you all!' It was a momentary relief to have been noticed, but they found her embrace too fervent and strange to be comforting.

Her letter-writing became compulsive and she would cram page after page with tightly-scrawled accounts of daily life, her preoccupations, fears and religious beliefs until the writing itself became the day's activity. Some days she would not have moved at all from when the children had left her sitting in her dressing gown at the breakfast table to when they returned from school in the late afternoon.

One of Sandy's rare memories is of his mother calling him into the sitting room to agree that Jesus Christ was in the room. Standing there, wanting to be helpful, all he could see were the blue swirls of the Persian rug. He felt desperately awkward but eventually said yes, he could see him, because there were slants of light coming in through the blinds and catching on the dust in the air. Maybe that was Jesus.

Other events stand out from this confusing time. A birthday party for Sandy, at which all the visiting children demanded fairy-bread sandwiches and nothing was quite right – Joan had made quantities of undecorated rock buns and done the pass the parcel up in an unusual way with newspaper. She turned up to watch Polly at a school athletics afternoon and was clearly unlike any of the other parents. Already marked out by their accents in an era when 'whinging pom' and 'snooty pom' were general terms of anti-English abuse, the children sensed there was more to Joan's difference than this. She was not like other people. She was no longer like herself.

Again to her mother, she wrote, 'The more confident we are, the more we are prepared to "risk" things being dull. It is so peaceful to be able to feel that entertainment is not essential, that you have not got to be clever to justify existence.'

In a bid for survival, she had shed her connections with her previous life, but it was a life that Jim was still part of and he despised her for opting out. Her horizon had contracted to a few hot streets and trying to get supper on the table on time. She was intent on being a good suburban housewife, yet doomed never to achieve the impossible standards set by her 1950s Australian neighbours. She might laugh about serving 'tinkly drinks on the veranda' but the only time they had a party it was a failure, with Joan handing round plates of burnt cheese straws and thick squares of soggy toast, Jim braced for disaster every time she opened her mouth.

However, the true extent of Joan's disintegration was not apparent to those outside the immediate family. Bill and Susan Sobey, who came out to Sydney with the CSIRO in 1953 and who stayed with Jim and Joan for several weeks while looking for a house of their own, had no idea of her problems. Susan remembers her as kind and generous and welcoming, keen to help them settle in. The two families got on well and saw a lot of one another, as the Sobeys bought a house in an adjacent street.

The children dreaded the fights, which would start almost as soon as Jim got in from work, but they too managed to pretend that all was well to everyone else. Moreover, Joan's deterioration was not consistent. Her letters to Jim's parents were a lot more measured and positive than those she wrote to her own mother. While life in Mosman was becoming very peculiar, she was capable of writing chattily about the children's schoolwork or some social event they had all been invited to. Sometimes she was very much 'there' – like

when she went to the toyshop to buy additions to their toy farmyard
and came home laughing because the shop assistant had not been
able to understand her accent. She'd asked, 'Have you got any
fowls?' and the woman had given her foals instead. She took Sandy
to see a documentary about the Great Barrier Reef at one of the
city museums; she helped the children make biscuits and
Christmas cards. She wrote, 'I feel I have the sweetest children in
the world.' But by 1953, from the family's point of view, Joan's
behaviour had become totally unpredictable. She was now so
disinhibited in her conversation that Jim preferred to turn invitations down than suffer the embarrassment of her suddenly talking
about sex or religion.

In a letter he wrote to his sister that year, he finally confessed
that he was struggling to maintain a normal family life:

> Joan, like her mother, creates a world of her own to live in
> which is unfortunately a most unpleasant one – and is rapidly
> becoming incapable of distinguishing fact from her own
> fictions . . . At present we are in the centre of a communist
> spy ring, I am involved against my will in anti-British activities
> and my mental health is being undermined by a process of
> hypnoses . . . I long for someone to talk to about day-to-day
> affairs, exploring Australia, the politics, the habits, customs,
> agriculture, caves, beaches and so on, to have a home back-
> ground with its own social life and interests instead of returning
> home to what is little more than a cryptic prison camp.

It was very difficult to persuade Joan that her fantasies were not
real when the political climate seemed to mirror her state of mind.
Sydney as a whole was seething with Cold War rumours about under-
cover agents, and Joan's paranoia was fuelled by genuine stories in the

news. One of these, which became known as the Petrov Affair, hit the front pages in April 1954 and centred upon the dramatic defection of an official based at the Soviet Embassy in Canberra. Vladimir Petrov, who was in fact a colonel in the Soviet secret police, had been operating in Sydney and Melbourne when he was befriended and prompted to cross sides by a Polish émigré doctor working for the Australian Security Intelligence Organisation. The media erupted in splashy headlines, sensational photographs, anti-Russian speculation and general panic about political conspiracies. Hidden dangers were all around, it seemed.

One night, when Jim was away on a work trip, she came tearing into the children's rooms and gathered them all into her bed. Gripping them tightly to her beneath the covers, she whispered, 'Shh, shhh, we have to be quiet. There's someone in the roof, they're moving about taking photos. Lie on this side so they can't see you!' Bewildered, Jane, Polly and Sandy lay in the dark until morning, listening to the noises in the roof space. Were they just possums thumping about or were they communist spies? They knew that something was seriously wrong but had no idea what to do about it.

Another time they woke to the sounds of a ferocious fight, with Jim shouting and Joan sobbing behind the closed door, which then burst open. Jim headed down the hall and went banging off into the night with Joan, naked, clawing after him.

It was only at this late stage that Susan Sobey began to worry. Joan took her into the back garden one day to explain that both their households were being bugged from the roof so she should be careful. Susan was at a loss as to how to answer. And since Jim was Bill's boss and such a deeply private man, how could she bring it up with him?

The ladies of St Clements must finally have realised that Joan was ill when she threw herself into the aisle after a Sunday morning service, weeping and imploring God to give her another child, like Sarah in the Bible. One of the congregation brought her home and tucked her up in bed with a large gin. The word breakdown was mentioned.

Shortly after this Jim and Joan went for a long walk together. Polly remembers them looking lovely, going off arm in arm. She felt proud of them and thought how young they looked. When they returned it was to announce that Mother was going to England for a while, for a holiday and to see her own mother, who had been ill. Of course she would miss them terribly and would come back soon.

They went to see her off at the airport, standing on the observation platform. Polly remembers her going up the steps to the plane in the pretty floral dress and little pink hat that she used to wear to church, now too big for her as she had lost so much weight. Sandy remembers that the plane was a Super Constellation. Jane can't remember being there at all.

They waved her into the sky and she never came back.

CHAPTER 7

GONE AWAY

I'm tired of walking in the dark,
With only a tall blank wall
Rising over me, grey and stark.
I'm tired of raising my voice to call
To they who walk outside –
The men who stretched so wide
A chasm between themselves and me
Because I signed my name as Christ.

from 'The Lunatic', J.A.E., 1930

One photograph of Joan survives from 1954, taken on a sunny
September afternoon in the garden at Partridge, the home of Jim's
parents in Iden, East Sussex. In the other pictures taken that day,
Dick and Judy are busy with shears and clippers, tidying up the
hedges around the cottage. Joan, by contrast, sits demurely on the
garden path, in a pale cardigan and bright white skirt, looking at her
father-in-law's turned back as he surveys the tree he has just
trimmed. Caught in the full glare of the sun, she turns away from
the camera, protected and mysterious.

There are no more photographs of her until the 1980s.

*

Joan arrived back in England in the spring of 1954 and enjoyed a period of recovery over the summer. She was forty-one, but this respite allowed her to relax and feel much younger. After a long, recuperative stay with her mother in Hampstead, she went on to visit various uncles and aunts, and Jim's parents, who noted that she was looking well and putting on weight. They treated her with great care, recognised her vulnerability and absolved her of her usual responsibilities. Brian and his second wife Betty were expecting their second child and invited her to stay with them in anticipation of the birth. She helped with the preparations, looked after her nephew and was pleased to be useful.

Her letters to Ellen from this time are sane and chatty, addressed to 'Darling Mother' and full of small-talk about her visits. She writes about how good it is to be back in the English countryside, how much she is enjoying English gardens.

Throughout these months, Joan believed that she was getting better and that it was only a matter of weeks before she would be reunited with Jim and the children. She missed them all and wrote to her mother, 'I am hoping to hear from Jimmy now that he will probably have more time to write letters. I have been thinking of him and the children packing things into the car on Monday morning, early, I expect, and driving off to Courra.'

Back in Sydney, however, Jim felt little more than relief at having her on the other side of the world. Family life had been so disrupted for so long that Joan's absence signalled a return to something like normality. Determined to keep the household running, he faced the situation pragmatically, buying basic shopping in bulk, drawing up a timetable for chores and hiring a home help. He was advised by Joan's doctors not to visit her immediately, so he stayed in Australia.

For the children, these were long, strange, painful months. Jim did not explain what had happened and they dared not ask. Neighbours would come up in the street and ask when their mother was coming back and they would reply, 'Soon. Yes, soon.' They missed her terribly.

In October 1954 Jim wrote to his sister Jill, the only person in whom he felt he could confide, 'I am satisfied that we get on better without Joan and am coming to the conclusion that Joan is happier in England on her own.'

On what evidence he based this belief is unclear. One of Joan's psychiatrists, Dr Thomas Main, reiterated Fairbairn's advice that family life would be the most beneficial course for her recovery in the long term, but by this time Jim held any psychiatric opinion in contempt. He wrote,

Main has told her to return to Australia where, even if she doesn't like the place, she will at least console herself with the children. Poor children. She will take what he says as something unalterable as holy writ & he ought to know this and be a damned sight more careful. I suppose if I was a noble soul of great devotion I would persevere, but I must confess to great relief in her absence. I particularly enjoy being able to visit friends without either having to explain why I left her behind or sit on the edge of my chair throughout the evening, waiting for the inevitable moment when some ghastly mixture of Freud & Jesus Christ is injected into the conversation . . . or when some remark of an innocent guest is pounced on & its motives ruthlessly explored through the pages of the New Testament & Havelock Ellis.

Jim was beginning to believe that he might be able to start afresh and provide a stable base for the children on his own. For him, the marriage had been over for some time. Joan's physical departure had only confirmed his lack of emotional attachment to her and the last thing he wanted was for his wife to come home and disrupt life again. He concluded,

> I have written Joan a brutally frank letter hoping it may induce her to think whether she really wants to come back. I am afraid it won't do any good & may do some harm but I so dislike the prospect of her return that I feel I must put it to her. Of course, if she insists there is nothing to be done until I get back to England, if I do, then I shall arrange by hook or by crook for two establishments, a flat in town & a cottage in the country.

Jim's 'brutally frank' letter was written in the first week of October 1954.

Joan was admitted to Holloway Sanatorium at Virginia Water, Surrey, on 3 November 1954, having suffered an acute mental breakdown.

The exact circumstances that precipitated this crisis remain vague, as Joan was alone at the time it happened. She had already begun to behave strangely a few weeks before, and had spoken of the Nazis trying to gas her through the kitchen taps. Unable to cope, her brother and his wife had left her in their house for a few days, with the instruction that she was to 'sort herself out' by the time they returned from their holiday.

In Joan's version of events, which she recalled as an old woman, she was in an upstairs bedroom when she felt suddenly overcome with panic and terror. She could not move her legs and had to crawl to the window and scream for help. Someone sweeping leaves nearby heard her and called an ambulance.

She was admitted to a local mental hospital, but when Jim's uncle and Professor Lionel Penrose (a family friend) saw the grim conditions of the place, they had her transferred to Holloway Sanatorium.

The Sanatorium was built at the end of the nineteenth century by Thomas Holloway, who had made a colossal fortune selling patented medicines. One of his ointments boasted particularly marvellous healing properties and sold by the million. He decided that he would spend part of his accumulated wealth on the construction of a sanatorium for the class of gentlefolk 'who fell between the Pauper's hospital and the Private institutions for the rich' – that is, the mentally ill middle classes.

By the time Joan was admitted to Holloway it was run by the NHS, but its extravagant architecture, elaborate interior decor and extensive facilities made it unique among mental hospitals. With a maximum capacity of five hundred patients, it had no official catchment area and took in a mixture of locals and people who knew of it as a place where the well-connected and respectable mad would go.

I try to imagine what Joan felt, seeing it for the first time on a wintry afternoon in 1954:

Arriving in a car with her father-in-law. Through the iron gates with a crunch of gravel and first sight of immense walls, grey clouds racing behind the looming Gothic water tower. Does her stomach cramp at the sight of this place, does her mouth go dry, does she hold her bag tighter on her lap? Or is it too extraordinary, unreal, the fact that she is heading up this long drive past an avenue of lime trees and tennis courts, where life seems to be continuing as normal in the shadow of this enormous building, people reading on benches in overcoats, hurrying across green lawns, smoking in a huddle in a doorway.

The car door slams, her bags are taken, her elbow taken. Up the front steps, past clipped hedges, a statue. To the great oak door where a porter greets them and they are welcomed into the muffled gloom of the reception hall.

And now what does she think, as a nurse comes forward and takes her name, someone else takes her coat, her companions embrace her and leave her standing at the foot of the red carpeted staircase? This place, not like a hospital at all. More like a chapel or the carved interior of an Oxbridge college, with gabled wooden archways set in scored panels and every surface, floor to ceiling, intricately painted. Barley sugar stripes in red, yellow, blue and green wrap round pillars and twist up and over doorways. The walls are decorated with flowers and heraldic patterns, every banister is turned and coloured and the rare flat spaces between each newel-post filled with creatures: a lobster's body with a lion's head, a griffin with scales, fantastic birds with rabbit ears. Does she notice these nightmare details, or is she concentrating on the assistant matron with her watch pinned upside down on her white breast?

Is she distressed or relieved as, beyond the mullioned windows, the car turns slowly back down the driveway and someone she has never met before leads her through a door, down a corridor to a room with a screen where she is asked to take off all her clothes and a man with cold hands examines her and writes the details in a book?

As with many of the large mental institutions of the day, Holloway was a major provider of employment for the local town but, beyond that, functioned almost totally independently. The water tower supplied all the requirements of the hospital and the Sanatorium had its own farm, orchard, greenhouses and vegetable plots. There were workshops and studios, two chapels, a shop, a cinema, a swimming pool, cafés, a hairdresser, laundries and a social club. A wide range of activities was organised to keep patients busy, from fruit-picking to sculpture, amateur dramatics to netball. There were tea dances and outings by bus. Long-stay patients might even be accompanied on holidays abroad if they had enough money to pay for a nurse.

January 2005
It is a shock to see the Sanatorium for the first time. My mother has described it to me, I've seen engravings and photographs, I've seen it on television but, leaving the station, looking up and seeing the tower and the gabled front for myself, I am caught off guard. It is so big.

From a distance it is the archetypal mental asylum, a rearing fortress of red brick and Gothic windows. It looks like the set for a film. But when you reach the entrance you realise it is no longer a hospital. After its closure in 1981 it lay derelict and vandalised until a developer bought and restored it in 1994. Now an exclusive estate of executive homes, renamed Virginia Park, it is a gated community of another kind, where the only people on foot are the nannies and cleaners of the wealthy. The main hall is now an indoor swimming pool, the chapel a badminton court. A brochure for the place boasts 'an enviable lifestyle on the grand scale'.

Joy Whitfield, my guide and host, was a student nurse at Holloway Sanatorium in the fifties. She still calls it 'the Sani' and speaks of her days there with huge affection. She believes that the treatment of patients was more humane than in other mental hospitals, and says that it was a wonderful place to work. Compared with the county hospitals, the wards were smaller, the corridors shorter. There were the inevitable isolation units, padded rooms and locked wards where chronically ill patients might spend years at a time, but for most people it was a good place to be.

I am hoping that Joy will suddenly remember Joan and tell me stories that will bring her vividly to life. 'Was she the one who used to write so brilliantly for the hospital magazine?', 'Was she the one who broke her arm, trying to escape over the railway line?', 'Joan Rendel? Of course I remember her! Who wouldn't?'

But there are no such stories; she doesn't recognise my grandmother's name.

We look through a bundle of curling photographs that illustrate hospital life at its best. The images have been carefully posed to give an air of calm and gentle activity. 'Anyone with their back to you is a patient,' says Joy, and immediately I start scouring the pictures with renewed hope.

Is Joan among these cardiganed ladies? Could that be her on her knees, choosing a library book from a trolley in a room decorated with silver paper stars? Or the woman in the striped skirt being shown how to use a loom?

Patients sit about in print dresses and court shoes, drinking tea with nurses in the day room or playing chess in high-waisted skirts, their handbags tucked carefully under their chairs. They all have the same hair, dark and crimped round the nape of the neck, and they all look well-dressed, if a little static and full of effort compared with the more graceful, vigorous nurses who seem to be having a much better time.

There are elderly ladies bending diligently over drawing boards in the art room; patients doing their washing in a tiled laundry full of spin dryers and ceramic sinks; someone in a smart suit being admitted by two smiling nurses, her husband's arm protective around her shoulder. There are satin eiderdowns on enamelled metal beds, daffodils in a vase.

In one photograph a woman sits alone in a small booth, making a phone call with her back to the camera, handbag at her feet. The receiver looks heavy in her hand. I picture Joan making a call from the same telephone, under the same unshaded light bulb. Ringing out.

At the time she was admitted Joan would have been referred to as someone living with a 'systemised delusional system'. Nowadays she would be diagnosed as a paranoid schizophrenic.

In brief, schizophrenia is a mental illness that manifests itself in a collection of extreme, alienating symptoms. These symptoms are usually referred to under two headings; 'positive' – those that *add* new aspects to someone's personality and behaviour, although they are rarely positive as one would normally understand the word – and 'negative' – those that *detract* from the sufferer's personality and damage their social functions.

Typically, a sufferer will 'hear voices', which might be talking about them in the third person or addressing them directly, giving instructions to act in a certain way. A schizophrenic might make apparently meaningless repetitive gestures or noises, or use words in a way that is confused or makes little sense. Hallucinations of touch are another possible symptom – feeling sensations based on no physical reality, experiencing 'something happening' to one's insides. And occasionally someone might even have 'visions', seeing things that are not there. Along with these symptoms, and dominating the sufferer's experience, is his or her severe thought disorder and distorted sense of reality.

A schizophrenic's perception is often paranoid; they believe that they are being persecuted, spied upon, followed, poisoned, made fun of, experimented upon. And the context of their persecution is often apocalyptic or a scenario in which the tyrannical political state is keeping them under constant threat and surveillance. Typical fantasies involve electricity, machines and technical devices. Obsessive religious delusions are also commonly experienced, where someone might think they are Jesus Christ, or acting as the Voice of God or being instructed by angels.

The illness is so destructive because the beliefs and behaviour it induces in sufferers cut them off from other people: friends and family, colleagues and people in the street find them unreasonable, bizarre, frankly mad. Paranoia and fantasy are often combined with hostility and suspicion, which only exacerbate their position.

The woman shouting angrily at the bus stop thinks that other people in the queue are reading her thoughts. The young man frozen for hours in a clothes shop is unable to choose a jumper because he thinks there will be deadly repercussions if he picks the wrong colour. But bystanders will think that she is drunk, possibly violent, that he is weird or trying to steal something.

The negative symptoms of schizophrenia often appear after the 'florid' or positive aspects of the illness have established themselves. After a while a sufferer might become withdrawn, lethargic, disengaged from their normal life. Communication with other people becomes difficult, they might lose interest in their appearance and stop washing or dressing properly. Their emotional responses blunt and flatten to the point where they seem to have lost their personality. And they find it increasingly hard to motivate themselves, to concentrate or to carry out tasks. This means they are likely to lose their job and, consequently, their financial security, possibly their home and any sense of being part of the social whole.

Without treatment from people determined to keep them even partially engaged, it does not take long for the schizophrenic to become a total outsider.

The causes of the disease, the ways in which it might be inherited, its subtleties and a possible cure, remain uncertain, even today. But the medical approach to schizophrenia has changed considerably since the nineteenth and early twentieth centuries. Where once the solution was deemed to be long-term incarceration in asylums such as Holloway, which would protect both the patient and the world at large, sufferers are now encouraged, as far as possible, to integrate with 'normal' society. Their positive symptoms can be controlled by sophisticated antipsychotic drugs to the point where the patient is able to function and where the negative symptoms are likely to be less severe.

In 1954, the main treatments for schizophrenia were still electroconvulsive therapy and insulin coma therapy. Joan was given heavy bouts of ECT over a period of several years, which she later blamed for her considerable loss of memory. The process involved having a substantial electric charge applied to the temples to achieve an artificially-induced seizure, similar to an epileptic fit. Joy Whitfield explained that a patient might receive ECT up to three times a week. In her opinion it was beneficial because, before the introduction of antipsychotics, it was the only available means of reducing some people's extreme symptoms. Perhaps it did have an effect, in that it made patients slower, more confused and thus more manageable. But it did little to dismantle their systems of delusion, only to stun them and knock out their memory.

Nowadays the procedure is no longer believed to be a useful treatment for schizophrenia. Greatly refined and used very sparingly, it is much more likely to be resorted to in cases of severe depression. When Joan received it, it was still crude and frightening. It was also open to abuse by unscrupulous staff, who used it as a threat and a punishment against patients.

Insulin coma therapy was seen as a more moderate treatment. The patient was injected with insulin, allowed to fall into a coma for a few hours and then quickly brought back to consciousness by the administration of glucose. Joan almost certainly underwent this treatment, although in the late fifties its clinical benefits were investigated and found to be minimal. Research revealed that patients were responding not to the coma itself, but to the close attention and gentleness of the nursing staff who brought them round afterwards. As the necessarily high dosage of glucose could induce vomiting, the patient was kept under close observation. In contrast to the miseries and confusion of much of hospital life, this peaceful respite, where they were given one-to-one care in a separate, quiet room away from the main wards, was genuinely comforting, although clinically doubtful.

Joan spent seven years at Holloway, at the time when the first antipsychotics were just being introduced. The hospital ran an early trial for Largactil in the late fifties and she may well have been part of that. She had a deep suspicion of drugs and would always refuse them if she possibly could. Early on in her stay, she wrote to her mother, informing her that she was receiving nothing apart from a 'tonic', but this could well have been medication in the guise of something else. In a letter to her mother-in-law twelve years later, remembering life at Holloway, there was no doubt that she had been given heavy medication:

> . . . frequently I was then distracted by the drugs they forced on me, affecting me so badly and making me feel so ill that most of my time was taken up by trying to persuade medical staff that at least my medicine should be changed – when I asked for it to be stopped they said that as long as I stayed at the hospital I must take whatever treatment was prescribed.

While her early letters discussed the possibility of Jim bringing the children over to be with her, no such reunion took place. Jim visited in 1955, alone, and returned to Australia. It was the last time they ever saw one another.

In a letter to Ellen, Joan wrote of feeling lucky to be at Holloway and of 'waiting gratefully until the family come home'. As time went on, however, and it dawned on her that they were not coming to join her, I imagine she was overwhelmed by grief, loneliness and confusion.

The children, meanwhile, were learning to live without her.

Jim was a man of his time and class. Brought up in the wake of the First World War, educated at boarding school and having spent all of his adult life as a scientist, he had never found it easy or palatable to talk about his emotions or difficulties. He had kept the problems of his marriage secret from his closest friends and relations, admitting only the bare minimum when he had no choice but to do so. His own way of coping was to ignore the worst and to hope it would go away. Rather naively, he assumed that this was also the best way for the children to deal with Joan's absence.

Since he had never explained what had happened to Joan, the children simply had to carry on without her. About two years after she had left, they finally asked him the direct question, 'Is mother coming back?' And he finally answered, 'No, she is not.' It was Jane who had to explain to Sandy, crying for his mother in his bath, that she was never coming home.

What Jim clearly did not understand was that, while they had to get on and deal with life and while they apparently functioned very well, the effect of these events on the children was devastating. Jane and Sandy in particular would spend the next fifty years trying to come to terms with the loss of their mother. But then Jim's own understanding of what had happened to Joan was fairly unclear. He did not speak of her illness as a scientist might speak of other diseases. In fact, at times he seemed incapable of accepting that she could not help what had happened. He continued to see it more as an extension of her perverted imagination, a collection of irrational traits that she had inherited from her mother rather than an identifiable condition.

Mental illness carried an enormous stigma at the time. Loss of control, behaving in an inappropriate manner, crossing boundaries were all excruciating embarrassments. No wonder he wanted it all to stop and, if that were impossible, simply to write an annual cheque for three hundred pounds in the belief that his wife would be given the best treatment available and kept at a safe distance.

Letters would arrive for the children in Australia, written in strange, spidery writing, full of urgency and religion and repetition. Joan sent Polly a Bible from Holloway in 1955. She also sent them badly-painted pictures done in the art room on scrolls of sugar paper – splodgy figures, a little boat sailing against a messy sunset – efforts that were embarrassing and frightening because they knew she could draw so well. What was so wrong with her that she had been reduced to daubing like a child? Her letters became so disturbing that they either handed them straight to Jim to be destroyed or ripped them up themselves.

Joan's mother, meanwhile, remained her most devoted visitor and correspondent. Ellen would go to Holloway regularly, liaise with the medical staff and run errands for her daughter. This was no easy task as Joan veered from being friendly and grateful to being openly hostile. Disinhibited by her illness, she felt no qualms about blaming her mother for the past and set about telling her exactly where she had gone wrong.

One letter in particular is uncompromisingly savage. Writing a year after her admission, Joan celebrates her own Christian faith, which was such a great comfort to her, while fiercely criticising her mother for not having more faith herself. She then condemns Ellen for putting too much emphasis on her relationship with Joan and Brian, and attacks her for destroying their childhood. It was Ellen's fault that Robert left and that the children suffered. She had failed to build a proper relationship with their father and had then done nothing to protect them from the distress of the separation, robbing them of their independence and stifling their development as individuals. Joan concludes that Ellen should talk to a psychiatrist – both about her own problems and her daughter's.

Over the next few years Joan would become ever more rejecting, and the letter signals the beginning of that hostility:

> I think you will surely see . . . that your relationship with me cannot add to my happiness and would always make it difficult for me to add lastingly to yours by our continuing to meet. I cannot help but notice that my self-reliance and cheerfulness increases when you leave me alone and that when you don't and you see a lot of me or try to keep an eye on me, as it were, through others, I am depressed and less able to live for others and for God.

At the same time, she writes that she is letting out the waistband of her skirts, feels very much at home, that she gets on well with both staff and fellow patients and that she is 'in excellent health'.

She also reiterates that she is waiting for Jim to bring the children back to England.

By June 1957 Joan was asking Ellen to find her a flat by the seaside and provide the capital so that she and a female friend (a fellow patient?) could move to the coast and open a restaurant or club together. 'When you have found something that is promising please come and see me immediately,' she demanded.

Details about the rest of this period of Joan's life are sketchy.

Her medical files have since been lost or destroyed and few people visited her. I imagine that the effects of illness and treatment, institutionalisation and the coping mechanisms she adopted to deal with the loss of her family gradually combined to distract and numb her. Depending on whether she was in a stable condition or suffering from acute psychosis, life could be either mundane or horrific.

She probably enjoyed the studios and gardens, the practical activities and some of the social events laid on at the Sanatorium. She probably prayed in the chapel. Maybe she finally got to dance regularly – the hospital hosted tea dances and various parties for the patients. But this was a mental hospital and, quite apart from living with her own miseries, it was a grim place to be, a massive building filled with disturbed, unhappy and sometimes violent people. Recalling nights at the Sanatorium years later, she wrote, '. . . sometimes the most terrible screams broke the stillness through the stench of heavily doped breath in a dormitory of ten beds in crowded lines and one would lie there gripped by terror'.

However civilised it appeared to be, the Sanatorium functioned like any other mental hospital of its time, minimising patients' freedoms and denying their sense of autonomy. Inmates lived to a strict regime; they got up at a set time, ate at set times, bathed when they were allowed to and adhered to rules and regulations. All physical space was shared space, to be negotiated and argued over. There was little to confirm who you were. If illness had not removed your sense of identity, then living in the institution most certainly would. There were no poems to prove that Joan had ever been a writer, no husband to make her a wife, no children to confirm her as a mother. Furthermore, Joan owned nothing in Holloway, since she had left almost all her possessions in Australia, arriving in England with a single suitcase. Friends and relations would send her odd items of clothing and maybe books and pens and writing paper, but she was effectively stripped of all the trappings of her former life. She had nothing to hold her to her past or to who she had once been.

Joan continued to live as an in-patient at Holloway until the early sixties. At one stage, encouraged by the occupational therapist to find a part-time job, she worked at a local hotel, but was unable to hold the position down for long. Jim divorced her in 1957, on grounds of 'desertion', and remarried in 1959.

In 1961 Jane returned from Sydney to go to art school in London and, with great trepidation, she went to see her mother at the Sanatorium. They walked around the grounds under grey skies. Joan was a very different person from when she had left Australia seven years earlier. No longer frenzied, she was slowed up and suspicious, although pleased to see Jane again. She claimed there was nothing wrong with her at all, that she had to stay in hospital only because her money would be stopped if she left. She said she felt trapped.

Then, on 12 September 1961, aged forty-eight, Joan discharged herself and disappeared.

CHAPTER 8

ON THE ROAD

> . . . *returning, she,*
> *Dwelling in sorrow and in hope went*
> *Spent and weary, heavy-footed,*
> *Along long roads, through hills and valleys*
> *Away from the main roads keeping*
>
> from *Amber Innocent*, J.A.E., 1939

Joan had vanished.

Ellen was distraught. She had the river dragged at Richmond and spent months looking for her. She eventually hired a private detective, who found Joan living in a field in Somerset with a man he described as 'simple'.

Writing to Leonard Woolf in May 1964, perhaps because he was one of her acquaintances who might have an understanding of mental illness, and one of the few who would remember Joan as a young woman, Ellen explained:

> We found her living in a caravan with what was described on the document as 'a rough man', the only thing against him, 'dislike of work'. They arrived here with no warning, destitute, having slept at a station. Albert is a Shakespeare clown to me.

He is a classic Russian idiot to Brian, Professor Penrose guesses he is feeble-minded. But they love one another as they share this strange borderland world, so bewildering to those living the normal daily way. Infinitely sad because out of touch, Joan there yet not there. It is not Joan because a stranger inhabits her.

The years spent in Holloway had changed Joan irrevocably. It was as if she had gone through a tunnel on a train, disappeared from sight and come out the other side a different person. The connecting threads of her life had almost completely dissolved. Community care did not exist at the time, so there was no follow-up to a long stay in mental hospital and no safety net should things go wrong. Like Amber Innocent, once she had left the gates of the castle she was alone.

I do not know what Joan did between leaving Holloway and before she was discovered in the caravan. I assume that she was homeless for many of those months, living hand to mouth, since she did not contact her mother and would have had little money. In a letter she wrote several years later she recalled sleeping under the shrubs in Fulham Park Gardens in London. Joan said she had known it was a dangerous place but preferred it to a hostel which she feared would have reminded her of nights in the Sanatorium.

She met Albert some time in 1963, but exactly how or where is another mystery. He was probably someone she picked up on the road. He could barely read or write, apparently had a child by a young girl he was still married to and lived partly on National Assistance and partly on odd jobs.

Initially, perhaps for a few months, they were comfortable together. Joan had someone she could look after, a companion, a focus for her love and energy. With a bit of money from Ellen, they managed to find accommodation in a string of Brighton boarding houses and spent at least a few weeks living almost normally. Writing to her mother in July 1964, Joan describes buying baked beans and bread for supper, getting quite brown in the sun and walking along the beach together in the evenings. She also repeatedly – and pointedly – mentions that she and Albert would like a van or a car, since having their own vehicle would mean he could get driving jobs and they would no longer have problems travelling from place to place. Ellen appears to have ignored the barely disguised suggestion that she could help them out with this.

In the same letter, Joan tells her mother that she has arranged for her allowance from Jim to be officially stopped through the action of a solicitor, and that she believes this was the right decision. She tries to explain how liberated she felt when the divorce was finalised, how it had taken her a while to realise that she was free to get on with the rest of her life, but that she has now started to do so. She feels quite neutral towards Jim and wonders whether her marriage to him was a mistake in the first place. She hopes he is happy but does not want to be reminded of him.

Joan's desire – which she was keen to explain to Ellen – was to live simply among normal working people who had no connection with her previous life. She wrote to her mother,

> I don't want any more communication with you, not because there isn't any love in my heart for you, there is, but I don't feel well as soon as I get in touch with you, and I don't suppose you do either with the strain of it all, so please let's leave it that we don't get in touch with you or you with us but just wish one another happiness and peace and freedom to live our lives as we want to.
>
> I find writing to you as I have to occasionally if we keep in

contact like this, a great strain – it reminds me of a life I no longer belong to or wish to belong to – people and ways no longer with me – you must realise that. Out of all the people I knew you are the only one I have kept in contact with . . . and it is truthful to say I feel my real self only when I am with Albert and his kind – I had already become close to others in his sort of life before I met him and I am happy if I don't try to live in two worlds if each of those worlds rejects the other because until they accept one another it means I am fully accepted by nobody until I make a full acceptance of one world or the other.

As a girl, walking through the gypsy encampment near Crouch, Joan had shared her mother's view that these people were truly free. Something of this romanticism remained in her wanting to live an authentic and simple life with Albert, but the reality of their time together was far from idyllic. With barely any money, Joan was forced to clean the stairs, hallways and lavatories of the house where they spent a few weeks in Brighton and then to juggle poorly paid menial jobs with constantly moving location. She had neither the physical nor the mental capacity to hold down a job for very long and she scraped from waitressing to washing-up, from factory to pub work, never managing more than a few days at a time. Jim wrote to his sister in January 1964, 'Joan seems to have racked up with a genial hobo. They seem to live like children from hand to mouth on the manna which drops from some unknown place as far as they are concerned.' His parents or Joan's mother must have written to him and explained about Joan's relationship but it was not the happy set-up he imagined it to be. Her new life was insecure and dangerous; when she and Albert were on the road or without a place to sleep they were sometimes robbed and beaten up. Albert could be a bully, often preventing Joan from taking work because he wanted her to stay 'at home' (wherever that was) and behave like a wife. Jim, relieved at the idea that Joan was now attached to someone else, mistakenly thought she was actually married and decided to stop worrying about her altogether.

After rattling about on the south coast for a while, Joan and Albert turned up in London, where they lived in a state of destitution, begging family friends for cast-off clothes and shoes and constantly shifting from one wretched place to the next because they could not pay the rent. At one point they were moving so often Joan would leave their latest address with a particular tobacconist so that Jane might know where she was. The lodgings available to them were grim and squalid, with the most basic sanitation and heating arrangements. Jane visited them in a basement flat in Paddington where the back wall ran with water like a fishmonger's slab and Albert sat thumping the radio because it wouldn't work. Joan was surprisingly resourceful in these circumstances. On one occasion Jane gave her a set of bright blue thermal underwear because she had been complaining about the cold. The next time she visited, her mother was wearing the vest as a top (now edged with gold braid and with arms stitched on from another garment) and Albert had the knickers – also trimmed with gold – to wear as swimming trunks.

No longer slow and contained as she had been directly after leaving Holloway, Joan had become extremely active and was always popping up wherever Jane most wanted to avoid her. When she was in hospital recovering from an operation, Joan arrived unannounced, bearing down the middle of the ward with Albert in tow, shouting at the top of her voice until she had to be removed by staff, leaving Jane crying with shock. Another time, she saw her mother and Albert by chance in the middle of a London street when she was out with friends from art school and dived down a side road to hide. If they ever arranged to meet up with her, Joan and Albert would insist on some dismal pub full of drunk down-and-outs. Albert's party trick was to pull a plastic turd out of his bag and plant it on the table.

Despite Joan's increasing hostility towards her mother, Ellen continued to write to her, to worry about her and to grieve for the person she had once been. Many years later, when she left a bundle of family papers to Reading University Library, she included the two letters Joan had written to her in 1964. Ellen had carefully typed them out and kept the copies with the originals, presumably to make them easier to read. They were precious, since Joan wrote only occasionally now, either to ask for something or to push her further away.

Over the first couple of years that Joan and Albert were together, Ellen periodically responded to their requests for financial help. She knew that the money would be spent almost immediately (and probably by Albert) but feared what would happen to Joan if she didn't send it. She tried to say she would send no more, but then surrendered to pressure once again. The temptation to keep the contact going, despite the uncomfortable knowledge that they were exploiting her, must have been very strong. Ellen was now old, frail and lonely. Whatever her failings as a mother had been, she also loved her daughter deeply and felt overwhelmed in the face of her illness; sending money was the one way she thought she might alleviate Joan's difficulties.

For Joan, the relationship with her mother remained impossibly complicated and she was always trying to bring it to an end, claiming that she did not want the money and that they must go their separate ways. Albert, on the other hand, clearly recognised a steady source of cash in Ellen and was probably unable to understand why

Joan could or would not extort more from her. Writing to her mother in October 1964, Joan explained how she had felt so much happier in the early days, before receiving any financial help:

> I felt freer in my heart in those days and somehow when you gave us money it has never really done as much as we always tried to feel it did – Money is important of course but I suppose it's the feeling of it not being our own which spoilt things as we spent it and it is very bitter as we know you want to help and for the help to make us happier.

Once, presumably when Albert's charms had begun to wear thin for Ellen, it seems that she attempted to send some money exclusively to Joan or to make some kind of qualified offer dependent on her leaving him. Joan was upset that her mother could even contemplate ignoring Albert, and in an angry letter insisted that they were in love and had promised one another that they would stay together. Perhaps prompted by him, she then demanded whether there might be some shares that Ellen could sell to free up some cash. And, she asked, was there not any family money that Joan was owed from the past?

Typically inconsistent, she concluded, 'Albert says that money is not everything. He said the other day that when he has no money in his pocket he is really happy. I feel like that too.'

Ellen was not the only one to distrust Albert. Jane disliked him and so did Jim's relations. He was not the benign simpleton they had initially assumed. His serious mental problems had made him suicidal on at least one occasion and he was almost incapable of earning any money. He was also unkind and unreliable, and he sometimes beat Joan up. Over time, she too decided that the constant financial scrabbling, his violence towards her and the miserable insecurity of their life together made the relationship untenable. After several break-ups and false starts the pair finally separated in spring 1966. A month or so later Joan told Judy Rendel that neither had felt any bitterness at the split and neither had told the other where they were going. It was with a sense of relief that she wrote, 'He must have thought of me as a sort of undeflatable dinghy that could survive all storms and even his attempts to, as it were, go overboard and pull me under at the same time. But I knew I couldn't carry on as things were . . .'

She headed back to the south coast alone.

What Joan sought now was a modest stability; a job, a place to stay and acceptance by ordinary people. Over the summer of 1966 she wrote a batch of letters to her mother-in-law from a small rented room in Dover. Detailing her daily trials and preoccupations, they seem to signal her last efforts to secure a place in society. Judy was one of the few people who remained loyal to her, despite having been railed at and distrusted during her breakdown. Jim's father Dick had recently died and maybe she felt doubly responsible about contacting Joan and sending her financial help now that neither he nor Jim were around. She sent her some bedsheets and various items of clothing – a fitted suit, a nice skirt, a petticoat, vests – and Joan wrote back, responding to this maternal attention, delighted with the clothes. The family contact seemed to strengthen her.

Joan was now fifty-five and keen to reinvent herself. Having briefly used Albert's surname when she was living with him, she started signing her letters 'Joan Curly'. She also decided to stop eating meat and cited George Bernard Shaw and elephants as inspiring examples of fellow vegetarians, renowned for their strength and longevity. From now on, she explained, she would try to wear only plastic and canvas shoes and to eat only free-range eggs.

She loved the sunshine by the sea, the sound of the gulls wheeling over the rooftops, flowers sent by Jane from her back garden in London. Her aesthetic sense was as acute as ever and, despite having almost no money, it was important to her that things were pleasing to look at. She bought a remnant of white material to make curtains for her room because, she said, the design on the ones provided by her landlord was so ugly it gave her 'a sort of mental and physical discomfort'. She also bought a white geranium in a pot.

Her letters to Judy are a mixture of everyday domestic detail, quirky Joan obsessions and playfulness, along with the now-familiar spirals of paranoid and religious argument that had started as far back as Edinburgh. In one she begins, 'I have been trying to make up a little rhyme about a punnet of strawberries, all written as if it's said with my mouth full!' In another she explains at length how she would love to run a series of experimental farms, not for meat but for the well-being of the animals – the sheep would only be sheared if it was very hot, otherwise she would just wash and comb their fleeces. But she soon veers into strange reconstructions of conversations she had in Holloway Sanatorium – encounters with people who may or may not have been real – and her horror that sex-change operations had been wrought on male inmates there. One of the themes that would preoccupy her for the rest of her life was the idea of disguised identities. Maybe Robert Easdale had not been her real father after all? Maybe she was adopted? Maybe she had met one of her aunts disguised in Holloway? Or was an old home help from long ago also an inmate? She wrote frenziedly about these possibilities, then reverted to normal chatty subjects or repeated worries about her finances.

Jill, Jim's sister and Joan's old flatmate from the thirties, would occasionally visit her, bringing fruit and Lucozade when she was ill. But Joan's own side of the family had almost totally given up on her. Exhausted by years of trying to maintain their difficult relationship,

Ellen now refused to reply to her letters, to see her or to speak to her on the telephone when she called, stating that she was too old to cope with the strain. Her brother Brian avoided any contact. Apart from her cousin Richard Adeney, who occasionally sent money, other relations were either too embarrassed or shocked at what had happened to want to help. She had been keen for them to leave her alone when she was in hospital but now that she needed financial rescue and familiar contact she could not understand why they would not change their minds. She had some idea that being shunned was part of a much larger conspiracy, which her whole family had been in on since childhood; she was sure that they had all connived to convince the authorities that she was mad and were now secretly urging one another to avoid her.

Even when young, sane and happy Joan had not been good with money. She had only ever earned small amounts through her writing and once she had given it up she had depended entirely on Jim's salary. It was only after her divorce that she realised she needed a national insurance number and had to apply for a card. Now in desperate need of assistance, she crashed from one appointment to the next, trying to apply for the dole with no real understanding of the welfare system and no one willing to explain it to her. The letters she wrote over a few weeks in the spring and early summer of 1966 detail miserable trips to the National Assistance Board, where she would outline her position to an unsympathetic clerk, promise to look for work, present her stamps book, which never had enough stamps in it and which numerous employers refused to frank, then trudge off to various hopeless job interviews. The system worked on points gained by having one's card franked. But for the years she had been with Albert he had somehow claimed any money that was owed to her (presumably by saying that they were married) and she had not had her card franked. One could apply for benefits if one did not have enough money to live on, but was penalised for having left a job voluntarily. You had to be available for work, and any money earned, however small the amount, was deducted from future benefit. Joan railed against her lack of education and the fact that she didn't even know how to type properly. In one letter she described going for eight job interviews in one week, and being told at each one that the position had already been filled or that they were looking for someone younger. They were no doubt lying, appalled at the idea of taking on this shabby, intense, muddled yet well-spoken woman in her fifties who had no employment history or qualifications. She would dutifully follow instructions and catch a bus to a distant location, only to be turned away and have to walk the miles back to her lodgings because she couldn't afford the return fare. Once, in early summer, she trekked out into the countryside to enquire about a raspberry-picking job, only to realise once she had got there that the fruit season was still several weeks off.

The situation became even more complicated when she fell ill because the Assistance Board then required an official doctor's certificate to confirm that she had been unable to work for genuine medical reasons. Typically, when she was laid low by an infection, she was not given the correct certificate by her doctor and was yet again turned away by the Board. Joan then had to chase the doctor – in person and by letter. He initially refused to re-issue the form, then became irritated by her persistence and finally sent her the correct certificate several days late, by which time she was penniless and frantic, and heartily disliked by the benefit office.

Some days she went without food. On others she could afford either a pint of milk and coins for the electricity meter or a meal in a cheap café. In one letter she describes going round a shop with her basket, having to put everything back on the shelves because she could not pay for it.

The Assistance Board in Dover had a policy whereby they stopped helping with rent payments over the summer months because they believed there was enough seasonal work to keep people going until the autumn. With her last four-pound payment given to her in May, the pressure was on for Joan to find work.

The jobs she was offered were always badly paid or involved complications such as having to get transport home because they finished so late. She thought about taking a live-in housekeeping position but was wary of the risk – if the job did not work out she would inevitably lose her home.

She was aware that she was an anomaly – a drifting middle-aged woman with no family ties or support. People were suspicious of her. She was also beginning to worry about the deteriorating sight in her right eye. It made her anxious to think she might be taken advantage of or that one day people would use it as an excuse to limit her independence. No doubt it also made her less employable. In the letter detailing her pointless journey out to the fruit farm she describes the shock of realising quite how damaged her eye really was:

> My eyesight is used to towns, whereas I noticed clearly how it had deteriorated in the country – it was not used to uneven ground and could not even get grassy banks and things into focus as it used to. It made me rather sad to notice the change, for somehow I had expected every blade of grass and shaft of sunlight to be clear as it was when I was younger!

She goes on to talk about the pleasure of finding herself in the countryside again, and one gets a brief glimmer of Joan as a much younger person:

. . . it was deliciously peaceful and I enjoyed it as I did another evening when I took a shorter trip out into the country and where I smelt the particular smells characteristic of Kent. It made me realise how much happiness I had felt in my youth, whatever I'd said about it, and this was a pleasant reassurance. It is always nice to realise that happiness does not begin as it were only 'as from now', however vitally important the present and future is.

The present and future were increasingly uncertain. Joan's letters to Judy stop in 1966 and once again the story peters out. For all her efforts, it seems she was unable to find a job. She then lost her room because, according to her landlord, she had brought a man back to the boarding house. Her brief bid for a normal life came to a sudden end.

I once asked Jill what had happened to Joan in the sixties. If she didn't have a job, how had she survived? Was she 'almost a prostitute'? Jill reluctantly said yes, but insisted that Joan had lived more confusedly than that, holding a muddled belief in Free Love, sleeping with people she found in the pubs round the docks and maybe getting food and a bit of money in return. It was a precarious existence. Jane wrote to her and saw her at irregular intervals, but had only a vague idea of how she was living. They would meet at Victoria Station; Joan would be waiting for her on a bench with all her possessions stuffed into a few carrier bags.

Her mental state seemed to deteriorate as the decade progressed, no doubt because the life she was living was so stressful. Nowadays she would be given antipsychotic drugs and encouraged to live as peacefully as possible. She might be given some form of social housing and periodic community support. In the Sanatorium, however much she had disliked the regime, she had been physically and financially secure, regularly fed and housed in surroundings that never changed. Life outside had taken its toll.

Jane found her increasingly mad, unpredictable and invasive. She had become a terrible combination of the ghost of who she had once been and a rackety, crazy stranger who would turn up in an old fur tippet and make embarrassing scenes in public. She once dragged Jane into a smart military outfitters in Dover and launched into a long, deranged explanation of her connection with Colonel Rendel to the nonplussed gentleman behind the counter. On another occasion she tried at great length, with much effort and no success, to wheedle free opera tickets from the box office in Covent Garden, standing in the foyer among the elegant throng, lecturing the staff about her musical brother.

Joan was convinced that Polly and Sandy would one day come and find her, as Jane had done. Meanwhile, she continued to write to them. Her letters to her children in the sixties were even more disturbing than those she had sent from hospital since she was now completely disinhibited in her use of language. Her illness had destroyed her sense of judgement, so that she would discuss the most shocking subjects in graphic detail. At one stage she started sending Polly a weird handmade comic book, full of explicit drawings with speech bubbles, expounding her theories and experiences of sex and religion. Another time, presumably when she was living rough and in danger of being robbed, she wrote, 'I keep my money rolled up and tucked into my rectum.' She described her submersion in a life that involved a lot of sex. She claimed to love this way of life and said that semen was good for the skin.

To Sandy she wrote, 'You can do anything if you try. You get used to things. If you have to wrap your shit in newspaper and burn it, you do it.'

Her children felt incapacitated by this kind of information. How were they to react? As teenagers and in their early twenties they dreaded her letters and would try not to read them in any detail, if at all. They rarely wrote back, not knowing what to write or where to send it.

Polly had begun to refer to her as 'my mad mother who's turned into a bag lady' and Sandy decided that he could cope with the idea of having no mother at all more easily than with the reality of a mother who had lost her mind. But Joan had ways of making her presence felt, albeit from the other side of the world. On returning home from football practice one evening in the early seventies, Sandy was shocked to find that the police had called at the house to check whether he really lived there. When he went to the police station the next day, the officer on the desk asked, 'Why don't you get in touch with your mum?' Joan had registered him as a missing person. Polly was telephoned by the police and similarly reproached for being neglectful.

In some ways I find it amazing that Joan's story did not end here, with one brutal encounter too many, or through illness or despair. But, despite everything she had been through, she remained incredibly strong. Her Christian faith kept her going but she also had an instinct for survival. In the past, when her situation had threatened to overwhelm her, she had always managed to give it the slip. As a child she had escaped into her imagination, as a mother she had known when to seek psychiatric treatment, as a patient when to leave hospital. She had finished the relationship with Albert before it was too late and now, facing destitution alone, she got on a train and headed north.

CHAPTER 9

_____

HER OWN PERSON

Don't cast me down
And let me drown
In pallid loneliness,
But love and bless
And give me company;
And let me always be
A vivid light
Obscuring night,
Among a heap
Of other stars that keep
Each other from blank emptiness.

from 'Want', J.A.E., 1930

Whether Nottingham was a deliberate choice or whether she was on the way to somewhere else and stopped off is unclear, but that is where she ended up. The people were kind, she said, and for the most part she was treated well by the city; it absorbed her, kept an eye out for her and let her be.

I imagine her getting off the train with her bag. Now in her late fifties, wearing strange, mismatched clothes, no hint of grey in her dark brown hair. She was probably still speaking with the strong London accent she used with Albert, the voice of 'real people', although she soon adopted a thick Nottingham growl. She used different voices, depending on whom she was with and what mood she was in. Sometimes, tripped into talking about the past, or because she was with the family or being grand, she would speak with her old Bloomsbury voice, but at other times she sounded like a local. She would slip in and out of these voices within a single conversation, suddenly changing from one to the other, transforming from rough vagrant to educated old lady in a matter of seconds.

She chose to call herself Sophie – or Sophia – Curly. Joan was part of the past she no longer belonged to, the woman who had married Jim and lived in Australia, the woman who had been admitted to Holloway. The name was a connection, a tether, to her mother, to memories and experiences she wanted to exorcise. Sophie Curly was the name for the person she was now, and it was the name she would use until she died. Jane thinks this was a deliberate combination of the intellectual and the sexual – Sophia being the Greek word for wisdom, Curly relating to pubic hair, 'the short and curlies'. It suited her well, although it took a while for the family to get used to.

On arrival in Nottingham Sophie had practically no money and nowhere to live. The first place to go would be a pub. Did she get herself a drink and then start talking to people? Did she ask someone to buy her a beer? Did she end up with a bloke at the end of the evening? Did he pay her?

It would have soon dawned on listeners that this woman from down south was not right in the head. Her theories about artificial insemination, child murder and evil scientists might have amused, disturbed then bored them. But someone must have taken enough interest in her to persuade her to stay, because the city became her home.

Information about her early days in Nottingham is scant and

fragmented, leaving one to guess at what might have happened to her in the late sixties and early seventies. In a letter to Jane she wrote, 'An abandoned car, if parked with care / Can provide shelter for homeless persons', suggesting that she slept rough for at least some of that time. She was still obsessed with sex, would talk endlessly about it and used to stand in the main square in Nottingham and preach free love from a soapbox on Saturday mornings. At some point she declared herself a Catholic and decided that she wanted to join the Roman Catholic Church. Although the local priest was willing to help her, and they had long discussions about the nature of her faith, she could not be accepted into the Church while she refused to renounce her strong ideas on adultery and what she saw as her God-given right to have sex with whomever she wished. She and the priest reached an impasse and, defiantly unrepentant, Sophie gave up the idea.

Episodes of anti-social behaviour, being drunk or being attacked meant that Sophie soon became familiar to the authorities. Social Services got to know of her, probably via the police. A bad patch would have landed her in Mapperley, the local mental hospital, and from there she would have been allocated some sort of accommodation, the first of her many council flats around the city. She still suffered from the positive symptoms of schizophrenia – as she would for the rest of her life – and they were particularly acute in the seventies and eighties. Constantly hearing voices and convinced that she was being persecuted, she found herself engaged in a daily battle with unseen forces who wanted her dead. She believed that Jim (whom she had now not seen for about twenty years) and other wicked experimenters were performing sex changes on people, killing unborn babies and preparing to kidnap her. She was sure that her boiler was emitting poisonous fumes and was convinced that the children in the street were chanting about her. They may well have been. It is difficult to work out what was real and what was not;

children *did* throw stones at her and call her a witch, maybe the boiler was making a funny smell.

A letter she wrote to Jane in August 1983 shows the extent of her paranoia, 'I take a wee piece out of everything in my larder and make it into a bird pudding or loaf – the birds who are my detectives eat it all. I think people don't dope food or infect eggs etc so much, observing this. Yet I find that I still need to smoke a little or occasionally I get symptoms of poisoning.' She goes on to elaborate on her current obsessions:

> Bring me a pen if you like because one can't have too many and in this flat petty pilfering goes on all the time. In every way it's too expensive in the dreadful torturing place, the agony inflicted on me from electronic activity, mental and physical pain and distraction from persons who evidently feel racially superior gives me only brief spaces when I manage to get on with all I have to do . . .
>
> The local children seem to have absolutely no other interest but Death, and death as related to one particular person, Sophie . . . I often wake in the morning to hear dirges on discs being played in this house, singing 'Sophie is bad' or 'Sophie is dead'. I think the filthy, perverted, self-elected 'psychos' who run all this lark must have loads of money, evidently made out of people's unheard intolerance and their hopes that one or two suicides will trigger off several more, just as Hitler wanted . . .

The tirade continues, for pages on end, in dense, lurching scribble. Sophie was the impossible tenant who disturbed other residents and infuriated landlords. She would accuse her neighbours of stealing from her or of being involved in criminal gangs, she would drop full bags of garbage from her balcony, customise rented furniture and abuse other tenants. Most of her hostility sprang from fear, as she felt under constant threat and was only acting to protect herself, but few, if any, of her neighbours understood this and most of them disliked her.

Throughout the eighties, much of Sophie's anger and energy was politically focused. She sustained a raging hatred for Margaret Thatcher, and capitalists in general, determined that she would somehow save enough money to go and live in the Soviet Union. The USSR was her vision of the perfect society, where she believed that the poor and old were properly looked after and where doctors and politicians remained uncorrupted. Her notebooks are sprinkled with Russian words – usually the days of the week – which she must have copied out from a dictionary. And she wrote strict instructions in various diaries as to what should happen to her in an emergency:

> In the event of accident or illness I do not want any of my relatives or friends to be contacted – I would only want to contact them myself if and when I wanted to. I cannot bear people fussing round behind my back or talking to authorities in Nottingham or anywhere. I have my own contacts with authorities.

> I like to run my own life & I do not try to run other people's lives.

> In event of accident, severe illness or death I would like KREMLIN, MOSCOW, RUSSIA to be informed at once and when I die I wish my body or any remains to be sent to KREMLIN, MOSCOW, RUSSIA.

> PLEASE.

John Richardson, the social worker attached to Sophie's case towards the end of her life, said he had never thought of her as someone with friends; she did not let people near and she was too peculiar to attract them. She had alienated most of her friends from her previous life – Naomi Mitchison, Jill Rendel, Professor Lionel and Margaret Penrose – although she might occasionally write to them. In Nottingham, she had drinking companions, she had favourite taxi-men, she had people who looked out for her, but she had lost the capacity to make close relationships: a two-way flow of interest for more than a few minutes was beyond her. She still, however, felt deeply attached to her three children and was kept informed of their lives and relationships by letter and the occasional visit from Jane. While Polly and Sandy remained in Australia, Jane decided to stay on in England after art school. She met my father while he was still a medical student and they married in 1965. I was born in 1967, my brother James two years later, my sister Clare in 1975 and my brother Andrew in 1978.

Polly, meanwhile, had also married and had two daughters. She and her husband moved out to rural Victoria, where she worked as a librarian and they built their own house stone by stone on the edge of a forest. Sandy bought a plot of land in New South Wales and moved to Kiama, a coastal town south of Sydney, where he became a solicitor. He too married and had a son and a daughter. Both Polly and Sandy wrote to Sophie and sent photos of their families, and she kept track of her clutch of grandchildren, even though we were not to meet her until much later.

Although Jane had taken my siblings and me to meet our grandmother as babies, she decided that visiting her as children would be too difficult. She wanted to protect us from Sophie's sexual preoccupations until we were much older, later explaining,

If you have a mother who you love deeply and who you feel is very special and she changes and goes away and is never the same again and yet has the same voice after all those years it's very difficult to deal with the sense of constant bereavement and distress . . . I couldn't be sure of myself, that the distress would be manageable, and I had determined that I'd do my best for my own children and be consistent and loving and reliable for them and I didn't want them to see me in tears or feeling weird . . .

I decided, however cruel it might seem, I wouldn't take the children to see her until I felt they were old enough to cope with it. I didn't want them to be ashamed or frightened of her.

Sophie's deep mistrust of people extended to my father, whom she accused at various times of being in collusion with Jim, of being a dangerous criminal and of having contacts with sadistic gangs. Most of the time, she refused to let him into her home and banned him from joining Jane on visits, listing a string of streets he was to keep away from. The fact that he was now a psychiatrist only compounded her dislike and distrust.

With her brother and sister in Australia and my father banished, Jane was left, at least until the mid-eighties, to deal with her mother alone. She was the first in line to liaise with social workers, doctors and the police, trying always to maintain a balance between protecting her mother and leaving her to live the kind of life she wanted. Sorting out practical problems could often be seen as interference by Sophie, who hated to be restricted in any way and had a sharp sense of when something might be happening against her will or behind her back. Her driving aim was to be free, yet her illness and increasing age made her vulnerable. At the same time she was wildly unreasonable and often hostile towards Jane. After weeks of asking for a visit, her daughter's physical presence would often be a disappointment. Sophie would be charmingly pleased to see her on arrival but swiftly lose interest as the day progressed, sometimes openly accusing her of neglect to people in the street or at the next table in the pub. It did not help that Sophie was continually trying to persuade Jane to leave her husband and live 'freely' with her in Nottingham, more than once insisting that she could help her give birth on the sofa and they could bring all the children up together in her flat.

The 'Baby Belling Crisis', as one particular episode became known, was typical of her determination to do things her own way. She had always been wary of gas appliances, fearing that they were unhealthy and that her enemies might use them to kill her. On moving in to a council flat in the eighties, she was horrified to find that she had been provided with a gas cooker. She first complained about it to Jane, who simply deflected her concerns, then went to the council to ask for it to be removed and eventually managed to get the gas supply disconnected by applying directly to the gas company. When Jane next visited, the cooker was out on the scrubby patch of grass that served as a garden, lying on its side with its feet in the air. Asked how it had got there, Sophie said blithely, 'By a system of planks and pulleys.' This feat of engineering, involving drawers from a chest, a large piece of wood and her dressing-gown cord, must have taken several long hours to accomplish. Rid of the lethal object, she then bought a two-ring Baby Belling electric stove, upon which she proceeded both to cook her food and boil water for washing. She also used it to heat the flat and left it on almost constantly. The resulting electricity bills, which she failed to pay, were so enormous that she had to get legal help to fend off the electricity board. Jane, Sandy and Polly eventually had to step in to bail her out.

Jane's policy was to intervene only when outside help was essential – when Sophie was seriously ill or in danger – and even then to do the minimum. A doctor who assessed Sophie in hospital after she had broken her arm was amazed at the extent of her delusions and astounded that she was not on medication. Why did she not take something to dampen down her paranoid thinking? When Jane explained that her mother refused all drugs the psychiatrist suggested that they could slip medication into Sophie's tea; it would be simple and effective, and Sophie would be none the wiser.

But that would have been acting exactly as Sophie *suspected* people of acting, something Jane did not want to collude with. In a landscape where the ground shifted constantly anyway, her policy was to remain consistently honest. She did not want to be doing anything behind her mother's back, even though Sophie clearly expected her to be doing such things. Had Jane put antipsychotics into her tea, Sophie might have been happier. Or she might not. At the time it seemed the wrong thing to do, although it meant that her fears and distortions went uncurbed.

Sophie lived in unmitigated poverty and it was very difficult to help her. She denied that she was ill, or ever had been ill, and she flatly refused any benefit or pension with Disability or Incapacity in the title. Why would that be of any relevance to her? Such things were a bad idea, she thought, as they encouraged people to say they were sick when they were not.

Until Sophie's last few years, Jane and her siblings were unable to subsidise her as she refused any offers of financial assistance from them, believing that it might be 'contaminated' by my father or by Jim. (An arrangement in the seventies, whereby Jane forwarded small anonymous amounts of money provided by Jim in Australia, had broken down because it was both complicated and duplicitous.)

Sophie might occasionally accept a five pound note at the end of a visit, barely enough to cover her beer and taxi for the evening, but she would resist anything more substantial. Practical gifts were usually rejected outright because there was no way of guaranteeing their purity or safety – a blanket could have been impregnated with chemicals, the soil of a pot plant might be bugged. Hence the annual dilemma posed by Christmas: how to give her something that she would keep and actually use. Sophie would say she needed a new coat or a pair of slippers but when presented with the items (painstakingly chosen to be the most innocuous, the most flattering, the most comfortable) she would suspect that they contained listening devices or invisible poison and she would unpick the lining, cut out the pockets or just throw them away.

Her severe mental problems did not seem to affect her enormous physical energy; she was extremely active and could appear on any doorstep at any time. There was an occasion in the early seventies when she tracked Jane down to Northumberland, where she was on holiday. Sophie turned up, trim and vigorous in fawn corduroy trousers, complaining that she was being stung in the legs by 'electric bees'. A decade later, in the middle of the night, she arrived at her cousin's house in Notting Hill, very dirty, clutching two bursting plastic bags and announcing, 'There's so much sex around these days, spunk flying all over the place!'

When one was with Sophie the world felt strange. Maybe it was spending time with someone whose perception was so warped by her fears, but normal things seemed to loom and magnify. Shopping centres became hellish, adverts spoke personal messages, milk smelt off. Encounters with other people felt exaggerated or as if they might be being filmed. My brother Andrew recalls sitting on a park bench with Sophie on a hot summer afternoon while a carillon pealed insistently and too loud, sliding off key, sounding madder and madder in the heat. Another time, two Asian women crossing a grey road seemed to flame green and purple as their saris caught the sun. We half-believed she could read our minds – if we turned up unannounced she might be ready and waiting, and not at all surprised: 'I knew you were going to come!' When we were still refusing to give her our address (Rose and Crown House, Bewdley), she would insist on taking us to drink at a Nottingham pub called the Rose and Crown. On one occasion when Jim was visiting us from Australia with his second wife, the telephone rang and Jane took a call from Sophie, 'Just calling to see how you all are, probably entertaining guests, no doubt.'

Sophie's letters reveal how the grind of survival kept her almost constantly busy. She had to feed herself, keep clean, keep her home safe and how she wanted it, write to her family, write to Scotland Yard, keep pressing the authorities about her situation. There was no let up in this labour. Until too infirm to walk, she would battle into town nearly every day to call at the Post Office, the Housing Office, the DHSS, the market, the police station, the pub. She was a recognised figure around the city centre, dreaded at various counters, the kind of old woman that people invent tea-breaks to avoid. I can imagine their hearts sinking as they caught sight of her struggling through the door with her plastic bags. But few could have imagined how long it had taken her to get dressed, to count her money, find, lose and find her handbag, locate her Post Office book and house key, leave and lock the house, walk to the bus stop, wait for the bus, struggle on board, negotiate and flirt with the driver (if she had forgotten her pass), struggle off again, get through the crowds, up the steps, into a queue, while all the time fending off assailants real and imagined, keeping hold of her possessions and her purse and making sure that she was listened to. As she got older, her increasing blindness and frailty made these trips into town even slower and more complicated, but she continued with them.

Sophie commanded respect as well as funny looks. People were often very gentle with her, like the assistant in a shoe shop who held her twisted feet with great tenderness as she was trying on boots. Or the optician who helped her down the steps on his arm after an appointment.

One of her regular visits was to a lawyer, Richard Hetherington, who practised in the city centre and whom she had adopted as her legal representative. With remarkable generosity and patience he took on Sophie's cause and continued to liaise between her and various authorities on a completely ad hoc, unpaid basis until she died. She would usually miss the appointments he gave her and turn up whenever she wanted to, demanding to see him at the end of the day and sitting in reception until he appeared.

Her requirements were bizarre and numerous; she somehow managed to get him involved in her need for warm winter vests one year, as well as embroiling him in endless negotiations between the family and the council over her electricity bills. Hetherington politely resisted her sexual advances and managed to remain seemingly unshocked by her lurid stories. Recalling her in 2004, he described her as 'the lady tramp' and, with her one bright eye, 'like a creature from Greek tragedy'. On several occasions he helped her out financially or gave her the taxi fare home, politely writing to Jane once the debt had reached nearly thirty pounds. He was one of Sophie's quiet champions (and one of the few who remained in favour with her until the end) whose tact, respect and professional help prevented her from being crushed by the System.

*

Sophie of course found it almost impossible to live on her pension and lurched from one financial crisis to the next, only just surviving by the skin of her teeth and because kind people occasionally bent the rules. She tried in vain to keep track of her day-to-day expenditure by writing down a running total in her pocket diaries and a series of handmade notebooks, which she carried in her handbag. These ingenious little volumes were made from chopped up bits of card and pieces of writing paper, stitched together with pink or red cotton. Reading them now, it is clear that her pension would trickle away over a few days, often leaving her with nothing, and that the wobbly sums in red and black biro could never quite keep up with her last trip to the pub. The problem was exacerbated by Post Office and Social Security closing times and holidays, which would occasionally catch her unawares and mean two days without food or not leaving the flat because she had no money left in her purse.

The notebooks give an impression of Sophie's constant activity, her incessant need and anxiety – as well as glimmers of her former life. Sometimes she has written a word vertically, or very large, or in letters with an outline or framed in a wonky square. There are doodles of fruit, an eye, a little figure with a shopping bag, a pair of legs in a landscape, drawings very like those in her childhood sketchbook. One entry playfully reads 'FRENCHEESEBRIE'. In another she writes, baffled, 'Later found I'd bought by mistake wine that is "low in alcohol and easy to drink". What does that mean? Shall return it to shop.'

The notebooks also reveal how vulnerable she was, living alone in poor housing in a rough area of a large modern city. She might be paranoid but on several occasions she was also the genuine victim of strangers who recognised an old woman capable of little resistance. An extract from spring 1990 follows her experiences over ten days:

Saturday p.m. 85p to last until Monday

9th April
P.O.
Knickers
Stockings or tights
Socks
Books
P.B case
Bread vegetables Fruit Brown-sugar Butter Coffee Milk
9/4/90
Later Stolen –
Large Bread
Good fresh English butter
Knickers about 2 pairs £4

Found them! But not the food
Could have been thieved soon after purchase at Canning
Circus at grocers – or at Yates' or Pumps or all depts finally in
Yates before getting bus home – or on bus –

10th April
Pubs to call tomorrow hoping my carrier bag of purchases
might have been handed in – Pumps, Yates, Rose & Crown.
Where did I have beef sandwich before tea in caff?

Call first bus depot then (if not there) Canning Circus

Small needle in my bed and earlier piece of broken mirror on
floor at foot of bed.

<u>16th April</u>
Rice. Brown flour. Potatoes. Bread Marmalade

<u>19th April</u>
So far have not been able to buy any of these things and am
very hungry.

74p left to last until Monday 23rd April
A man broke in through my window after I got home on
Monday night & he demanded I must hand over to him all my
money or he would kill me – & he said 'I do not <u>want</u> to hurt
you'. I gave him all I had left of money I drew on Thurs. last
week because P.O. was closed on Bank Holiday.
I gave him or rather he took as far as I could see about twenty
five pounds & left me only 74p which he said was for food. I
managed to edge away & pull cord to central control & he left
immediately through the window.
I do not want him to be hurt. I felt he was only acting like a
soldier & I was sensible to obey his orders because he was
threatening me with a knife. I feel sad that there was no time
to talk and that I might have been able to persuade him not to
take so much of my money which is such a small pension. I
think from what I hear on the radio that prisons are not any
way to help in what is a violent situation in the World.

<u>Thursday 19th April</u>
Am in Social Security, ticket 59, & hope they will be kind &
lend me some money towards money taken at knife point.

I had no Christmas presents and no Easter presents. I entirely
depend on my pension from Nottingham Social Security.

I feel I would rather die than be supported by Conservatives & capitalists and I am frightened that on death my X husband & Americans might kidnap me.

I am persecuted.

Once, a good landlord, before I became a council tenant, said I had a persecution mania. I said 'why have I got a persecution mania?'

My landlord replied, 'Because you have been persecuted'.

<u>Midnight.</u>

On Friday a.m. after at last eating some good food & supping tea on getting home. Saw Social Security & after a while they gave me fifteen pounds seventy three p. – which I am to repay them by arrangement in my Pension Book. Feel thankful.

Sophie's preference for male company made her vulnerable, as did her persistent naivety when it came to sex. She was a poor judge of character and would often misread someone's motivation, suddenly finding herself in a dangerous situation that seemed to have come out of nowhere.

On one occasion she was raped by three young men who set upon her in a churchyard. Afterwards she would not condemn them, terrifying as the ordeal had been, saying that they had not really known what they were doing and that it was more about them than her. Another time, she called the police with a complaint that a neighbour had tried to strangle her in her own home. She had consented to have sex with him on her sofa but things had 'got out of hand' and she had been in fear of her life. The authorities were not entirely sympathetic.

*

For much of the time Sophie refused to talk about the past. The present was demanding enough. If Jane mentioned people from the thirties and forties, in an attempt to stimulate interest and memories, Sophie would usually cut the subject dead, as she did in a letter dated 6 October 1983: 'It has become rather sad in the autumn lately and I really don't like nostalgic decaying parks and gardens & talking about antiquated depressed intellectuals.'

Nor would she be drawn when one tried to talk to her about her writing. She only occasionally mentioned it in letters, usually dismissing it as something that was no longer relevant. 'I'm glad I stopped myself doing that because really it was so lonely,' she wrote in September 1983 and, almost a decade later, 'As for writing poetry, I never have the urge to do that any more – it just wouldn't be me to do that sort of thing.'

Ellen had died in 1977, having long been estranged from her daughter, and Sophie barely spoke about her beyond the odd bitter anecdote in which her mother was always the villain. A paragraph Sophie wrote in 1993, however, reveals that the emotional link between them had never been completely severed:

For some years after my mother Mrs E died, I used to wake in the early morning having heard myself calling, 'Mother . . . Mother!' and then my trembling voice would say to myself, 'Oh, she's not here. She died.'

Even though . . . I had lived nowhere near her for many years, subconsciously I was aware that she was alive & 'there' and I used to think sometimes I never did enough for her perhaps in her old age but I felt happier if I didn't see her too often.

She had similarly lost contact with her brother Brian, but was keen to have news of him and pleased to receive the occasional newspaper cutting about his work.

It was only on very rare occasions that memories from a long time ago would come floating to the surface and Sophie would talk briefly about the past as if she had suddenly seen it through a window. One letter, written on 10 December 1985, swerves uncharacteristically back to her childhood, arriving at a distant time as if by accident:

My very dearest Janie,
No I didn't buy this writing paper. Somebody gave me four pieces . . . I fold paper like this in some moods because in my teens one could buy paper that was like this in boxes & it made one feel secure – i.e. another thing that one's less likely to lose. In those days I sometimes bought scented writing paper & wrote to Geoffrey on it.

It was the days when also some ladies still used, the Edwardian slightly lower class women were united in using 'Papier Poudre' – on hot days one would see them smearing their over-heated faces with papier poudre from their handbags, then they had them changing their veils again from their dark navy blue straw hats onto their faces and handing the papier poudre around to other females –

'It's very hot, isn't it?' – but they all looked as if they enjoyed the heat & the sun sprinkled in through the edges of drawn William Morris curtains and a sweet breeze blew in through the French windows at the back of the house & where moss was somehow always damp and cool & there might be old deckchairs which after sherry we would go out & sit down on and go on with well-tempered versions of family news because of course there was only a tall but slender hedge between our garden and the neighbours!

Despite her determined and, in the main, successful attempts to blot out the life she had once led, there were some things, engrained through early experience and pleasure, that still bound her to Joan Adeney Easdale. Her childhood passion for nature was still with her as an old woman in inner-city Nottingham; she noticed the weather, the changing seasons, the way the sun came into her room. In February 1992 she wrote, 'I love seeing what wild animals come round here and I wonder how the hedgehog family are getting on in Brook Street and occasionally I think of the back garden which turned very wild when I lived in Ena Avenue and I used to see kind of visions there of some prehistoric animals.'

In July 1995 she described watching an approaching summer storm from a crowded pub:

Day after day dawns after a hot night-time into an even hotter day. Blue changes into noon after noon after noon of dry trees waving where the wind comes from a glaring grey.

In the Bell in Market Square yesterday evening we all watched the clouds coming lower & darker, waiting while the rain began, accompanied by one burst of thunder over the city.

Girls in light summer dresses & some in bikinis & boys & men in blue briefs quickened their pace, some scuttling onto buses, while we customers supped our lager or wine etc, with a few of us smoking. But the storm never really took shape over Nottingham last night, though it did in many places.

Apple orchards always look lovely in the evening sun after a storm in summertime.

She missed the country but was a city person by now, a familiar sight in any Nottingham pub, peering out from beneath the enormous leather Rasta hat someone had once given her, and which she wore like a collapsed football on her head. She loved the company of younger people, the humour and stimulation of pub conversation and the feeling of acceptance she got from drinking with strangers. She felt truly at home in some of the roughest pubs in the city, among washed-up heavy drinkers, people who had lived hard lives and drank to forget, people who would not make judgements about her. When my cousin Dinah came over from Australia in 1996 she and I went to visit Sophie (now sixty-three) and ended up at the Blue Bell, where she was obviously a regular. Dinah tried to buy her a sherry (as requested) but the bloke behind the bar laughed at her: 'Is that for Sophie? She doesn't drink sherry! Get her a bitter!' and pulled her a pint. 'Don't know how she does it,' he said, shaking his head in grudging admiration, 'Walked out of here last night totally wasted.'

To an outsider she probably looked poor, dishevelled and peculiar, but even as a very old woman Sophie took great care over her appearance. She minded intensely what she wore and would curl her hair before going out to the pub, twisting it round pipe-cleaners for a few hours and sometimes adding a paper bow or a piece of ribbon. She liked overtly feminine things – the colour pink, soft textures and velvet – and if she saw a piece of lace in the market or some taffeta of the right colour she might well buy it and go without food for a few days. Her letters to Jane often featured very specific requests, like this list written in May 1992:

Will you please, daughter Jane Susan Robertson, Rose & Crown House, send me the following, in cash or kind:

A bag of 1 apple, two bananas, a small peach tree and some
handkerchiefs.

Socks, number 6 shoe, & not in bright colours & they must
be cotton.

Herbs (some to plant in garden) & brown rice, brown
macaroni & spaghetti (not tinned).

Pink or Pinkish & Brown (never grey) slippers, size 6, to
wear in house.

Very wide Indian or European sandals, Chinese or Italian,
continental size 6.

2 or 3 prs large size nylon knickers with lace, not in bright
colours. Pink, white or gold. Not blue.

2 genuinely long pink or black petticoats, nylon or similar.

Short sleeved, salmon pink jumper, woman's size.

Long sleeved size twelve black lambs wool cardigan.

Oily French perfume in <u>small</u> bottle, not spray. Musk or
similar, not fresh or stale but lingering and thick.

Garments regularly got left behind in pubs or on buses, pieces got
nicked or she might suddenly take against something and throw it
out. She once took umbrage against a pub landlord because he
banned her for dropping her drawers in the middle of the bar: 'I
don't know what all the fuss was about,' she protested. 'They were
clean on this morning!'

Despite her encroaching blindness, she would spend long hours
darning her clothes or adapting them to be more comfortable or more
glamorous. Sometimes, with a few adjustments, a dubious gift could be
rendered acceptable, as she explained to Jane in January 1992:

I now realise I can turn the white woolly tights into simply
long knickers – and I can wear the bottoms as bed-socks

which I always need in the cold at night. So that is solved.
And I need to concentrate on <u>buying stockings</u>. I bought
(and had to enlarge) a rather twee black lacey suspender belt
with a red bow to show which was the front of it . . .

One of Sophie's many lingerie projects was what she called her
'freedom bra', a loose, vest-like top that offered ample ventilation
but no support. Convinced that this garment would be a best-seller,
she presented a hand-stitched prototype to the manageress of the
local Marks and Spencer, who accepted it with mute astonishment.

Sophie rarely had time for distractions beyond the demands of
everyday life, but a few scattered references in her pocket diaries
allude to things that briefly caught her interest along the way. She
noted down the address of the Vegetarian Society and the meeting
times for the Charlie Marshall Blue Coat School Debating Society.
Did she ever actually make it there for 2.30 p.m. on a Sunday?

Another entry reads, 'Martin Reith's talk referring to tribes of different Celts. Essence of Celtic religion which can be studied at
Edinburgh', which sounds like a radio programme she and Naomi
might have tuned in to in the thirties.

There are also a few highly critical mentions of trips to the theatre, organised by the warden of the sheltered housing she later
lived at. *Salome* is dismissed as 'An absolutely useless bit of stage-
work. A waste of time,' and *Les Liasons Dangereuses* on the 7
December 1993 as 'good cast wasted on very dull play'.

At various other times she became interested in handwriting
and calligraphy – a letter might arrive even less decipherable than
usual because she was practising writing with her right hand in
order to keep both hands and both sides of her brain exercised. In
one, she mentions that she has ordered some books on twentieth

century comedy from the city library. In another she says she want to paint again.

Sophie remained combative, paranoid and delusional until the end of her life, often imagining that a stranger she had seen on the street was Sandy or Polly, and that certain people were characters from her past, sent to spy on her in disguise. But in the last few years she mellowed slightly, enough to begin to let people support her in a way that she had never previously allowed. She still talked about genetic experiments and conspiracies against her but the physical onslaught of old age seemed to focus her energies on self-preservation. She consented to medical care if the need was critical (even submitting to several stays in hospital) and she allowed her children to pay her bills. After years of resistance and worries about bank robberies, she also conceded to having a bank account set up in her name, which they could pay into and she could use for taxi money and other essentials.

This gear-shift seemed to coincide with increased contact with her family. In the late eighties, just as Sophie had always believed they would, Polly and Sandy came to see her. Sandy had been liaising with her lawyer on various matters long-distance for some time but decided to meet his mother properly in 1986, when he and his wife Diane were over on a visit to England. It was not easy, but in many ways it simplified things; Sophie was overjoyed to see her son again and he was relieved to have reconnected with her. Three years later Polly visited for the first time and recorded the reunion in her diary:

> Jane went forward to kiss her, saying something like, 'look who's here!'. When she recognised who I was, she fell into my arms, we hugged and hugged and she kissed me & looked into my face to see that it was really me and said she was so glad I had come at last because her sight was getting worse and she

thought she would soon be blind.

At first she seemed like a complete stranger. She was so much littler than I remembered, and she had no teeth any more . . . As we sat on her bed and talked, I could gradually see the mother I had known looking out fleetingly, in an expression which would be gone in an instant.

Again there was a sense of completeness, of circles finally made. These visits were momentous for both sides. Although they stirred up complicated feelings and distressing memories, and were painful for what they could not achieve, at the most basic level they validated Sophie's unwavering belief in love.

There were limits to this sense of normalisation, however. It was some time in the early nineties that Sophie came to stay with Jane for a weekend. The visit would have been inconceivable a decade earlier, but Jane had by now given her mother our address and phone number and could see no real reason why she could not stay for a couple of days. This was, however, an ambitious undertaking and one which Jane now refers to as 'a complete disaster'.

Sophie started asking, 'Are we nearly there yet?' while Jane was still negotiating the outskirts of Nottingham, when they had only just embarked on the two-and-a-half-hour journey to Worcestershire. Once at Rose and Crown House, Sophie found that it wasn't as rural as she had hoped – it was not as isolated as Crouch – and she kept demanding to go to the pub. She did not want to 'waste time' shopping, felt anxious at being in the house and was then scornful of our local, which was clearly not rough enough for her to feel at ease. By the end of two days, Jane was exhausted and Sophie ready to go home. Far from being a healing experience, the visit had only emphasised the impossibility of making things better.

*

Sophie broke her hip in a fall in October 1990. While recovering in hospital, she finally agreed to consider moving into an old people's home, swayed by the argument that it would be safer for her and the suggestion that it might even allow her to live more happily than on her own. Of the homes available, however, only a few would consider her because she was funded by Social Services and her track record in council housing had not been good.

At Forest Lodge Sophie found herself among the very old, the very poor, the senile, the demented. Compared with most of the other residents she was still highly astute and vigorous. While her companions languished in the shared lounge, Sophie would be upstairs, getting ready for a night on the town. While they offered no resistance to the roar of enforced television or a visit from the mayor, she would defiantly muster all her energy to go out shopping for coloured thread, to eat eggs on toast in a café and visit the police station before stopping off for a drink and staying out until closing time.

Within days of arriving at Forest Lodge Sophie was planning her escape. She felt trapped, she disliked most of the other residents and she panicked at the idea that this was where she was going to spend the rest of her life. She wrote to Jane, suggesting an alternative solution: why couldn't old people attend three different homes on a rota, so that they got variety and a break from each place? Those 'stickers' who didn't want to move could stay in one place, but the 'mobile resident' could enjoy change and variation and would only have to remember to bring their pension book. In another letter she asked Jane to investigate the possibility of a vegetarian home, possibly in France.

The idea of permanence clearly disturbed Sophie and she did everything she could to kick against it. Her survival strategy depended partly on getting out of the building and partly on stating and re-stating how different she was to everyone else her own age, as if this were some kind of protection against senility. She was horrified by what she saw as the lassitude of her contemporaries and their loss of faculties, apparently unable to grasp the fact that most of them could not help their situation. In letters she described them as almost alien, lolling about in armchairs all day while she was off 'canvassing hard for the Labour Party'.

She wrote an account of her new surroundings on 6 April 1992:

I am in my bedroom writing now & I love to have the window open. At least there is the semi-wildness of birds & squirrels out over the railings & dogs meeting strange dogs or regular pals, being exercised by their owners or helpers . . . Across the park there are sometimes young footballers taking exercise & occasionally I hear them calling, 'Sophie Curly is there – Yes, she is,' 'No – she is dead – No,' 'No,' says the other lad, 'she's not dead, I've just seen her at her window. Yes, it was Sophie.' . . . So actually I don't feel so lonely in my room as in the lounge.

In contrast to her own room, the communal areas were anarchic and frightening:

. . . to have some semblance of living alone is some help – it stops actually the fear at sudden harsh screaming voices in lounge or dining room – the scowls, the dreadful deliberately 'pulled' faces and the obscene insults. Edwina, the lady from Eastern Europe or borders of Russia, and I try to sit silent as another old lady at our table suddenly snorts and scowls viciously fixing her eyes, usually on me, then mumbling, I have no idea why, 'Y' dirty bugger!'

I may be rearranging my things at my place at the table to avoid, if I can, her hugely breathy coughs which seem focussed to go straight into my food or coffee or tea. It is daily hell. Occasionally the old lady leans so slantingly one way or the other in her chair that, as it's got no arms, she falls crashing to the floor, hooting & yelling.

Finding herself back in an institution seemed to stir up comparisons with her days at the Sanatorium, for the same letter shows her almost nostalgic for the facilities of the mental hospital she had so hated thirty years earlier: 'Of course I sometimes think if only I was in a council dwelling of mixed age groups & with a day & night canteen, and 24hrs a day wardens on for the whole establishment which could be larger than this & with workrooms for carpentry & art & sewing & rug-making attached.'

Sophie wrote like a front-line journalist, keen to record every failing of her fellow residents, every detail of her new life, as if by doing so she could keep a grip on the situation. She vacillated between periods of misery at her predicament and times when she could find genuine pleasure despite it. She lived for getting out. The pub had always been her refuge from hardship and loneliness but, once she was living in the home, it became her lifeline. Within days of having a tumour removed from her bowel in 1991 she wrote that she was already back walking and going out in the evening:

> . . . probably on Saturday I am going out with a nurse of 16 and her boy-friend who looks wild but nice & dresses out of the ordinary & I wonder if I will be looking after her rather more than she looks after me but probably everything will be OK even though the boyfriend recently gave her a black eye because she went out with her sister (and who else?) presumably without him.

This was the kind of social contact that made her feel alive and kept her going. She wanted to be involved with the mess of life and, as John Richardson said, she was not content with small-talk; she demanded intellectual stimulation and was always on the look out for a decent discussion. She wrote to Jane, 'I do occasionally, oftener than one would expect, meet artists & poets in pubs & on the way to them, and that gives gleams of understanding that is ageless.'

One of her drinking companions was a Trinidadian called Anthony Robinson, himself a writer and poet. Sophie would sit with him and sometimes his friend George Johnson ('my boys', as she called them) on long Sunday afternoons in the Lion. Robinson says she occasionally talked to him about her writing, but only briefly. He remembers her saying, with a languorous wave of the hand, 'Oh, I passed my poems to some obscure publisher.' Johnson said she talked about how handsome the black GIs had looked in the war, how she would have liked to go out with one if she had not been married.

It was in the Poacher's Arms on a summer evening in 1992 that Sophie first met Julian Griffiths, a local solicitor. He was drinking in the front bar and they struck up a conversation. Remembering her in 2005, he described her as 'intriguing' and 'very eccentric, intelligent and sensitive'. He took her home to meet his wife Pippa and their family, and they all sat in the garden together, talking and drinking. They found her fascinating and from then on Sophie would go round for meals sometimes.

It was a long time since she had shared anything resembling family life and so it must have been a strange, perhaps painful, pleasure for her to have Sunday lunch round a big table with children laughing and playing. They learnt that she had had a terrible marriage, that she had a son and two daughters whom she hardly ever saw. She told them that her husband had been a eugenicist. She never mentioned her writing.

Sophie continued to be unhappy at Forest Lodge. Used to running her own home, however eccentrically, she was now compelled to wait for meals or ask if she wanted a cup of tea. She became afraid and began to talk more and more about death. Flippant remarks made by staff, like, 'You won't be happy until you're dead, Sophie!' and 'You should get out of here before you're as bad as the rest of them!' only deepened her insecurity, as she took them literally. As usual, her despair was not consistent but it was obvious that she was distressed. In one letter she wrote, 'I continue to feel, day after day, like a frightened rabbit, simply crouching in terror, unable to move but awaiting my ghastly fate.'

The final straw came when she wanted to put a Labour campaign poster up in her window but the management would not let her, for fear that passers-by might throw stones at it. Furious on her behalf, Jane asked for Sophie to be transferred to somewhere more suitable, and it was at this point that John Richardson was appointed as her social worker.

Richardson was another of Sophie's champions, although she did not always welcome his involvement. He chose to ignore her fantasies and focused instead on the practicalities of improving her life and maintaining her independence. His plain-speaking verged on bluntness, but it was exactly what was required. Writing to Jane after Sophie's death, he admitted, 'Even though I respected your mother, I cannot pretend I always liked her. At times I felt more like her equerry and certainly when she moved into Ben Mayo Court I seemed to follow her around, picking up and carrying bits and pieces as we went round buying things.'

Sophie was always trying to angle for a lift into town or to get him to come in to the pub with her. It was a constant battle to outwit her manipulations and deflect her weird ideas, while maintaining a firm grip on what was needed.

When John Richardson managed to get her a place in Ben Mayo Court in September 1992 it seemed the perfect solution. It was a brand new building, only recently opened, and it offered independent living in a secure environment, with a warden on hand should residents need assistance. Pippa and Julian helped Sophie move her furniture and belongings into a fresh, bright flatlet on the third floor.

Within days, however, Sophie wanted to leave. She was offended by the fact that the place was not actually run by the council, as she had been assured it would be. She despised most of the other residents and vaguely suspected the warden of being someone else in disguise. The warden, in turn, became exasperated with the way Sophie used her buzzer almost constantly to call for attention. She would call up central control, the emergency helpline, to verify the date or to tell them that she had arrived home safely from the pub.

Residents started to complain that Sophie had borrowed teabags and not replaced them, taken someone's walking stick and not given it back, that she had been abusive in the corridor. Then came reports that she would roll home drunk late at night and ring every bell in the building trying to get back in. She was accused of shouting obscenities, and of propositioning one of the male residents in the lift.

It was obvious that Sophie had no intention of fitting in with other people's rules and a petition was got up to evict her, the discussions behind her back only fuelling her paranoia and distrust of the management. Relations worsened and within months she had been issued with a Notice to Quit by Nottinghamshire County Council on grounds of 'nuisance' and having acted 'in a threatening or offensive manner'. As Richardson said, she had burnt her boats. The only option open to her, since she was too frail to live alone, was to go to yet another residential home.

CHAPTER 10

BLACK ANGEL

'Will you die, Amber?' said the stone.
And she answered,
'No, I have to live'.

from *Amber Innocent*, J.A.E., 1939

A cold November afternoon in 1995 and I am wandering around the streets of Nottingham, looking for her. The home told me she had gone out. Didn't know when she'd be back. Try the pubs.

I try the Cricketers behind Kwiksave. Push open the door and everyone turns. Drifts of smoke hang in the middle of the room, caught in pale sunlight. There's a click of pool balls from the dark at the back. A few men sit alone at tables, a few at the bar. Everything is maroon.

She was here earlier. Try the Poacher's.

Out again into the cold, litter wrapping itself round the corners of walls. A bingo hall, traffic. The pub is on a hill, opposite a multi-storey car park. I brace myself. Hubbub, the smell of lunches eaten an hour ago, smoke. I ask the barman. He laughs and points, 'She's over there, by the window. Sophie! Someone come to see yer!'

She is tiny, lost in a boy's outsize puffa jacket that comes almost

231

to her bare knees. Long white hair, slightly drunk, head held a little to one side. She doesn't see me until I'm right up next to her table and then she beams and grabs me to her.

Sophie moved into Ash Lea Court in December 1993. It was a nursing home near the bottom of the pile, run on the bare minimum but with just enough caring staff to provide a sense of security. The physical surroundings were dismal, with mean rooms, worn lino, cheap light fittings and the most basic decor. There was the inevitable shared lounge with big chairs jammed around the walls and the telly on loud and the smell of gravy. Residents sat staring into space or wandered about in the corridors.

What made it bearable was the staff, who recognised how Sophie wanted to live and allowed her the freedom she demanded. She might be eighty, but she could come and go as she wished and they even gave her a key to the front door. While for others less mobile and independent this laissez-faire approach might have tipped towards negligence, it suited Sophie's particular character and needs. She would head off for the evening on her two sticks and if she had not returned by midnight or breakfast time the next day the nurse on duty would simply shrug and say, 'Ah, that's just Sophie. She'll be back. She's like a cat. She'll come home when she's hungry.'

Often, of course, Sophie chose to interpret being left to her own devices as 'systematic neglect' and she would then demand special attention – a trip to the shops or a lift to the pub. Much of the time she was humoured by the staff, who seemed to be quite fond of her. She knew a lot about them, kept her ears open, got to hear about their home lives, at some points felt almost that she was their friend. This made it seem all the more harsh when they refused to take her on holiday with them or to have her back to their own homes for a meal. The situation was not ideal, but by this stage there was no alternative.

Sophie's letters from Ash Lea Court are long, rambling and often desperate. In those last few years, she became increasingly anxious and discontent, and yet more likely to write with unbroken sanity about her situation than she had for decades. A letter from 29 August 1996 reads,

Friday? I don't know what week or when.

Dear Janie,
I do hope you are well. Days fly past here so quickly & new staff keep arriving – some very nice.

My buzzer starts working and everything feels orderly and making sense and then – plonk! – everything gets topsy-turvy & one has to go hobbling up & down to find staff – the place seems empty except for a terrible smell on top floor & may be one very old resident sleeping in a row of empty chairs on all walls & his head thrown back & on another floor, another giving an occasional twitch – then in a corridor a male nurse whizzes past rigidly carrying a commode pot to the sluice to empty it – somebody in a lounge calls repeatedly 'Can I have a cup of tea, please? Can you hear me? Are you – is – is anybody there please – I'm deaf – can I 'ave a cuppa tea, please? Are you there? Tea, please. How long will it be, can you tell me – You say somebody's gone down to make some? Can I 'ave a cup of tea? I can't stand up because my trousers won't do up. Is it bed-time please? Can, is she coming soon with that tea? Can I have some please – Hullo – who do you say you are? Sophie? Yes – I know you. Can you get me a cup of tea, please? Can't you go in the kitchen? Yes, that's right, I'll wait while you go down & ask if they're bringing some tea.'

Len the kind and swift and much loved nurse seems always on the move – he says 'Oh, I shall be on every floor tonight, I expect – you can have this tea now – I must go now – Betty's not very well – I know, we do need more staff, really—' and puff, and some brow and hair-mopping – & off he flies.

In her sixties and seventies Sophie had raged against class differences, against car-owners and people who could afford new things. In her eighties she saved her anger for staff members who were lazy or superior. She was fiercely critical of anyone who took too long over their tea break, failed to respond quickly enough to her buzzer or pinched her food if she was late back from town.

As she became frailer and was less able to escape the company of her fellow residents, they too became a source of irritation, worry and sometimes even terror. Sophie imagined that some of them were characters she had known many years before, who had been deliberately reintroduced into her life. There was one softly-spoken woman she thought might have been Virginia Woolf, but also a particularly unpleasant old man who frightened her. On arrival at the home he had apparently announced 'I feel like murdering somebody in this place, and I'm going to murder you!' (looking straight at her) and for months afterwards Sophie lived in fear of him. He would wander about and rattle her door – they had adjacent rooms – and on one occasion he punched another old woman in the face.

Sophie had already survived several bouts of serious illness: meningitis in 1987, a broken hip in 1990, bowel cancer in 1991, pleurisy in 1992 and numerous other breakages and medical crises, which she had always come through triumphantly. But throughout 1996 and 1997 her health worsened rapidly and she became prone to nose-bleeds that left her anaemic and very weak. Her brother's

death a year earlier, in October 1995, had come as a devastating
shock and her letters began to reflect an increasing preoccupation
with mortality. In 1996 she wrote, 'I think and think about the
next world and other worlds and only occasionally I feel I could
attain to a spiritual body fashioned to adapt to such a future life.'
In another letter she referred to 'a few flashes and dim revela-
tions', which were her only clues as to what might be waiting for
her. The doctors found lung cancer in early 1998 and it was clear
that she did not have long to live.

On my last visit I pushed open her door with dread. She had almost
disappeared inside her nightie and hardly made a bump under the
bedclothes.

'Oh, it's you!' she cried, 'You're the one I wanted to see most!'
She felt like a small bird when I tried to hug her.

We talked about a lot of things: the rain, the man next door
who kept shouting, 'There's no hope for me! There's no hope for
me!', her days at the BBC – 'I wrote plays, you know' – and my
work. All this interrupted by mouthfuls of mashed parsnip and her
wracking phlegmy cough and a cup of tea and needing to be moved
up the bed.

My diary entry for that day, 13 January 1998, reads,

Good things were that she allowed me to help her and touch
her and hold her hands. And there was fresh air coming in
through the window and she had a silver paper ribbon in her
hair and she said I had lovely eyelashes. And I made her laugh
(once or twice). And I felt we were close and probably closer
than we'd ever been.

And I went out and bought her a bottle of sherry and some
pink lipstick and some Kleenex in a box with pictures on it –

and she was delighted with all this & put the lipstick on immediately and some on her face as rouge.

But it was also very sad and the grimness of the place unavoidable.

And no one came to empty her commode all afternoon. And I noticed that her shit was black, soot black and frightening. And her bed was dirty.

By the end of my visit I felt pulled apart.

If that was my goodbye I am grateful for it. She said she was tired of it all (indicating the world, lifting a corner of the curtain and half-looking outside, into the rain).

Later she said she knew she didn't have long left and hoped we'd see one another again but would I pray for her, and she wished me success with my acting. I felt it was her blessing.

It seemed she would die any minute but she held out for months. There was time for Polly and Sandy to come over separately from Australia. Polly wrote in her diary of seeing her again, 'It was somehow hard to talk and all sadness.' Knowing that this was the last time they would see one another, there was none of the exhilaration she had felt when visiting nine years before. The banalities of struggling out to the pub collided clumsily with the seriousness of what was happening. She wrote after the first day,

The goal of Mother's life is 'to get out' but she looks far too wasted and frail for the speed and vigour of the city and when we get there, after wangling her up kerbs and through doors and over steps and round bar stools, and finding a table with no draught, she hasn't the stamina to sit on a bench along the pub wall . . . She whispers to herself, 'Oh dear, oh dear . . . oh dear, oh dear . . .' She may swim up again, helped by a shot of anger, 'It's terrible! I don't know what to do about it!' and then sinks down and rests . . . She seems to get the most out of arrivals and farewells. The confirmation of our affection.

But as so often before, Sophie rallied. Sandy's abiding memory of his last visit to see her is of her triumphant entrance up the steps and through the swing doors of a rather flash Nottingham pub. He felt the 'Ride of the Valkyries' should have been playing as she slowly and determinedly made her way to bar on her two sticks.

Of course, as he and Jane headed home along the dual carriageway later that evening, the Wagner came blaring over the car radio.

Sophie's last trip to the pub was just three weeks before she died.

She had more than once talked about going to heaven in the arms of a black angel. By a strange but typical coincidence her drinking partner and friend Anthony Robinson had become a nurse at Ash Lea Court. It was in his arms that Sophie finally died, at six o'clock in the morning on 10 July 1998.

The home reassured Jane that her mother had died peacefully, but when I spoke to Anthony in 2004 he said that she had been frightened and fought death to the end. 'No, I'm sorry,' he said, 'Sophie died hard. Very hard.' At one point she had even thrown herself out of bed in the struggle.

The death certificate recorded the cause of her death as chest infection, anaemia and, against all odds, old age.

There were more people at Sophie's funeral than one might have expected and the different parties seemed surprised to see one another. It was as if we were all characters who had been in the same play, but never in the same scene until now: our immediate family, Brian's daughter Jo and her partner, several nurses, staff members and residents from the home, Anthony Robinson, John Richardson, Richard Hetherington, Julian and Pippa. Sophie was buried in the city graveyard with views over Nottingham, flowers from our garden in Worcestershire lying next to bush flowers sent from Australia. We played the music from *The Red Shoes*, I read a verse from *Amber Innocent* and my brother James read 'Eternity', a poem she had written aged seventeen:

> The profuse orchestration of the night
> In the wood
> Is felt in the thick leaves and the owl's flight;
> Understood.
> When the wind sends the jet leaves fluttering
> And the clouds send the wet stars guttering.
> Like a hood
> The huge sky spreads over the throbbing earth,
> And the moon's eye watches our death and birth.

After the burial we all went for beer and sandwiches in the back room of the Poacher's.

EPILOGUE

I still catch sight of her in a crowd, think that she's just ahead of me in the bus queue or sitting at the bar with her back to me as I come through a pub doorway. She has been dead nearly ten years now but I don't think this will change.

Researching her life, I'd catch similar flashes of her as I tried to piece the story together. Coincidence and elusiveness combined to make it a tantalising process. On my first visit to the BBC archives at Caversham, for instance, I found myself staring at the cover of her talk on Mrs Beeton, reading and re-reading the front page until I suddenly realised what I was looking at. It was stamped with a date . . . I was reading it exactly sixty years to the day since it had been broadcast.

Months later, trying to track down the script of her Mrs Beeton play, I had despaired of ever finding it because two searches at the archive had come up with nothing. It had no doubt been lost during or immediately after the War, when huge quantities of programme material had been destroyed. Disappointed, but not wanting to give up, I wrote a third letter, asking if they would make a final search – the archive assistant found it. Joan wasn't in the index, she'd somehow slipped through the filing system, but her play had been there all the time, unread for decades.

She is remembered by her three children, her eight grandchildren and has five great-grandchildren she didn't get to meet. There are people in Nottingham bars who will still laugh with amazement if you mention her. A few friends and acquaintances scattered between Edinburgh and Sydney. John Richardson wrote to Jane, 'I still miss her, even though I didn't see her that often. I still find it hard to believe she's not around any more.'

In one of the last conversations Jane had with her father before he died, Jim remembered Joan as 'a gallant creature'.

What gets left behind is a mixture of people, bits of paper, ways of doing things and traits that are so subtle you can hardly grasp them. I know I owe her tenacity and independence. A love of words. I make fruit pies in the way Jane taught me and Joan taught her, with a pastry rose and leaves on the top. I have a thing about dressing-up clothes. Colour. I write a lot of letters. I'm untidy.

The thing I value most is a way of seeing – or *looking*, rather. My visual sense comes from Joan through Jane. I remember being a child and going for a walk in the country, trying out an old box camera I'd been given. I wanted to take a picture of a field of cows and my mother said 'Look at the udders . . . take one of the udders.' So, aged six, I took a picture from underneath, with a line of barbed wire crossing the top of the shot, most of the cows' faces cropped out and a portrait of their udders. That was what Joan would have seen too.

My own daughter Zoë was born on 14 February 2006, when I was halfway through writing this book. I occasionally catch a split-second flicker of her great-grandmother's determination and vulnerability as it crosses her face. When she frowns she looks like Joan aged two. She is a visceral connection with what has gone before and I feel closer to my grandmother because of her. I no longer have to guess at Joan's happiness as she holds Jane on her knee in that wartime photograph. I understand completely her panic in the face of mounds of damp laundry, a wailing child with tooth pain and blank pages demanding to be filled.

At the same time, the differences between our experiences of motherhood, of life, are huge. I don't have mental illness to contend with. Or war. And, unlike her, I do have a washing machine. There's a limit to the parallels I can make.

On her gravestone, four names circle a Celtic cross. Joan Adeney Easdale. Joan Rendel. Sophia Curly. Sophie. And underneath: Poet, Mother, Free Spirit. Even so, it doesn't say quite enough – or rather, she manages to evade the summary and refuses to be set in stone, slipping sideways to somewhere else.

I cannot protect my grandmother from the loneliness of her story. I cannot make it better or bring her in from the cold. But in writing it down, joining the pieces up, I hope I have told what happened, shown her to be an extraordinary person and given her a space to dance in.

Amber
innocent

Joan Adeney
Easdale   The Hogarth Press

AMBER INNOCENT

AMBER INNOCENT

JOAN ADENEY EASDALE

THE HOGARTH PRESS
52 TAVISTOCK SQUARE,
LONDON, W.C.1
1939

First published 1939

PRINTED IN GREAT BRITAIN BY THE GARDEN CITY PRESS LTD.
AT LETCHWORTH, HERTFORDSHIRE.

To
J. M. R.

AMBER INNOCENT

I

Speaking into the folds of the curtain,
She would not be able to hear in her voice
The height of the ceiling nor the width of the room.
" Dusk has come," said Amber.
And afraid lest a small chink might reveal
A ribbon of sky more grey
She drew the curtains closely together.

The warmth of her breath on the velvet
Made in the shadow a momentary bliss.
Deeper she buried her face and her face
Seemed all of her. Her lashes brushing the pile were
    part
Of some sequestered woodland dark.
She lived in her face. Her body might be
A negative pillar alone.

She knew that her brother-in-law sat
In a chair behind in the world.
Most likely his eyes were sizing her shape
From her neck's dun curve down to her still shoes.
But Amber was all in her forest's shade,
It was only her face that held herself.

" God left the Churches at the Reformation,"
Said Mark from his chair in the world,
" But even in houses we need lamps."

Softly he spoke, and gone were the shades of the
        forest,
For tongues can utter smooth as velvet, too.
So her face drew away, for his words had entered
And broken the heat into hate.

Amber turned back and trod in the world.
" I thought only the curtains were dark,
I forgot the room," laughed Amber with laughter
Round and unreal, which she could not feel.
But within her person—
For now she had stepped down from her face
Into the whole length of her body—she was crying,
" Dear God,
            Dear God,
                    Dear God, protect me ! "

She went for a lamp, a round moony lamp,
Which one of the servants had placed in the hall.
This rule they observed,
But none of them knew they hated their master.

As she lifted the lamp from the table
Where another lamp shone on the surface,
Amber heard the tiny moan of a child-voice,
Ill, and far away in the turret.

Megathy had woken !
The reflection of the moony lamp told her,
With the wide, anxious face of a mother—
Megathy cried !

Slowly she walked, she walked slowly,
In case the cry of the ill child should come down again,
Unheard, from the winding stairs of the turret.

The moony lamp spread wide and became the whole
    room.
Without it
There would be no tall organ with gilded pipes,
There would be no white walls encompassing
Like a raiment her praying self.

But Mark would always be sitting in his chair of wicker
In which he twisted his fingers while talking.
White his face, like a document. And closed his mind,
Save for one faint essence that issued from there,
Of cerebral war-gas and conscious decay—
A will that is snapped over self and must therefore
Fly off, as elastic, in everyone's eyes.

Opposite Mark was another chair. Empty,
Always there, an empty chair.
His late wife footed the carpet-piece
With the regular wear of one who sits yet has restless
    feet.
She who had been pale-spirited, threadbare of purpose,
Had now firmness of opinion.
For this do the living bestow on the dead.

" Megathy calls," said Amber, seeing behind her eyes
The broad, female face of the moony reflection.
The lamp itself in her hands had no meaning,
It identified nought but the blossoming room.
O the blossoming room now spread transfigured !

And shadows revolved the while she walked.
She was in the world again, but the world had changed.
The forested curtains bordered this clear white
    meadow
Made by the moony lamp.

" It is for you to go," said Mark. And he was there,
For his voice spoke and the mirage broke.
Small is the mind, but waterfalls crash there,
Boulders are loosened and topple on crystal,
Breaking the blown-glass visions to blackness and dust.

2

The turret door had closed, and while Amber mounted,
Emotions now feathered themselves as birds and flew
    up
From her bowels to her breast, from her breast to
    her throat,
And from thence travelled before her a little while.

At every other turn of the turret
There was a round window holding a view of the
    grounds,
And each of these, despite the descent of dusk,
Were clearly yet distantly defined
As the small scene shown through the bottom of an
    inverted tumbler.

In the first window
A nuttery flowered like gold, suspended fountains,
And a hay-stack, shadow-shelved, breathed quietness,

While chalky hens were poised in the act of scratching
For invisible grain.

In the second window
An ilex tree was stitched in pearly silks
At the side of an olive lawn, where croquet hoops
Rusted in gentility.

In the third window
Fields unfolded beyond a reserved shrubbery
Whose oiled leaves tapped not the iron railings,
Black and arrow-headed.

In the fourth window
The sky, immeasurably deep, depicted infinity,
And the high-tuned bat when slipping jagged-wise
     through
Could pierce nothing.

" This way shall I go to-morrow," said Amber at
     every window,
But reaching the next she would think, " no, it shall
     be this."
And leaning into the cold, round frame of the fourth,
She all but submitted herself to the deepening air.
But murmured there close a voice from her blood,
" Go not heavenward yet."
She listened, and did not go far on that ethereal sea.

Assertion of self was no less a pain
Than the frozen limb that feels again,
As Amber stepped back from annihilation,
And the blue was a sky with a bat flying through.

Shod with terrestrial claims to her feet
She mounted the steps to Megathy's door,
And echo of moony reflection illumined
As the lone child whimpered again in the room.

A candle burned, with a short-wicked spluttering
flame,
In a bracket upon the wall,
Making a darkness to move over the cupboard,
A darkness that was a man coming forward and back
In the fever-dew of Megathy's mind.
The child lay crumpled on the floor,
With yellow hair stuck to her brow,
And blue veins traced the dampened neck.
Her tears made gold wheels round the candle flame—
Bright spokes of gold stretched fair as sun,
Thus joy in sorrow is begun.

When Amber came
All space dissolved between her entering
And lifting up the child in arms that seemed
Large wings that shadowed shadows from the view.
Her bed and hair she smoothed till sobbing ceased,
And then, the pale child watched her aunt across the
room,
Touching, folding and arranging shapes.

The short sound of water poured into a white basin
Wherein it became green as the underneath of leaves.
Unbuttoning her dress, she slipped the clothes from
her shoulders,
Lifting them slowly into powerful emergence.
She leant over the water and met her face,

A little removed she watched herself.
The familiar when met is stranger than strangers.

Her long brown face
Was an untracked space,
And the honey-brown eyes
Were prescient wise.
Green shades among
The gold hair hung.

The cupboard held a dress of garnet silk,
And dressed in this she'd rise on stolen pinions
To wing a world where all could be eclipsed
Within the feathered floss of vain illusions.

Suddenly, her spreading wings would drop.
With frail wings cut, she'd stand and think
Till thinking wove all opposites as one
And she would end where once she had begun.

" The serpent eats its tail," she said.
Megathy saw the eternal ring,
And Megathy thought she saw everything
From the downland country of her bed.

Soon the ill child was lying alone again,
With a darkness leaping forward and back over the
    cupboard.
In slipshod shapes
Old men in capes
Were saying prayers, hypocritically bowing.

And an old nail
Was the Lord's eye—God's watchful eye,
Or a hornless snail,
Ready to move at Megathy's will.
But sleep was spun at a spider's pace
And God and the snail and the bowing men
Were drowned in the sea of a dreamless space.

Amber trod the darkened stair,
The elemental lion's lair,
And grope she must
For long experienced darkness proves no better known.
O weep, weep, weep! Is the pulse's beat.

Eyes, what use are eyes
When darkness robs them of their sight
And too much light makes blind again?
Yes, either numb or else in pain,
The old grey wall told her finger-tips,
The choice is sleep, or waking—pain.

Then silent became the wall and stair,
The stone spoke not and the girl crept quietly down
Till a beam cast wide on the rugged stone
And a candle came to claim its gleam.

The old servant Medly drifted upwards.
Like a hesitant leaf, or a sigh's half utterance,
She wafted back a measure scaled before
In a range between reality and dream.
Her face was bowed under a knitted shawl,
A strange, unfinished visage in the shade,
Insatiable to scrutiny or stare.

And in this wise her trembling shook the glass
Of milk she carried up for Megathy,
Till nearly all was spilt in riverlets of pearl
Between her fingers and the creases of her shoes.

3

In the glistening gloom
Of a long white room
They dined in hazy, separate reaches.
Severed in hate,
With the glasses and plate
In the table doubled and pooled with peaches.

But Mark pursued,
Tried to intrude,
With sword-eyes searching her virgin shore.
But Amber withdrew
And went into
Herself, and shut the door.

Then he spoke,
Taking smugly-smacked lips from the rim of his glass,
And his voice thrust.

" No lacquered eloquence shall falsify our speech.
I shall not talk of music in your voice
Or coins in your hair.
Nor shall I say though both our hearts are flints
That love's our Pyrodes.
Let moons be moons nor even turn to blue
If we should find tranquillity together."

And rising from his chair, eyes bleared like bruises,
He made his way through candle glamour, *down*
The lime white room, his sepulchre.
And O the clangour of his arteries bid him *drown* !
Yet on he talked,
And smiled to see him build a bower
Of petals peeled from off a flower.

Amber rose and left the table too,
Where toppled bottles bled on crusts of bread,
And broken walnut shells with pale brazils
Were floating mirrored in the waxy wood.
They went into the other room
Which was no meadow breaking into bloom
But melancholy now as a marble tomb.

Still Mark spoke, and satirized their state,
With throat grown dry as a droughty river bed,
And sought precision with a drunkard's care,
Till Amber interrupted him and said,

" To-morrow, Mark, I go."

The wicker creaked, and Mark sat down.
His hands hung veined, and in themselves
Expressive of an evil perspicacity.
His face was bowed, and duskier so,
It almost hid a smile which sealed itself in torpor.

" To-morrow, Mark, I go."

She went to the organ and made and lost
Her own long sigh in the gilded pipes,

And her playing blackened the hollow air
With swollen sounds of dolorous music,
Lost in a column of echo outwitted,
Outwitted and foiled in a column of echo.

There was pain in reaching the surface again.
The clocks all struck in various places,
And long and short were the lifted spaces
Between the chimes of their different voices.
Some were sonorous, deep as a gong,
Others were high as a hedge-king's song,
But one was thin as a golden hair
Plucked in the regions of the air.

Then midnight entered, meaningless,
And no ghosts threaded the turret stair.

4

Do you know the sound, the wraith articulation,
Made in the sleeper's throat before full waking comes ?
Is it our going back into the bodily vessel
From unremembered voyaging in the universe
And mystic instillation from our ancestry ?
Ah, mortal ! Back again. Renew your inward
        wrestle,
At last the time will come when pestle breaks the
        mortar.

So Amber stirred, but made no further moan,
And with unlifted eye had knowledge of the dawn,
Through a presence of stealth and silence that must
        break

19

In the creaking of the furniture and boards
At the precise moment of the winds' interchange.

This was the morrow. No matter which.
To-morrows have reality of myths,
And Amber's morrow dawned in May or June
Though yesterday was February or March.
For what are man-made charts of sun and moon?

The child Megathy still ailed,
She was not ill yet none could call her well.
She chose to go in shade and shrunk from touch
Like small anemones in pools.

In the turret room, or where she played
Among the bitter shrubs that were green to blackness,
She grew tall and white as a slender stem
With thin existence in the undergrowth.

Nothing was changed, except the flowers were more
        advanced
And trees put out their leaves to screen the nesting
        birds,
Who watched with steady, supplicating eye
The hand that moved the foliage when no winds blew.

The lugubrious worm lifts up his head
In exposure to the thrush.
The thrush hops up, the worm is dead,
And the nest is gone from the bush.
Ah weep, weep, weep! and vigil keep,
There's life in grief's persistence.

And Amber fled up the gravel drive
This morrow's morning.
Yet she could pause in the sun to view
On every twig the drop of dew
Wherein an inverted garden grew,
Till a startled bird broke the air with a cry of warning.

Then on she walked, a little ahead of herself
In eagerness for reaching somewhere,
And she met a fanatical gardener
Spreading nets over beds of pale green strawberries.

The sun was so low it lit the undersides
Of the delicate tendrils and leaves,
Making the hard and bloodless fruits luminous.
When he bent,
It streaked the creases in the gardener's breeches
Of soft peach corduroy,
And sent a rose reflection under his nose and chin
Till the down glistened.

Through the arch of his legs
He saw Amber approaching. An immense figure
Which, had he thought, might have been a goddess.
She lengthened to the upstairs windows of the house
And out of sight, except for her legs and shoes.

So when he straightened up and turned
It was surprising he should loom so tall.
She seemed to pass
With face set on some far destination,
Yet no, she stopped beside him, too, and spoke,
" Give sunflower seeds to Megathy

For her own garden plot.
Or, if not,
Sow on the unsuspected grave."

For in the turret window of her mind
Stood Megathy's ghost. A pale fragment of a face
Watched there, whether she lay abed or no.
Thus Amber counted for the child's death
In cold collected thoughts she could not credit.
But can a mind prophesy ?

Megathy lived. While Medly ceased to be,
Dissolving on the eddies of the air.
No more remained for curious eyes to see
But a brown husk, all shrivelled in the chair
Beside the other's bed.
And people thought a corpse could give
True evidence of death.

Stray essences of Medly distilled themselves in
    Megathy.
From that time onwards the child seemed ancient and
    weary.
She had an old face, which held secretly an all-
    comprehensive grief,
Her brows were crossed like battens on a door against
    hope,
She had no wish to do anything.

The gardener touched his forehead and smiled.
He forced no buds to look for flowers
And lakes were water with no depths to drag.
So Amber's smile in freedom interchanged,
Where smiles with intimates estranged

For very fear of deeper revelation
When too much self-exposure is defiled.

The gardener had made her whole.
She revelled in sufficiency new-found,
A confidence which mingled with the sun
And flowered in flowers and grew as tall as trees.
She was a globe all sensitive to sound
And yet unhurt to hear the world go round.

The gardener stooped to drive more pegs,
To stretch more nets
And pride himself on unpecked fruits.

To Amber, the outskirts of the garden were labyrinths
        unlearned,
No matter how constantly explored.
Paths, once found, might vanish again
To reappear on some far distant evening,
As fleeting fragments of a dream
Are loosened from the riprap of a stream
For brief disclosure on the surface of the mind.

Gates marked private, prim and padlocked,
Through which elusive glimpses mocked
Of sheds, discarded rollers, and sacks of sulphur there,
These and many paths, confusing in their twists,
Duck-ponds and stables emerging from the mists
Of early morning—all conspired to waylay Amber.

Sun in the dust,
Sun in the glass,
Delirious dust,
Grains of glass.

Ash on the floor
The floor of the train,
Sand by the door,
A world in a grain. . . .

" World without end," said Amber, " Amen."

Somebody loosened
And let up the blind,
Like a thunder-clap
In Amber's mind !

Who is Mark that he may enter
And seem in the ash,
The hand-worn leather
Or the window-sash
And rattle there like so many bones ?
Who is Mark that he should trouble,
Extend a hand
From out the past,
As the explosion of a bubble
Or gases off some festering pool ?
Let ash be ash and nothing more but ash !
And sash and leather be leather alone and sash,
Not living metaphors of Mark.

A woman behind a newspaper.
Amber saw only her hands, pale and nervy-fingered,
That clasped the edge or, rustling, lingered
On a snake-skin bag.
A railway dame,
Her legs in a rug, and a great big newspaper
Concealing her doubtful mug.
But, who knows ?
She's nifty, she suddenly harks back to dreamland,
She's a childhood contraband.

Cuttings heaved, embodied sighs
And fell again beside the train.
Fields and woods were caught within
The mesh of wires that cut the sky
And borne beyond the reach of eye,
As post on post drove like bars across the mind.

Amber saw a red house. Only a red house
Seen and gone again
In the rush of country falling past the train.
But it was a red house seen through the leaves
And waxy points of chestnut trees.
This was a memory of seasons,
Part of the leaves, part of the likeness of the house
To another house. So listen.

" How large was the wash-house down there,
Down below stairs at home ?
O big, very big, like a big damp drum
With all of them talking inside.
The copper peeled all round,
Like flakes of chalky skin,

And I would do this in the dark—
Hide and peel with a pin.
My brother could squeeze into difficult places,
My brother brought news of the mangle—
Pushed notes between the baskets—
And told me to go on peeling.

I lifted the lid for Dina—
Dina the negress washer,
And steam rushed up my arm
So I dropped the lid and ran.
Dina the washer chased me,
I screamed and screamed in the shed,
And still the negress chased me
With her apron blown over her head.

Now when was it Dina left the wash-house,
Down below stairs at home ?
O soon, very soon, and she kissed me and cried
In a voice as deep as the big damp drum.
' Dina's the last of the slaves,' they said,
' It's long since they ceased in a civilized world,
Dina's the last of the slaves.'
The mangle groaned, the copper peeled,
And the new washerwoman was white.''

The carriage windows became ebony black
And Amber turned to search their depths.
But these evil mirrors had no other side,
She only met the carriage looking back,
Her own face, as a papier-mâché mask,
With holes for eyes full of tunnel-black.

And what lay in the further dimension,
At the back and above her large shoulder ?
Passengers merely, but
What of the dame ?

She loomed large and blurred as through a telescope,
And her fingers were *black*.
" O !
Dina, it's you, with the steam and the soap !
It's Dina, the slave, the negress come back—
O !
Dina, your apron's blown over your head ! "

As if Dina heard what Amber had said,
Her apron stirred with a crackling sound
As if she were ready to start the chase
And last of all reveal her face !

How bright are beads of fear.
How tingling, jingling bright,
Dancing in her head and powdered in her hands.
Amber looks for light,
Looks for light to come creeping down tunnel,
And Dina's waiting for the given moment,
The highest pitch of fear,
To rise with a crackling sound,
To come with a leap and a bound—
O shiny fear ! Hard as sparks up funnel,
In my hands,
In my head—
O !

Dina !

Out of the tunnel, the girl emerged
Into a liturgical carriage light,
And the long line of dovetailed hours,
The flat space we call a day,
Passed with sensations interlaced
As a counter-point of pulse and thought.

Shifting from a hot and thundery sleep,
Amber saw a twilight's silver-grey
Curtaining fields—the last before the city,
And like widows' weeds the willows' leaves drooped
    down.

The other passengers were insignificant
And therefore vanished, all save the dame
Whose self was now transferred into her duplicate
And sailed outside, illumined by the carriage light,
With trees and cattle sliding through in dim aquarium
    glaze.

6

Black and furred, the night reigned,
Sceptreless, for the moon had waned,
And the stars that studded a city sky
Were lustreless farthings, the air was dry.
Lights, there were lights that scorned the dark,
Like globular eyes they tracked men down,
And only an earwig in the park
Had a private place in a bar of shade.

Lights, and the lights, those globular eyes,
Closed at last, as close they must,
For even the grimalkin sleeps with the sun.

And the droning air, dry as chaff,
Shakes and shudders with heat and rattle,
Splits at the oaths of the roadmen drilling
And shovelling sand, sand and tar.
In blue malignant fumes and gases,
The braying, grey metallic asses
Conveying magnets or messiahs
Throb in lines, while bands pass drumming.
Behold ! cries one, Christ's second coming !

Black busbies in the midday sun
Stifle and glitter with tar and the rifle.

The roadmen pause and scratch their heads,
Lick the sweat from off their lips,
Then dark the purple tongue rolls back
And cleaves to the roofs of their sanded mouths.
Their shaking sinews drive the drill,
Renewed again are din and rattle.
The roadmen say,
" We'll beat the bloody band in battle."

Distant now, the red coats seem
A thin stream of hæmorrhage.
The asses bray and the block disperses,
The drum-beats miss like a dying pulse.
The battering-rams and the roadmen's curses
Are lost in a sudden vomit of steam,
And withering flowers stench on hearses.

29

Make way, there. This lady must attend the dead.
Her money spent on wreaths, there's none to spare for
    bread.
You're living, you speak, you still have strength for
    breath.
In time, maybe that even you will scrape and save
Enough to pay the parson for a decent grave,
And men will raise their hats when you achieve your
    death.

Faces blank and screwed in contortions,
Faces of fear, faces of mirth,
With muttering mouths that bring to birth
Twisted truths, mental abortions.
Faces, faces, all are branded
With the mark of existence, a crooked cross.

The band has reached another street.

Black busbies in the noonday sun
Stifle and glitter with tar and the rifle.

7

How long, how long in this burning street
From shade to shade the railings laid,
Or canopy of shops—how long, how long,
With glazed, translucent eye of trout
To tantalize with slabs of ice, the blow-fly
To sicken with its undulating buzz—
And the limp chickweed an old man sells
For the canary that expired an hour since in the sun ?
How long, how long ?

" Pence for recompense," said Amber,
Putting forth her hand.

The face she scanned
Was severed by the sun and shade.
Her look was answered by no look at all,
For utter darkness lay beneath his cap,
And his mouth shifted like a flakey gap
Torn across the whitewash of the wall
He leant against. Three yards ahead
Amber turned to find he was not there.
The agèd are difficult to see
Because, for the most part, they are already elsewhere.

At the next corner she met him once again.
" Pence for recompense," said Amber.

He took the money, and this time he spoke—
The plaster fell away, the plaster broke,
" Thou'lt gladden the heart of no man," said he,
Or did she answer for him, was it she ?
Closely she peered, but his vision smeared,
And trying to keep pace with the fading face,
She cried, " Mark ! is it Mark ? "

Through the gap in the wall the voice blew,
Saying, " No, not Mark, nor even Simeon."

" Simeon," said Amber, " Simeon, Simeon."
And the name could stay the deadening smash
That Mark had made in the window-sash,
That Mark could make in ash and anguish—

So comes the air to flowers that languish.
But who
      is
         Simeon ?

The name had made a fair oasis in the burning street.
She moved, it seemed, continually from shade to shade.
A water-cart shed crystal water
And music issued as it sprayed,
Like chimings from a faint celeste.

A stab, like the flight of a bird, entered her breast,
And her breath caught and quivered in her throat
As the beatings of wings.
As quickly, the name of Simeon was forgot,
But the enchantment flowered and scented all the air,
The seed from which it sprang mattered not.

Again, as when the gardener smiled
And she had grown as tall as trees,
She was enthroned.
Amber was tenant of her own mansion,
And armoured thus could venture carelessly
To think of things that used to frighten her.
The negress washer—
Now if that sack of coal were her,
As coalmen did,
Amber poured her down the hole
And shut the lid.

The coal dust rose, and even Mark dissembling
Might now be met, nay summoned to her side.

But scales are delicate, and one weight more can break
    them.
Fiends are light sleepers, and one step more can wake
    them.

Mark, in his malignancy, entered now
To take possession of her mind in heavy hate and fear.
Mark became manifest in many things,
Not dust alone, but heat and tar coagulation.
He festered in a dog's discarded bone
Left in the gutter with the grit and grime,
And when a monstrous copper bell
Swung out from some tall tower above the town
It seemed he struck in each discordant chime
And broke what secret harbouring she had.

There are some who, velvet-tongued, persuade
    reserve
To fall away like petals from a fruit-tree,
And there are those who suffer death to the secret
    recesses of their heart
As fruit, new-set, is bitten by the frost.
Thus a whole season's learning is defiled
And a dream imparted is for ever lost.

Forget !
Forget, then, what flower had been her joy.
Forget !
Forget the one who did alloy,
Who, summoned, came, in fearful magnitude,
Who, thought of, entered only to intrude.
For though severed by what men call miles
The time had not yet come when she could challenge
    Mark.

Amber thought quickly of this and that.
Lousy sparrows clattered noisily
On house-tops,
Shops
Wafted threads of coffee and tobacco,
With sudden smell of bread from side streets.
And then a cat,
Like an emanation from the underworld,
Slunk up iron steps of an area.

He paused, his pouched belly hanging,
And looked down the street,
With chipped ears twitching at a sudden clanging
Of buckets below stairs.
Delicately he sniffed soiled sawdust as Amber passed
    by.

She felt no sympathy towards the cat.
He was soiled and superior and abstract.
His remorselessness only made her vengeful,
And though he cringed he remained intact.

Amber's covenant was with the feathered creatures
And those who dwelt in shells or under bark,
The insects who moved between the grasses,
Weighed down the flowers or, flying, stitched the sky
With steel needles, like the dragon-fly.
With these, and with small fish in curtained pools
And animals that burrowed under ground
She felt akin.

            No wonder then,
In trying to remember where she had slept

The night before, she seemed to recall
The secret sensation of an armoured insect
And all it felt to be a little horny beast,
Sensitive to every grain of earth,
Glossy, hard, with pinchers raised . . .
For she had been the earwig in the park.

8

The sun was sinking.
                        In an upstairs window
A tailor's dummy underwent transfiguration.
A crimson tape-measure crossed the bust
As an order, such as queens wear,
And her diamonds were the scintillating dust.
Paper-covered books curled,
A needle slid towards the scissors on the sill,
Shadows unfurled
Like rolls of dark crêpe across the counter.

For so things happen when the tailor turns the key
And goes away, and no one's there to see.
None can witness when a change is wrought
Till afterwards. Few have heard
The last tick before the clock stops short
Or seen the crack appear upon the ceiling.

9

Amber entered a cobbled mews.
The blue stain of dusk ran down the walls

And voices rose through the hollow air
Like bubbles in a vessel of water.
The blond ghosts of hay were lifted,
They drifted, and lodged in the folds of her dress.

Faintly she seemed familiar with this place,
Yet when she turned her thoughts to trace
How and whence it was, her thinking blurred,
As pools become opaque when they are stirred.

She knocked at the nearest door
And waited, wondering what she waited for.
The door had once been painted green,
Now it was blue, and blemished here
Where stray fingers had burst the tempting blisters.
Its countenance was lined. It had the wear
Of every caller's absent-minded stare.

The latch was drawn, and he who opened
Stood poised in enquiry. A kindly man
With a brown beard, and a tentative mouth,
While his eyes could preserve
A gracious yet quite masterly reserve.

" Mr. Emanuel ? " said Amber,
She might say any name,
It would all be just the same.

" They call me Lapwing," he replied,
And bid her come inside.

There is a space called the threshold,
Immeasurably long or unaccountably short,

But it is crossed, and all that is remembered
Is where we have left and where we have arrived.
But Amber did not cross, she stepped in to the
   threshold.

" Have you journeyed long ? "

" Yes, and Christ how tired I am."

The light switched on. A burning white
Slew the values of her sight.
A quick omniscience, an utter blankness,
Revealed eternity rolled in a second.
The man, the hall, the stairs and all
Had diminished beyond the reach of vision,
Or else enlarged till atoms were
Holes within holes—again, oblivion.
And this is all there is to know.

. . . Amber had fallen upon her face—
The floor was so cold and lovely a place.

10

Mrs. Lapwing sat working at a sewing-machine.
Her deft fingers drove gold silk towards the needle
Like straw into a chaff-cutter,
And a rustling cataract of silk or straw
Fell down the table to the floor.

The room of course had been a stable once.
It seemed the bitter smell of horses lingered.

Someone had left a bridle on a beam, which none took
    down,
And the lamp made all the stars upon it gleam.

All this Amber watched from where she lay
Upon a couch. The flowers of the cushion
With feathery hairs, shielded and gave her a hiding
    place.
Her body was mountainous, cold and alone,
She could scarcely believe it to be her own.

Mrs. Lapwing was busily turning the handle.
Stopping, then turning, and suddenly stopping again.
There seemed a safeness,
A kindly reassurance in the noise,
In her features' sharp intentness and her poise.

She was pregnant but gave little thought about it.
It was her last bearing, and no more than trees
In their last summers savour their state
But submit to their secret sap,
Did she reflect upon the fruit within her lap.

Above her head, a rack which had some other day
Been used for hay now held large lustre plates.
They shined
And partook of the same luminosity
With which her pointed features were doubly out-
    lined.

Then, as snow falls down upon the tiny soundless
    world
Within a crystal globe, the air grew wild and glittering

With minute particles of golden silk or straw.
Whose hand had made
The room to shift till all its calmness was dismayed ?

II

Amber stayed in the cobbled mews
Many a measureless day and night.
Each nuance of the house was not
More mazy than the sea.
The stain of rust,
The rain of dust
Or powder from the gentle wood-rot
Showed the workings of the worm
Or other hidden tenants.

Domestic tides swelled from room to room
With rush of voices, brush or handle-broom.
The lustre plates from out the hay-rack
Were used and washed and then put back.
All things were moved and known to Amber
Except the bridle on the beam.

The household hub was Mrs. Lapwing.
From her the busy wheel revolved.
The days were full of substances
To touch, to see and talk about,
Yet, strange, at night these all dissolved.

Each evening Amber climbed a ladder to a loft
Wherein she would sleep, or sleepless, sit and think
Until she reached the dangerous brink

Of unlearned meditation
And placed the tail within the serpent's head.

To the ladder's foot the girl had come
And touched the ladder's sentient rung
Till as a lyre so lightly strung
It answered to her hand and sung,

" Regard how steep ascensions vary,
For practice never taught a man
Except to be as he began
And even grow more wary."

One evening
The ladder veered athwart at wide, dissenting angles,
As scaffolding inside a vast cathedral dome is slung,
And Amber, she, an astral steeplejack,
Must needs attend to every step and never dare look
    back.

Another evening
The ladder soared erect into the refined ether
Where colours range in blessed namelessness,
The purest state of being,
With no constructed eye to sanction with its seeing.

And while she scaled her secret rainbow
How easy death appeared, how frail the tissue
And how fair the issue.
O sweet would be relinquishing, the casting off of
    manacles
And fusion with her deity.

Wherefore remorse at parting with identity
When life itself is full of minor deaths—
The frost that sears the unborn fruit,
The voice that blasts the visions of blown-glass,
Or, velvet-tongued, betrays by gentler means ?

But fear prevailed, of failing breath,
Extreme distemper and dreadful dissolution.
Her blood reforged the slackening fetters
And bid her say,
" Teach me not first-hand, death."

So Amber gained her room.

12

Autumn days ensued, and equinoctial gales
Loosened tiles, cracked chimney stacks
And blew down vagrant feathers out of old birds'-
    nests
Or suddenly tore the straw from crates and packing-
    cases.

At night owls hooted, and their wavering notes
Held the heart in sadness with their invocations.
For had not Amber heard them in the ilex tree
Or on the castellations of the turret at whose foot
They cast hard vomit of dead mice and bats ?

Mark had employed a keeper and the owls were shot
And strung in rows beside sequestered paths,
Where all the ground was dotted with small grain,
Where charcoal burned and woodmen cut their laths.

41

This was before Megathy was motherless,
Before, indeed, she had been born,
When Mark, yes Mark, was a youthful man,
Sensitive, and greatly moved by books,
More moved by books than men.

He was a lover of the spring's defenceless flowers,
And having picked them joyed to pick apart
First calices, then stamens, pistil last,
And on their inmost cells he breathed soft perfidy.
These things he showed to his wife, to Amber and
        their brother who
Was not yet killed. They wandered in the fields to see
Mark pick his flowers in spring,
And watched the dreadful things he did, his gentle
        murdering.

Now Mark could hardly bear to see
His wife and Amber hold in painful, women's palms
The pleated mushroom, with its gloss
And satin skin against their trembling fingers,
They were nervous violators of the phallic bloom.

But he said nothing, and kept these secret implications
        to himself
With many others, some which tortured him.
His restive brain
Played subtlety too long and turned the rapier in.

His was the talent and the curse
To split creation and to weld again
All fragments to a whole within his brain,
Depriving them of native honesty.

He could perceive things as they are, yet would not let
    them be.

These were holidays within the war,
Springs when nature was beloved the more
For her indifference. When hazel's green
Was greener yet than it had been before
And soldiers tenderly forgave the bud
Of sap-insistent blackthorn in the blood,
And women wondered how many more springs
Would bind the hedges with false promises of peace.

" Keeping alert to the horror you're in
Is the best hair shirt for anyone's skin."
So said Amber's brother who was not yet killed.

" To be gentle and feeling and yet not die,"
Said Amber's sister who was to die.

                    And Amber thought,
" If she goes, it will have to be I
Who'll be gentle and feeling and yet not die."

13

Many a measureless day and night
Passed like a bird in changeful flight.
Winter came. The cobbled mews
Glistened like pear-drops.
Snow fell, the muffin bell
Rang, and stationers' shops
Put out their Christmas trees.
" Situations Vacant," read Amber.

43

Places, places, waiting to be filled.
Occupations. Somebody kicked out, somebody killed.
A funeral passed. Slowly, because of the ice—
" Situations Vacant," read Amber,
" Wanted.
Births. Deaths. . . ."
No, none of these,
Then, " Lost," read Amber.

Lost—a gold watch lost,
A cocker spaniel puppy lost,
Five pounds reward. Lost, a lady's hand-bag.
Lost, a silver earring, a switch of false hair—
A black cat lost, a private polar bear.
An opinion, a maidenhead, a parrot in a cage lost—
Lost, a game of cards, a husband or a memory.

Who is he to speak of loss ?
The loser ?
Then he's the chooser.

Another man has the gold watch on.
He knows, or he does not know, whose it is
But the watch still goes, and the switch of hair
Is the find of a programme seller,
A present for mother. The cocker spaniel puppy
In the Shadow of the Knife, is sacrificed to Science
And saves a chancellor's wife.
Virginity is not acquired by he who takes it
Though opinions are sometimes adopted—
As for the bear, he was never there,
The parrot was confiscated,
And the husband was found with the chancellor's wife.

14

Through the letter-box fell a thin ray of light,
Pale and mysterious, crossing the hall to the foot of
     the stair.
Mrs. Lapwing occasionally walked through it,
It broke on her white stockings in a blur, a dim
     blossom of light.
Amber watched from the top of the stair.

She wore shoes like Pierrette. Were her tufted bobbles
     the light-blooms ?—
Mrs. Lapwing, moving, deft as a mummer she—
She was not tragic, she had a common-sense magic.
The door ! Inrush of light !

Framed in the doorway sideways,
Mrs. Lapwing stood in a frosty gleam,
Sharp-featured as usual, but waiting,
Overwhelmed, but facing,
Working watching the clock and the calendar.
She was like a rock when it moves in a thousand
     years, or—
The rod strikes the rock and the water gushes and
     breaks.
In his own time, the piping infant springs,
A weeny manacled man.

The miniature figure, the self's precursor, unmanacled,
Danced in the thin ray of light,
A perfect form,
And Amber said to it,

" Dance before the net is made
To net you in,
Dance before your joys are diarized
And your mother says ' Tell me everything.'
Dance before your suffering is her ire
And she like a she-wolf bites your paw off
To think to put an end of, to think you'll have no
    more of
Pain, but only pap, sweet pap
And no more pain, so safe,
So safe in momma's lap."

Unforgiving, Amber feared again, with scheduled dread,
To see herself one day to suck
The secrets from the infant she had fed,
To bite the hand off to forestall the trap
And bathe the blood with lily-soothing milk,
Hers the solace luxury, the boycott silk.

But there was something in Mrs. Lapwing's look,
Something different, something floored.
As if she were getting old, and getting old
Would not as most get old hook care to care,
But poise mid-way, and not wear sorrow
Like a ribbon on her breast to teach the rest
To guard against to-morrow,
Nor feed on infant smiles, as fear beguiles
And teases up the wick to burn
And champion up faint hearts, till all is burnt.
She'd do without,
She'd let young sympathy lie cold
Till it shall wake, slowly, to schooling of many people,
And learn to love unasked.

46

15

*Letters to Amber went to various wrong addresses. At last
the G.P.O. did them all up in a letter packet and delivered
them to the Lapwings.*

Through the letter-box, through the thin ray of light,
Shot a letter packet. Slower than light, it seemed to
    drop
As a fat white spider, clasping to its belly
A round egg, a smooth, untinted lollipop.
But it stayed on the mat, tied up,
As though its own web were its binding fetters.
Amber, peering, saw strand on strand of string
Tying tight a wadge of battered letters.

They were all from Mark.

16

Excerpt from Mark's letters

" No angel so appraised another angel's face
As did a fiend by contrast love it,
And good was never better understood by good
Than those kind seers schooled in evil.
You are afraid of those who know you,
You would consort with strangers rather,
And so you leave me."

The first rebuke. Amber answered it,

" Because you encroach, as strangers never would,
Not because your closeness understood as you think
    closeness should,
Not because you were close as you would be, I left you.
I left you because your closeness is not knowing,
Because your knowing is not knowledge
And therefore never kindness.

You speak of evil, I will speak of good.
Good is that which lets alone,
Good stands near but stands apart,
It has no thing to call its own
And so sees clearest to the heart.
I prize more dearly
The stranger's small act of disinterested kindness
Than all the love that's bred in blindness of kith or
    kin."

Amber saw Lapwing as he let her in—
A whirl of days in the mews—

" It is the eternal stranger that I seek."

(Excerpt from Mark's letters)

" We have reached the time when thoughts return to war,
It is the natural sequence of our age.
The tawny warrior, the corpulent veteran,
The meek emasculated, the hen man,
The man like me who schemes a dark reprisal
And calls down calumny on churches—
Now is the time when memories wage
And coagulated veins begin slowly to move again
Over the darkened minds."

48

Strenuous thieves, in the night, in the day,
Stole his charity away,
Left only his assessing.
Perhaps
His digestion ?
Let us say that thieves—fiends, jump into physical
    complaints.
" I lost my stomach in the war," said a man of Mark's
    generation,
" O it's there, but it plays me tricks,
It won't let me forget it."
Some men in their sickness turn to the Saints and the
    Prophets.
Does that matter ?

" It does not matter," thought Amber.

Strenuous thieves, in the night, in the day,
Demanded employment or compensation.
Mark bargained with his fears.
" If I have thee and pay thee more, I can dispense with
    t'other,
And from thy surplus wage thou canst pay off thy
    brother,"
He said gutturally. In the long white room, with his
    alkali,
In the glistening gloom,
He dined with his thieves.

He had experienced fears beyond Amber's experi-
    encing,
But she answered him,

" The churches reflect our human state.
If they give us nothing
It is because we bring them nothing.
We give them no oil, and in our darkness
We cry, Why is there no light in the churches ?
O the cocks have flown to find themselves new perches.
And so with the peoples,
They say the steeples are so high—
Too far from us—

And the preachers outreaching reality.
What is reality ? I dreamed last night
That the cuckoo from the cuckoo-clock
Expelled the weather-cock
And took his place, determined to make himself heard.
Greenwich Time is more necessary than direction, said
      the bird.
And then he did not show but had, the wind,
And putting on his small prebendal hat
He flew away to gather up his stipend.

The church reflects our human state.
The truest thing reflects the truest,
Or like a window looked through either way
Takes in and passes out the light.
So, if we could be windows,
Windows without bars to shadow—— "

Amber fell upon her knees
And said,

" O self, O shadow, self,
Dispense !

Dispense enough for me to see and seeing, give—
And yet be only tough enough to let me seeing, giving,
    live."

17

In the spring, but many springs ahead,
Megathy left the turret house and came to the town.
She sought Amber, and meeting Lapwing on the stair,
Passed him, as if he were not there
And this were not his house.

In Amber's room she sat by the window,
Banning approach with her steady frown.
She sought Amber, but said nothing.
She soon went, but she came again later,
" Come for a walk," she said.

In the park,
" The serpent eats its tail," she said.

" No," said Amber.

" That was your song once," said Megathy.

" I was wrong, or not quite right."

" And now you are right ? "
Megathy turned sharply, though she spoke quietly.

" Not quite."

" Ah, invest with care, even in piety,"
Said Megathy smiling,
Smiling, smiling.

Amber made no answer.
Silence, an alliance of difference
Spread between them.
Silence, a sharp-edged gem,
A diamond cutting glass,
Glass cutting ice, ice and glass broken together.

Silence, what was the inference ?
Megathy thought she scored,
Megathy's mind was a score-board.
Up a peg, down a peg.
Peg over peg. Win or lose
According to wits. But play long enough
And it's sometimes a draw,
A cancel out. Then back again
To loss or gain. What are we playing for ?

" I hate life," said Megathy,
" I hate it.
I have no wish to do anything.
I feel I have learnt all I want to know
And I don't want to know any more,
Creation was a mistake,
It's rotten to the core.
Shall we go and row on the lake ?
I wish I could drown,
But it's only three feet deep.
I want to lie down
And go to sleep

And never to wake,
But that would be boring,
Everything's boring,
Everyone dies.
Why do we live ? "

Megathy did not stay for an answer,
She vanished from Amber's side.
A sudden darkness fell upon the park.
" Where are you, Megathy ? " called Amber.
There was a faint sound of laughter,
Or was it sand and gravel falling
As men dug trenches in the park ?

Megathy had gone,
But Amber made her answer.
To the dim shades of the railings and the sound of
    spades
And to the listening sky,
She made her answer,

" Say that we are scribes to the written page,
Yet what we write shall never be blotted out.
Say that we are here and that we have gone before
And as we shall be are we now and were we.
So should we be more careful.

Say that the bread upon the table is also in the van,
And the wheat in the bread is also in the field
And in our mouths as it is sown.
Then would men not despise the moment, which is
    also eternity.

Not until we acknowledge the moment as eternity
Shall war cease and life have meaning."

18

Amber returning, she,
Dwelling in sorrow and in hope went
Spent and weary, heavy-footed,
Along long roads through hills and valleys,
Away from the main roads keeping.
Keeping to lanes and footpaths
Through orchards painted white
And new-strung hop gardens,
Past ponds with no leaves floating,
Hazels mirrored and the ring-doves' flight.
Coo-curoo, coo-curoo, the soft doves said.

Nothing was changed, but all seemed stricken still,
As though the air like a winding-sheet wound round
         about
And all it touched was dead.

The field's uneven ground
Took all alike the sun's smooth passage,
The cloud's indent, the lark, the rabbit,
Or the hawk intent, the sheep munching
And the jackdaw on her back.
Across all alike did the sun pass—
Passed the sun fast as the clouds rolled back—
Then, as a bunch of weapons suddenly thrown down,
The shadow of the railings fell at Amber's feet—
Black and arrow-headed.

Branches of fear, sprouting from her hands,
Sprouting from her head, grew and fell downwards
Breaking with her heart's disdain.
She moved forward and alongside the railings
Till she found the gateway and entered the garden she
    had known.

Broken and fallen were the branches of fear
From her hands, from her head,
Trailing loose in the grass.
But foreboding invisible sounded,
As distant thunder, an imaginary voice, or a heart-
    beat—
Foreboding invisible sounded
With her heart's disdain.

A hurl of darkness came,
A sleeve, as mourners hide their faces
Yet show more clear their mourning.
Manifold the visions. Amber saw
Climb up the sky a pale and ghostly cavalry,
And then again, the heavens seemed
With pale clouds dotted as stones to mark
The burial ground of some inglorious dead,
And as she looked the face of that frail continent of
    air
Veined white with cracks, splitting the smallest star,
And shimmering—A resurrection
That hesitated. Slowly, the vision
Faded, as distant thunder rolled,
Echoed by the valleys, and a footfall
Vast as the sounds of all that night, came near.

But suddenly the world grew smaller, the sounds, the
    shapes,
Were man-size, and two small creatures met and spoke,
Amber to the gardener, the gardener to Amber.
" Where is Megathy ? " said Amber.

He spoke, with a face resolute to adopt no fitting grief
Nor to forestall grief, nor to soften grief.
Bare the statement, bare the face,
A face in the moon's trace, cool of all colour,
The face that had smiled once now said,

" Megathy has killed herself."

Everything speaks of death to those who hear,
In all life lies elegy, singing.
Death, in the absence of credulity, even in death by
    violence.
That absence is the mockery, that mockery death.

" I found her in the field, face up,
The grass was short enough to see her lying.
As I was setting traps I saw her,
No, as I was taking traps up
From the hedge, I saw across the hedge
The field, her lying in it, I found her in the field.
With a bottle of poison in her hand, I found her
In the field."

19

The one lamp lit. The hall, listlessly awake.
Amber stood near the open door,

Stood and stared till the lamp went out,
And many the chimes of clocks she heard,
One o'clock, two o'clock, three o'clock, four.

She waited in the garden cool,
Where a pigmy fool
In cap and bells, pranced, gesticulating, in a tulip bed,
Hugging his pumpkin sides in canny laughter,
All silently, wagging his head, finger to nose,
Whilst one huge tear welled and swelled
And fell, fell down his front.
Cool, the wind shook the lilac leaves,
The tulips nodded in the night, and the joker joked,
Wisecracking in a dead world, grimacing, weeping,
    wooing the air. . . .

" Mark ! " cried Amber, " Mark, come out ! "
                     And again she cried,
" Mark, come out ! "

And Mark to his thief said,
" Thy master's absence forgive,
His absence shall be brief.
On his return he shall be wholly thine
And thou his guest for ever.
What ? Come with me ? Nay, stay
And I shall repay thee amply,
Thou shalt have me as annuity, I swear it."

Mark came to the door, stood there, as the thunder
    rolled.
This was the final and unfeigned
For which all else were deputies,
This was the moment when unstrained

The tension of a lifetime broke—
Or, is Mark so in love with thieves
The favourite follows at his heel
And cleaves to the last, with no repeal ?

Amber and Mark sat together at the end of night,
And with dawning invincible
It seemed the earth was pulled and driven as a chariot
Pulled by its runaways—skylarks
Mounting in the light of morning.

But in this dawn which draws the shapes of life,
The master hand sculps death, even as it crumbles.
So Amber saw Mark's face as one who fumbles
To build against the oncoming sea,
So did she see him falling,
So did she see him—dead.

20

Into the garden sprung a white lion.
His paws were soft shielding claws like iron,
His tail a distaff or a torch held high.
He came all armed for strife
But knelt at Amber's feet in mild docility.

And when she climbed the turret stair
The same white lion was there.
It might be said that he who was eaten by lions once
        cannot be eaten again,
But the white lion rends even as he renders,
And it seemed not once but over and over again
Amber was slain.

Then the lion was slain,
Then Amber was slain,
And yet there was no rancour, bale or canker of the
    anchorite's
Promulgating rebirth.
Victor and victim were one, without excise.

Then, as a dream awakened from, a dream forgot,
Amber forgot the white lion's fight.
She said as she climbed the turret stair,
" For me make no exordium."
And she reached the turret room.

Where the room ? Where ?
The sunlit air did float a ghost of stone and slate
    somewhere.
The turret top was but a bare barbarian half-mast,
A broken battlement of care, a rattle in the wind,
A blown-up bight, a carcass of uncurfewed night
Evinced by the clear day light—
Cement for cerement covering it.

Then Amber cried, vehement,
" O all those gone before !
Pray for us—not we for you !
Forgive us not for what we do !

My friends ! Where are you ? "

None spoke but the stone.
" For you, Amber," said the stone,
" For you, alone, what is there ? "

" I have no soul's indemnity for a ruined truth,
No fine redemption,
No martyr's mattock for my head.
Like all men, I am my own sooth,
And I shall never say, nor was it ever said
I have aught to fear but my own enmity which
Is the perpetual augur threatening innocence.
For the expungement of this and this alone shall
    Amber live.
With this and this alone let my head be bowed
And boughed about."

But the stone would flout.
The sides of the precipice were sheer.
Who has not thought of death when it comes near,
Near as a ruler's inch ?
Who has not said, why should I flinch at death ?
But instead of death, think, what is the ruler's inch ?

" Will you die, Amber ? " said the stone.
                 And she answered,
" No, I have to live."

March 1932—March 9th, 1939.

60

ACKNOWLEDGEMENTS

Anyone who knew my grandmother will have their own idea of who she was. And they will remember things differently.

My version of the story could not have been written without the cooperation of my mother Jane Robertson, my aunt Polly Woods and my uncle Sandy Rendel, each of whom would have written something else.

I am immensely grateful to them for trusting me and letting me get on with it, for giving me as much material as they possibly could and for opening themselves up to the past once again.

I would also like to thank my father Dr J. A. Robertson for his sustained interest and for being my general sounding-board on many things, including psychiatry. Thanks too to my brothers; to Andrew for his support throughout, to James for taking my photograph. And to my sister Clare, who has been particularly stalwart in providing reassurance, hysterical laughter and an expert critical eye.

In chasing my grandmother up and down the country and across the world, I have been helped by many others, without whom it would have been a much paler experience and this a far shorter book:

For family background, photographs and memories, thanks to Richard Adeney, Tom Evans and, in particular, to Jo Easdale (cousin and champion sender of encouraging postcards).

In Edinburgh, thanks to George and Hazel Newell, who welcomed me like someone they knew and took me to the important places.

In Australia, many thanks to various members of the family I rarely see but who are all connected to the story in some way: Dinah Woods and Jules Evans; Emma and Charlie Silveira; Barry Woods; Diane Rendel; Kate Rendel and Grant Hayes; for having me to stay, cheering me on and making my research trip so rewarding. Thanks also, and in particular, to Bill and Susan Sobey, who made the past come alive and were so generous with their time.

Also to Elizabeth Rasmussen, who let me in to the house after all.

Back in England, I am extremely grateful to Joy Whitfield for her extensive knowledge of Holloway Sanatorium, for giving up a day to show me round and answer my barrage of questions. Thanks also to the Egham Historical Society and to Jill Hyams at the Surrey History Centre.

In Nottingham, huge thanks to John Richardson, for a lot of information and practical help and for the sporadic phone calls.

To Richard Hetherington and George Johnson and, in particular, to Anthony Robinson. Also to Julian Griffiths and Pippa Mac Keith, who not only let me ask them a lot of questions but had me to stay out of the blue.

I am also extremely grateful to the following people who answered my enquiries, put me in touch with others, gave me information, talked with me about my grandmother or showed me how to do things: Sally Mitchison; Lois Godfrey; Denny Mitchison; Avrion Mitchison; Dorothy Sheridan; Mark Charlton; Keverne Weston; Amy Rosenthal; Helen Rix; Stephen Barkway; Shirley Hodgson; Jonathan Penrose and Pippa Rendel. Thanks to Broderick Smith in Castlemaine, Australia, and the boys at the Computer

Centre, Clapham, for rescuing me on the technological front.

Special thanks to Kathryn Hughes for pointing me in the right direction to find Joan's BBC scripts and correspondence, and for unearthing *In Pursuit of Mrs Beeton* and the story behind the broadcast.

I would also like to thank all those who helped me in the various libraries I used: the archivists, librarians and assistants at the London University Library; the BBC Written Archives Centre at Caversham (especially Jeff Walden); Special Collections and the Mass-Observation Archive at Sussex University (in particular Adam Harwood); and Special Collections at Reading University Library, where Verity Andrews has been unstintingly helpful and positive. Thanks, too, to Nicholas Graham and Suzanne Lankford at the University of North Carolina, the staff at the British Library, the British Newspaper Library, the Sydney Records Centre and the Family Records Centre, London.

I am extremely grateful to my agent David Miller for responding to the story in the first place, for taking a punt and being so enthusiastic throughout. And to my editor Lennie Goodings, who understood it from the beginning, knew exactly what was required and remained unfazed by my timing. Thanks also to my shrewd and speedy desk-editor, Zoe Gullen. Along with Linda Silverman, Jenny Fry, Viki Ottewill and everyone in production at Virago, they have made it happen.

I am indebted to my friends for their moral support and forbearance but special thanks (for various reasons) are due to William Eaves, Lucy Hackney, Olivia Lacey and Sarah Malin. Also to my acting agent Sarah Barnfield.

And I could not have finished the book without sterling help with Z from Aneta Bosch, Rupert and Antonia Bailie, Bill and Shelagh Hill and Alice Barclay.

Finally, thanks to Paul Hill, for his patience, understanding and constant support over an awfully long time. For his brains and sense of humour. For reading it first and not letting me get away with anything. For making me realise I had to write it and for taking Z out of the house while I did.

A NOTE ON SOURCES

Much of the material for this book comes from conversations and informal interviews with people who met or knew my grandmother. I have also quoted extensively from her letters and notebooks, most of which remain within the family.

In addition, I have quoted from letters written by my grandfather James Rendel, which are held by the family, and from Polly Woods's personal diary and a written account of her childhood, which she has generously allowed me to read and use.

John Richardson has given me kind permission to use his own letters about Sophie.

Letters written by Joan to her parents-in-law were only unearthed at the last minute. I had in fact slept several nights with my head just inches from them in the spare room of my Uncle Sandy's house in Australia. The filing cabinet of correspondence had lain untouched for years, and I returned to the UK none the wiser. It is thanks to my Aunt Diane that this treasure trove was finally remembered, opened, copied, read and included.

The letters written by Joan to her mother, spanning the fifties and sixties, are held in an archive of personal and family material that Ellen Easdale left to the Special Collections at Reading University Library. This also includes Joan's Crouch sketchbook and a series of photographs of the family and their friends in the thirties.

Joan's correspondence with the Hogarth Press is also kept at Reading, in the Hogarth Press Archive; access to it is thanks to Random House. I also quote from Vita Sackville-West's letter to John Lehmann, which is contained within this archive.

Letters from Ellen and Joan to Leonard Woolf are held in the Leonard Woolf Archive in the Special Collections at Sussex University Library.

All material and correspondence relating to Joan's BBC work, including her scripts, is held at the BBC Written Archives Centre, caversham. I am most grateful for the BBC for access to this material.

Ellen's unpublished journals, spanning the years 1930 to L934, are held in the Senate House Library at the University of London.

Extracts from the wartime diary of Naomi Mitchison are taken from *Among You Taking Notes*, edited by Dorothy Sheridan and published by the Phoenix Press in 2000.

I also quote from *The Letters of Virginia Woolf*, edited by Nigel Nicolson and Joanne Trautmann (Hogarth Press 1978).

Other books I found helpful or relevant to the telling of my grandmother's story include: *Thrown to the Woolfs* by John Lehmann; *Leonard and Virginia Woolf as Publishers* by J. H. Willis; *A Checklist of the Hogarth Press 1917–1938* compiled by J. Howard Woolmer; *The Nine Lives of Naomi Mitchison* by Jenni Calder; *J.B.S – The Life and Work of J.B.S Haldane*, by Ronald Clark; *The Short Life and Long Times of Mrs Beeton* by Kathryn Hughes; *Asylums* by Erving Goffman; *Palaces, Patronage and Pills* by John Elliot; and *The Restoration of a* Masterpiece, Octagon Developments' brochure for Virginia Park.

Every reasonable effort has been made to credit sources appropriately. If I have made any errors or omissions, I will endeavour to correct the mistake at the earliest opportunity.